CHANGING GENERATIONS

A Story for Developing Reading Skills

Longman ·

Fredricka L. Stoller
Northern Arizona University

Nina Rosen
Santa Rosa Junior College

Changing Generations: A Story for Developing Reading Skills

Pearson Education, 10 Bank Street, White Plains, NY 10606

Editorial director: Allen Ascher
Executive editor: Louisa Hellegers
Acquisition editor: Laura Le Dréan
Development manager: Penny Laporte
Development editor: Andrea Bryant
Director of design and production: Rhea Banker
Associate director of design and development: Aliza Greenblatt
Managing editor: Linda Moser
Production manager: Ray Keating
Production editor: Martin Yu
Electronic production editor: Rachel Baumann
Senior manufacturing manager: Patrice Fraccio
Manufacturing supervisor: Edith Pullman
Cover design: Miguel Ortiz
Cover photos: Ericka O'Rourke
Text design: Barbara Rusin
Text art: John Dyess

Library of Congress Cataloging-in-Publication Data

Stoller, Fredricka L.
    Changing generations: a story for developing reading skills /
Fredricka L. Stoller, Nina Rosen.
       p. cm.
    ISBN: 0-13-727280-4 (alk. paper)
    1. English language—Textbooks for foreign speakers. 2. Conflict
of generations—United States—Fiction. 3. Family—United
States—Fiction. 4. Readers. I. Rosen, Nina. II. Title.

PE1128.S843   2000
428.6'4—dc21   99-059025

1 2 3 4 5 6 7 8 9 10—MV—05 04 03 02 01 00

Dedicated to enduring and ever-changing generations

To our parents
Betty and the late Leo B. Stoller
Rose and Leo Kapler

To Nina's daughters
Lola, Sasha, and Katrina

Contents

To the Teacher

Changing Generations: A Story for Developing Reading Skills is a high-interest reader and a reading skills development textbook for intermediate students of English as a second or foreign language. It combines a highly motivating fictional story with a principled array of reading skill and strategy development exercises that translate reading theory into practice. By using pre-, during-, and postreading exercises that provide practice in reading skills, strategic reading, and critical thinking, students are more prepared for the reading demands of the real world. Speaking, listening, writing, and vocabulary-building activities are also integrated so that students will have a complete language learning experience while using *Changing Generations.*

Changing Generations is a versatile text, designed for ESL and EFL students. It can be used in reading classes, integrated-skills classes, or pull-out classes. It is also appropriate for language institutes and language classes offered at high schools, adult schools, community colleges, and universities.

What's special about *Changing Generations*?

Unlike most reading textbooks, *Changing Generations* tells a continuous story, creating an authentic reading experience for students. The story line engages students of all ages and backgrounds by exploring a universal human experience: the generation gap. The story line raises a variety of real-world issues that will be familiar to students: family dynamics, growing up, parenting, societal problems, and generational differences. The family depicted in *Changing Generations* is American and lives in the United States. As students read about some of the ways in which this American family deals with generational differences, they are able to consider how similar issues are dealt with in their own families, as well as in the families of their classmates. Because students are reading about issues that may have parallels in their lives, they are drawn into the story, which in turn aids the development of their reading abilities.

Changing Generations includes several other special features that are not often found in reading textbooks. These include the following:

- The **Learning about Your Book** section, at the beginning of *Changing Generations*, allows students to (1) become familiar with the format of the book; (2) predict the contents of the book, building up expectations and excitement about reading the story; and (3) practice a prereading strategy commonly used by skilled readers.

- **Graphic Organizers**, such as grids, Venn diagrams, and charts introduce students to strategies for demonstrating relationships among characters and concepts in the book, in addition to summarizing and synthesizing information from the text.

- **Original Musical Scores**, included in three chapters, recycle vocabulary, revisit important concepts from the story, and give students the opportunity to improve their English syntax and pronunciation (including intonation, stress, and vowel reductions).

- **Word Recognition Exercises** help students develop the automatic and rapid word recognition abilities that are characteristic of skilled readers.

- **The Whole Story**, at the end of *Changing Generations*, gives students the opportunity to engage in authentic pleasure reading by rereading the whole story, without exercises or teacher intervention.

- The **Certificate of Completion: Reading Award**, provided at the very end of the book, is an award for students who have successfully completed *Changing Generations*.

What inspired *Changing Generations*?

Changing Generations was written with the goal of providing students with positive reading experiences and opportunities to develop their reading abilities. The authors were motivated by their students who expressed a desire to read about topics relevant to their own lives. Students who helped pilot *Changing Generations* found connections between the story line and their own experiences, motivating them to continue reading, engage in animated discussions, pose provocative questions, and think critically. The positive experiences our students have had with *Changing Generations* have resulted in increased self-esteem and confidence as readers of English.

How is *Changing Generations* organized?

Each of the fourteen chapters of *Changing Generations* consists of a portion of the continuous story line and related exercises. As the story unfolds, students work with exercises that were designed to develop general and academic reading skills and strategies. By using both familiar and new exercise types, students are encouraged to go beyond rote, mechanical learning and become engaged, active learners in the process.

Each chapter begins with a **Getting Ready to Read** section, intended to bring students *into* the text. These prereading exercises serve four purposes: (1) to help students access background information that will facilitate comprehension of the story, (2) to provide information that will prepare students for a successful reading experience, (3) to expose students to a range of strategies that skilled readers use to familiarize themselves with new reading material, and (4) to stimulate student interest in the story.

The **Reading Carefully** section of each chapter takes students *through* the story and encourages purposeful extensive reading. This section begins with a short task, such as asking students to consider questions while reading or asking them to underline information as they read. Following this is a portion of the **Story,** which is divided into sections for easy reference. Words and phrases within the story that may be difficult for some students have been glossed.

Changing Generations includes a variety of postreading exercises that take students *beyond* the text by checking comprehension and requiring students to extend and apply what they know and have learned from reading. Each chapter contains these postreading exercises:

- **Reviewing What You've Read** checks students' comprehension and encourages students to apply different reading strategies, such as rereading the text, checking predictions, sequencing events, answering questions posed before reading, and verifying information in the text.

- **Reading between the Lines** guides students in making inferences about the text, which helps improve higher-level thinking and reading abilities.

- **Discussing What You've Read** guides students in discussing the story line and related topics, in pairs or small groups. Through these collaborative exercises, students recycle important vocabulary and concepts gleaned from the story.

- **Writing about What You've Read** provides students with practice in meaningful writing, using a variety of activities, such as summarizing and synthesizing information from the story and writing letters, essays, and other student-generated materials.

- **Connecting the Story to Your Life** assists students in connecting their personal experiences and opinions to the text. Through a range of activities, students express their own ideas in English, practicing meaningful vocabulary and benefiting from extended language use.

- **Building Your Vocabulary** reviews and extends vocabulary, through exercises focusing on synonyms, antonyms, phrasal verbs, descriptive adjectives, idiomatic expressions, compound words, irregular verbs, and collocations.

How should the Word Recognition Exercises be used in class?

Separate from, but connected to, each chapter are the Word Recognition Exercises. For optimal results, have students complete the three word recognition exercises developed for each chapter before asking them to read the story carefully. Use the first exercise as a warm-up; then have students strive to proceed faster and more accurately during the second and third exercises. These exercises can be completed with a limited amount of classroom instruction time. All that is needed is any clock (or watch) with a second hand.

Introduce the Word Recognition Exercises procedures with the practice exercise on pages 155–156. Then have your students follow this easy six-step process:

1. Direct students to begin a Word Recognition Exercise when the second hand of the classroom clock is on the 12.

2. Tell students to look at the key word in the left-hand column and then move their eyes to the right as quickly as possible to identify the identical word.

3. When students encounter an exact match, tell them to cross out the identical word and then quickly go to the next line.

4. When finished, direct students to look up at the clock and record their exact time (in seconds and/or minutes) at the bottom of the exercise. Or have students call out "finished" or "done" so that the teacher, who is watching the clock, can state each student's time aloud.

5. Ask students to correct their work and then record the number of correct answers at the end of the exercise.

6. Finally, remind students to record their results on the Word Recognition Progress Chart on page 199. Reassure students that scores are likely to fluctuate.

Word Recognition Exercises can be a lot of fun. Students can set goals for themselves and gain speed and accuracy with each chapter. Help students understand that as they strive to improve accuracy and speed, their scores are likely to fluctuate. That is, as students improve their speed, their accuracy may falter. Similarly, when trying to improve accuracy, the time students need to complete the exercise may increase. It is acceptable to make mistakes when trying to improve performance. When students obtain a perfect score (20/20), encourage them to work faster with the understanding that the accelerated pace may lead to mistakes. Basically, the goal is to improve both speed and accuracy over an extended period.

While using *Changing Generations*, what can the teacher do to help students become better readers?

1. Remember that students only improve their reading abilities by reading. Give students time to read silently in class.

2. Developing readers benefit greatly from reading material more than one time. Provide students with a legitimate reason for rereading this text (and other reading materials). For example, begin a lesson by asking students to skim the story for the main idea. Then ask them to read the same passage for a more thorough understanding. When discussing the chapter, ask students to return to the text to scan for details or confirm classmates' answers.

3. Good readers make use of different strategies to accomplish a range of everyday reading tasks. For example, good readers predict what a passage will be about after looking at the title and accompanying illustrations; they guess at the meaning of unknown words or phrases; they connect the contents of a reading passage to their own background knowledge to make sense of the text; they connect one part of a passage to another; they reread passages for a variety of purposes (e.g., to clarify a misunderstanding or to get more details); they ask questions to focus and guide their reading; and they summarize what they have read. Reinforce good reading habits by introducing students to strategies such as these, giving students multiple opportunities to practice strategies in class, and asking students to describe the strategies that they are using to make them more aware of their reading behaviors.

4. When reviewing answers to postreading questions, ask students to identify the section number of the story containing information that helped them answer the questions. This helps students practice scanning for a purpose.

5. Remember to provide students with sufficient time to read and process questions in the text. Encourage students to go back to the text to find correct answers rather than answering quickly by relying solely on memory or random guessing.

6. To ensure that all students participate, ask them to write down answers to questions before calling on someone to respond. In this way, all students participate and receive feedback that supports their development as confident, successful readers.

7. Integrate graphic representations—such as semantic maps, flow charts, compare/contrast matrices, cause-effect tables, Venn diagrams, graphs, and outlines—into reading instruction. Graphic representations help students process written material by revealing organizational patterns as well as key concepts and their relationships. Use graphic representations to introduce a new chapter or review a passage that has already been read.

8. Developing readers benefit from print-rich environments. Try to surround your students with written materials. Create bulletin board displays that recycle concepts and vocabulary previously introduced in class. Stimulate students' interests with provocative reading materials that reinforce and supplement class activities. Post student writing to create accessible reading materials for classmates and support students' creative efforts.

9. Reading is one of the best ways to improve students' vocabulary. Remember, however, that new vocabulary items (words, phrases, or idioms) need to be recycled, in a range of contexts, before students actually use the new words and phrases accurately and with confidence. Make a point of recycling important vocabulary items from the text in your conversations with students, in sample sentences that you put on the blackboard, in worksheets that you generate, and on your bulletin boards. Systematic recycling of important vocabulary helps students improve their command of the language, thus helping them to become better readers.

10. Set high expectations for all students and assist them in achieving those expectations. Students often rise or fall to the level of expectation of their teachers. Provide all students with concrete feedback on their efforts and accomplishments.

11. Relate the contents of *Changing Generations* to students' personal backgrounds and experiences. This enhances the learning and reading skills development that take place in class.

12. Encourage independent reading beyond the classroom.

To the Student

Changing Generations: A Story for Developing Reading Skills was written especially for you—students who want to improve their English. As you read, you will improve your reading abilities and build your vocabulary. You'll also improve your speaking, listening, and writing skills.

The theme of this book is "the generation gap." As you read *Changing Generations*, you will see how an American family deals with generational differences. At the same time, you will also see that the issues of this family are issues that families throughout the world face. *Changing Generations* addresses many topics that may be familiar to you: family relationships, growing up, school, work, clothes, music, friendship, food, dating, and society. As the reader, you will have a chance to decide how the lives of American families are similar to, or different from, your life.

We want your experience with *Changing Generations* to be a positive one that will prepare you for the real world. In addition, we hope that by reading this book you will gain a greater understanding of American culture and discover some of the experiences that all cultures share.

Acknowledgments

There are many people who have helped to shape *Changing Generations*. First of all, we would like to thank the numerous students who read various drafts of the book and offered their comments. Special thanks go to students at Santa Rosa Junior College who piloted our first version of *Changing Generations* and provided many helpful suggestions: Oleg Belkov, Alejandra Gonzaga, Rafael Hernandez, Arturo H. Herrera, Miriam Kirk, Yvonne Lee, Juan-Miguel Mascote, Bertha Monroy, Rocio M. Padron, Jose L. Sanchez, Marcela Torres, and Jessica Wang. We would also like to thank Marianne Arden, Gelsey Bell, Andrew del Monte, Casey Giordono, Margarita Montes, Sasha Rosen, and Camille Stewart, colleagues and community members who provided support, energy, and imagination.

Our gratitude also goes to our superb editors Andrea Bryant and Laura Le Dréan, both of whom have been a pleasure to work with so closely. Last, but certainly not least, we extend a heartfelt thank you to William Grabe and Richard S. Rosen, for both their input and patience. Writing *Changing Generations* has been an adventure; we hope it provides an adventure for ESL and EFL readers as well.

Learning about Your Book

1. What is the title of the book? Write the whole title on the line below:

_____

2. Read the title of the book again. What does the word *generation* mean? Choose the correct definition.

    a. Communities near the mountains

    b. People in the same age group

    c. Workers in the state government

3. How many generations live together in your home? _____ Write the name of one person from each generation.

    a. _____

    b. _____

    c. _____

4. What does the title tell you about the story in this book? _____

_____

5. What are the authors' names?

    a. _____

    b. _____

6. Find the Contents page and answer these questions.

    a. How many chapters are in the book? _____

    b. On what page does Chapter 5 begin? _____

    c. What is the title of the eighth chapter? _____

    d. Who do you think the main character of Chapter 12 is? _____

    e. What is Chapter 3 about? _____

_____

    f. Look at the titles of Chapters 13 and 14. What are these chapters about?

_____

_____

g. What kind of exercises begin on page 155? _____

h. What kind of certificate is at the end of the book? _____

i. On what page does the Whole Story begin? _____

7. Look at the Whole Story. What is different about this section of the book?

_____

8. Look at the pictures below. They tell you something about the story in *Changing Generations*. What do you think the book will be about?

A Weekday Morning

Getting Ready to Read

A. Look at the chapter title and the illustration.

1. When does this chapter take place: on a weekday or on a weekend?

2. What do you see in the illustration?

3. What do you think Chapter 1 is about?

B. Prepare to read Chapter 1. **Scan** Section 1 of the story on page 3. When you scan, read quickly to find specific information. Answer the following questions. Stop when you have answered all the questions.

   1. Who wakes up at 6:15 A.M.? _____

   2. Does she wake up with an alarm clock or a clock radio? _____

   _____

   3. Does Sandy like the music? How do you know? _____

   _____

C. Now **skim** Section 2 of the story. When you skim, read quickly for the main idea. After skimming the section, answer the following questions. Stop when you have answered all the questions.

   1. Does Sandy's father like or dislike the music Sandy listens to? _____

   _____

   2. Why does Sandy's father feel this way about the music? _____

   _____

   3. What does Sandy like about her favorite music? _____

   _____

   4. Is Sandy's father happy or unhappy this morning? How do you know? _____

   _____

D. Now that you've scanned and skimmed Sections 1 and 2 of the story, try to answer Question A3 again. Expand your answer.

_____

_____

Reading Carefully

Before you read the story carefully, write down one question of your own. What do you want to know about Sandy's family and their weekday morning routine?

_____

Now read the story carefully. While reading, look for the answer to your question. In addition, think about these two questions:

   1. What kind of relationship does Sandy have with her mother?

   2. What kind of relationship does Sandy have with her father?

CHAPTER 1 | *A Weekday Morning*

Section 1 The radio clicked on. The rock music was loud. Sandy heard the music and woke up **like a bullet.**[1] She looked at the clock. It was 6:15 A.M. Sandy sang along with the words. She was listening to her favorite radio station.

Section 2 "Sandy," shouted her father. "Sandy, turn that music off." Steve Finch came into her room. "Why do you have to listen to such **weird**[2] music? It's the same thing over and over. I'm not sure that is really music. It does have **rhythm,**[3] though. Hmmm. No, it isn't really music. It's terrible. It is definitely terrible music."

"I like that music, Dad. It's my favorite group, Green Waves. Listen for a minute, and I'm sure you'll like it. It has a really powerful message. Didn't you ever listen to music like this when you were younger?" Sandy went over to the radio to turn it up louder.

"No, no, don't do that. I can't stand it. The music I listened to had a message too. But the words were clear and the groups didn't use **offensive**[4] language. Turn the radio down so your mother and I can't hear it. I'm sure that music is hurting your ears as well as your brain. Now would you please turn it off and get ready for school? You'd better hurry up!"

Section 3 Sandy walked into the bathroom. She turned on the shower. At first the water felt cold. This helped her wake up. Then the water got hotter. "This shower feels great," she thought. "A place where I can be alone and sing. No one bothers me in here." She grabbed the soap and washed thoroughly; then she shampooed her hair. If she stayed in the shower too long, her mom or dad usually banged on the door to **hassle**[5] her. Time to get out of the shower. She grabbed a towel and dried off.

After her shower, Sandy brushed her hair. She put on her old green T-shirt and some jeans and wrapped her sweatshirt around her shoulders. Then she put on her makeup and a pair of earrings.

Section 4 She looked at the clock again. It was late, and she didn't know what to have for breakfast. She poured a glass of milk and ate a piece of toast while standing by the sink. Her mother, Jane, came into the kitchen.

"Sandy, why don't you sit down and eat breakfast? It isn't healthy to eat breakfast standing up."

---

[1] **like a bullet:** very fast
[2] **weird:** odd, strange
[3] **rhythm:** a regular, repeated pattern of sounds in music, speech, or text
[4] **offensive:** rude; likely to upset people
[5] **hassle:** to argue with; to bother; to annoy

"I know, Mom, but I'm already late for school. I don't have time to sit down and eat."

Section 5 "Did you finish your homework, dear?"

"Yes."

"Do you have your flute?"

"Uh-huh."

"And your lunch?"

"Yup."

"Did you brush your teeth?"

"Mom, I haven't finished eating breakfast yet. I'll brush my teeth after I finish eating."

"You should brush your teeth when you wake up and then brush them again after breakfast. Sandy, why are you wearing that old T-shirt? It has a hole in it. I know you have some nice blouses in your closet."

Section 6 "Mom, please stop."

"Stop what, dear?"

"Stop **nagging**[6] me."

"Sandy, are you wearing eyeliner?"

"Yes, Mom, I've been wearing eyeliner for months. Isn't it pretty? It's called French Lilac Blue. I just love it." Sandy pretended not to notice that her mother was a little **annoyed.**[7]

"Sandy Finch, you're too young to wear that much makeup. Please go upstairs and wash it off."

Section 7 "Mom, I'm fifteen. I'm old enough to wear makeup. Believe me, all the girls at school wear makeup. They have tattoos and pierced ears, noses, tongues, and everything. Listen, Mom, I don't have time to talk about this now. I'm late and I've got to go. See you later." Sandy kissed her mother quickly on the cheek, picked up her school books, and ran out of the house.

Section 8 Sandy ran to catch the bus. While she was running, she thought about her older brother, Bill. Bill was away at college, and Sandy heard from him often. When they talked, they shared their problems. But she hadn't heard from him for a while. She missed him. Since Bill had gone to college, her mother nagged her much more than before. And she was arguing with her mother a lot more than usual too.

---

[6] **nag:** to bother constantly
[7] **annoyed:** upset; a little angry

Reviewing What You've Read

A. Think about Sandy's typical weekday morning. What happens first (1st)? What happens second (2nd); third (3rd); fourth (4th); fifth (5th); sixth (6th); seventh (7th); eighth (8th); ninth (9th); tenth (10th)? Put the sentences in the correct order.

_____ Sandy makes a quick breakfast.

_____ Sandy kisses her mother good-bye.

first The clock radio goes on at 6:15 A.M.

_____ Sandy begins to sing along with her favorite music.

_____ Sandy gets dressed.

_____ Sandy takes a shower.

_____ Sandy wakes up like a bullet.

_____ Sandy puts on makeup and earrings.

_____ Sandy's mother nags her about makeup.

_____ Sandy catches a bus to school.

B. What happened this morning at Sandy's house? Read these statements. Are they true (*T*) or false (*F*)? Correct the statements that are false.

Example ___T___ *Sandy woke up at 6:15 A.M.*

_____

___F___ *Sandy put on a red T-shirt.*
Sandy put on a green T-shirt.

_____ **1.** Sandy's father woke up to his favorite music.

_____

_____ **2.** Sandy took a shower before school.

_____

_____ **3.** Sandy put on a skirt to wear to school.

_____

_____ **4.** Sandy ate breakfast at the dining room table.

_____

_____ **5.** Sandy had a glass of milk and a piece of toast for breakfast.

_____

_____ **6.** Sandy's mother was annoyed because Sandy was wearing a lot of makeup.

_____

_____ **7.** Sandy kissed her mother good-bye on the cheek.

_____

_____ **8.** Sandy's mother asked a lot of questions.

_____

_____ **9.** Sandy picked up her school books and walked to school.

_____

Discussing What You've Read

A. Sandy and her parents had a few disagreements this morning. What did they disagree about? Circle all the words that are related to their disagreements.

homework	Sandy's brother	earrings	breakfast
clothing	setting the table	smoking	dating
friends	brushing her teeth	makeup	tattoos
drugs	going to bed too late	noise	respect
money	making the bed	music	movies
pierced ears	offensive language	being late	hair

B. Work in groups of three or four students. Look at the words each of you circled. Are they the same? Then discuss these questions with your group.

    1. In your opinion, which family disagreements are the most serious? Explain your answer.

    2. Which disagreements do you think are most common in families?

C. With your group, discuss and answer these questions.

    1. Sandy's mother said, "Sandy Finch, you're too young to wear that much makeup" (Section 6). Why did Sandy's mother call her "Sandy Finch"?

2. Sandy's father doesn't like rock music. He doesn't like loud music and he dislikes music with offensive language. What kinds of music do you think he might like? Check (✔) more than one answer.

_____ jazz	_____ rock and roll	_____ opera
_____ classical	_____ blues	_____ rap
_____ country	_____ pop	_____ folk
_____ heavy metal	_____ disco/dance	_____ reggae
_____ gospel	_____ bluegrass	_____ salsa

3. What is "Green Waves"? _____

4. What are the names of musical groups or musical performers that you like?

_____   _____

_____   _____

D. Look back at the "Reading Carefully" exercise on page 2. Discuss the questions with your group.

Writing about What You've Read

A. What do you know about Sandy? Her mother? Her father? Her brother? Look back at the story and complete the chart.

Sandy	Sandy's mother	Sandy's father	Sandy's brother
15 years old plays flute			

B. Compare your answers with a classmate's. Add information to your chart to make it as complete as possible. (As you read the rest of the chapters, you may add more information to this chart.)

Connecting the Story to Your Life

Compare your life with Sandy's life.

1. Sandy wakes up to a **clock radio** every weekday morning.

   a. How do you wake up in the morning?

   b. What time do you wake up on weekdays?

   c. What time do you get out of bed on weekends?

2. Every morning when she wakes up, Sandy **sings along with** her favorite music.

   a. Do you sing along with your favorite music?

   b. What is your favorite music to sing along with?

   c. When do you sing along with your favorite music?

   d. Where do you sing along with your favorite music?

3. Sandy's father **can't stand** the music that Sandy listens to.

   a. What kind of music can't you stand listening to?

   b. What kind of music does your family listen to? Can you stand it?

4. Sandy ate breakfast **standing up.** She said that she didn't have time to **sit down.**

   a. How do you eat breakfast: standing up or sitting down?

   b. How much time do you usually spend eating breakfast?

5. Sandy **had** toast and milk **for** breakfast.

   a. What do you usually have for breakfast on weekdays?

   b. What do you usually have for breakfast on weekends?

6. Sandy **argued with** her parents **about** several things.

   a. Do you think that it is acceptable to argue with your family? Why? Why not?

   b. What do you argue about with your family? Do you argue about different things with different family members? (Look at the list of topics on page 6 to help you answer these questions.)

Building Your Vocabulary

A. Chapter 1 includes a lot of useful vocabulary. Look at the following page. What do the highlighted words and expressions mean? Circle the letter of the correct answer. Then answer the questions that follow.

1. Sandy's mother asked a lot of questions. At one point, Sandy said, "Stop **nagging** me." Later Sandy thought her "mother **nagged** her much more than before." What was Sandy's mother doing?
   a. She was telling Sandy over and over again to do things.
   b. She was giving Sandy helpful suggestions and advice.
   c. She was arguing with Sandy in an angry voice.

   Who nags you? What do they nag you about? _____

   _____

2. Sandy's mother was **annoyed** with Sandy. What does this mean?
   a. Her mother was proud of Sandy.
   b. Her mother was upset with Sandy.
   c. Her mother was happy with Sandy.

   Who gets annoyed with you? Why? _____

   _____

3. Sandy **pretended** not to notice that her mother was annoyed. What did Sandy do?
   a. Sandy made believe that her mother was not annoyed.
   b. Sandy believed that her mother was angry.
   c. Sandy noticed that her mother was annoyed.

   Describe a situation when you pretended not to notice something. _____

   _____

4. Sandy's father said, **"You'd better hurry up."** What did he mean?
   a. He wanted Sandy to move faster. He didn't want her to be late for school.
   b. He wanted Sandy to eat her breakfast sitting down at the table.
   c. He thought Sandy was feeling better now that she was awake.

   How often do you have to hurry up in the morning? _____

   _____

5. Sandy often **hears from** her older brother, Bill. What does this mean?
   a. Bill calls Sandy on the telephone or writes her letters.
   b. Bill comes home from college on the weekends to talk to Sandy.
   c. Sandy listens to Bill when he's in town during the holidays.

   Who do you hear from often? _____

   _____

B. Chapter 1 includes many phrasal verbs. A **phrasal verb** is made up of two or more parts that function as a single verb. *Hear from* is an example of a phrasal verb.

Note the differences between these phrasal verbs:

turn on = start   turn off = stop   turn up = increase   turn down = decrease

1. Think about a typical morning at Sandy's house. Use *on*, *off*, *up*, or *down* to complete these sentences about the story. Identify the section of the story that helped you complete the sentence.

> **Example**   *Sandy's father wanted her to turn the music off . (Section   2)*

    a. When her father complained, Sandy turned the radio _____ rather than turning it _____. (Section _____)

    b. Sandy wanted to turn the radio _____ so her father could hear Green Waves. (Section _____)

    c. Sandy turned the shower _____ after she walked into the bathroom. (Section _____)

    d. After she washed her hair, Sandy turned the shower _____. (Section _____)

2. Look around your classroom and answer these questions.

    a. What classroom objects can you turn *on* and *off* <u>but</u> not turn *up* or *down*?

    _____

    _____

    b. What classroom objects can you turn *on* and *off* <u>and</u> turn *up* or *down*?

    _____

    _____

Jane and Steve

Getting Ready to Read

A. Look at the chapter title and the illustration.

1. What do you see in the illustration?

2. Where are Jane and Steve?

3. What are they doing?

4. What do you think they are going to talk about?

B. In Chapter 1, Sandy and her parents had some disagreements. Do you think the cause of the disagreements is a generation gap? Read "What's a Generation Gap?" on page 12. Is there a generation gap in Sandy's family? Explain your answer to your classmates.

What's a Generation Gap?

As children become teenagers, families often experience a generation gap. Teenagers want to be independent, make their own decisions, and do things on their own. They want to separate themselves from their parents. This separation can be painful for both parents and children. During this time, children may need to reject family traditions or beliefs. They may also reject their parents' opinions.

Although the separation may sometimes be painful, it is a necessary step in a teenager's growth and development. Teens become adults as they begin to have their own opinions and develop their own identities. The generation gap that occurs is a natural process.

Families experience different types of generation gap problems. Sometimes parents don't like the music that their children listen to or the clothes they wear. Parents often disapprove of some of the food that their children choose to eat. They may also disapprove of the TV programs and movies that their children watch. These days some parents are uncomfortable with computers and video games, yet their children love using technology. Sometimes children don't want the advice that their parents give them. They don't like their parents' rules either. These types of disagreements often create a generation gap.

A generation gap, created by these differences of opinion, may exist between children and their parents, their grandparents, or even older brothers and sisters. A generation gap may exist between other groups too. For example, there can be a generation gap between students and teachers, young and older musicians, or traditional and modern artists. People all over the world experience a generation gap in some way.

Reading Carefully

Before you begin to read the story, your teacher will ask the class to "count off" the question numbers 1, 2, and 3. The number you count off is the question that you will answer. Put a check (✔) next to the question. Think about your question as you read the story. Underline words, phrases, or sentences in the story that will help you answer your question.

_____ 1. What aspects of the generation gap are Jane and Steve discussing?

_____ 2. How do Jane and Steve plan to solve their problems with Sandy?

_____ 3. What problems have Jane and Steve had with their son, Bill?

CHAPTER 2 | *Jane and Steve*

Section 1   After Sandy had gone to school, Jane Finch sat down to drink her coffee. It was quiet at the table. She sipped her coffee slowly and began to read the newspaper. She was **distracted.**[1] She was trying to read, but she was thinking about Sandy. Her husband came in to join her.

"Would you like some coffee, Steve?" asked Jane.

"No thanks, honey, my stomach has been acting up. I feel like there are ten thousand **knots in my stomach.**[2] It's probably that awful music that wakes me up every morning. I can't stand the music Sandy listens to on the radio. I don't think I'm old-fashioned, but hearing that tuneless, offensive language over and over **makes my blood boil.**[3] There is no message to the music either. I can't believe that Sandy really likes it."

"You know, honey, different generations have different tastes," said Jane. "Remember some of the music we used to listen to?"

Steve smiled as he remembered. "You're right. Maybe I'll just have some apple juice and toast today. Maybe eating breakfast will help me get rid of some of the knots in my stomach."

"I'll get you some juice," she said, starting to get up.

"That's okay," said Steve. "I'll get it. You're reading."

"I'm not really reading. I'm distracted. I've been thinking about Sandy too."

Section 2   Steve went to the kitchen to prepare his breakfast and returned to sit down with his wife. She gave him a section of the newspaper and they both tried to read in silence for a few moments. Then Jane looked up.

"Did you notice how much makeup our fifteen-year-old daughter was wearing this morning? When I asked her about it, she told me that she's been wearing eyeliner for months. I can't believe I never noticed. I suppose we should feel lucky because makeup is our biggest problem with her. I've noticed other teenagers walking around town with tattoos and rings all over their bodies: from their eyebrows, their noses . . . what's next? I suppose they're expressing their identity. It's very different from how we expressed ourselves."

"Is it so different?" asked Steve. "I remember when I **defied**[4] my parents and grew my hair long. Remember, it was so long I put it in a ponytail!"

---

[1] **distracted:** not paying attention
[2] **knots in (one's) stomach:** to feel nervous, uneasy inside
[3] **make (one's) blood boil:** to make angry
[4] **defy:** to refuse to obey; to oppose or resist

"And you almost got **expelled**[5] from school," added Jane.

"That's true. But my ponytail could be changed. These tattoos are permanent. It is different. Tattoos seem **radical**[6] to me."

"Actually, tattoos can be removed," said Jane. "Not as easily as a ponytail, but they can be removed. It seems that every generation has a need for self-expression. I wonder what our grandchildren will do in the next generation."

Section 3   "What worries me about today's music," said Steve, "is that it has a very negative message. Sandy hears that message, and it could have a negative influence on her. I don't know what's happening to our little girl. She's changing and I'm worried about her. Makeup, terrible music. Who knows what will be next? We need to have a talk with her. The newspaper often has stories about teenagers who are in trouble and their parents hardly know anything about their problems."

"Oh, I don't think the music is so terrible; I like it," said Jane.

"You like it? I can't believe it."

Section 4   "You know I like loud, wild music. When we first began dating, you didn't like *my* musical taste either. Anyway, you're right. We need to speak with Sandy, have a talk with her," said Jane, nodding her head. "Remember the problems we had with Bill when he was her age? Oh, so many problems, and his music was much worse. And he played it all night long. I remember when he was up all night listening to music and we didn't even know it. I don't want to have all *those* problems again. The difference between Sandy and Bill is that we can talk to Sandy. Bill would never talk to us. He would never tell us what he was thinking or what he was doing. Even now, he still doesn't communicate with us."

"You're right. We haven't heard a word from Bill lately. I hope he's doing all right in school," Steve said.

"Of course he is. He's a good student; he's intelligent and capable. I wonder if he has called Sandy lately. He usually **keeps in touch**[7] with her," said Jane.

"Let's check with Sandy. Maybe she knows something we don't. You know, Jane, you're always so sure that Bill is a good student, that he's intelligent and capable. But college isn't easy, is it? I think that Bill may be staying away from us because he doesn't want us to know that he's **less than perfect**,"[8] said Steve.

"That's very possible. We need to connect with Bill. We haven't talked to him in such a long time. I worry unless I know everything is okay."

"Well, let's make sure everything is okay, and then we'll both feel better," said Steve.

---

[5] **expel:** to send away
[6] **radical:** very nontraditional; very different from normal
[7] **keep in touch:** to stay in contact
[8] **less than perfect:** having some mistakes or problems; not perfect

Section 5   Jane looked up at the clock in the kitchen. "Oh dear, I'm late!" she said. "Let's not forget to have a talk with Sandy and to ask her about Bill. Right now I have to run or I'll be late for my first appointment." She kissed her husband quickly, picked up her briefcase, and started to go out the door.

"Bye, honey," said Jane.

"Bye, dear," answered Steve.

Jane Finch got into her car and drove to work. She worked as a **chiropractor**[9] in an office near her home, helping people with body pain and injury. As she was driving to work, she was thinking. She was thinking about Sandy and Bill. Bill and Sandy. Her two children. They were each growing up and they were changing. They were becoming adults, and, in her opinion, they needed her.

Section 6   "Sandy is becoming a woman," she thought. "Soon she'll be dating and going out all the time. I want her to continue to do well in school. I want her to continue practicing her flute. She's a good student and she's very musical. I don't want her to forget about school and music. Some girls waste their time talking on the phone day and night and watching TV. How can I tell her these things? I wish my mother had told me. And yet I don't want her to get angry with me. If I'm too strict, she'll **rebel**.[10] I always worry that she'll rebel and go too far. So many young girls get wild. They drop out of school and get into all kinds of trouble. Sometimes they even run away from home. I thought it would be easier to raise a daughter, but sons and daughters are both difficult; they're just difficult in different ways. Bill has his problems and Sandy has hers. I must keep talking to her, so that she grows up with a sense of values, with self-esteem. Could she find that on her own? Does Bill have a sense of values? Does he still need my **guidance**?[11] I couldn't really talk to him when he was living at home. He always thought I was nagging."

"Mothers need to guide their children even though it may seem like they're nagging. Someday my children will be glad that I told them how important it is to study, to stay on the right track. I believe in the old saying: Mother knows best."

Section 7   Jane knew what she wanted to say to Sandy, what she had to say to Sandy. She was so glad that she and Sandy could still talk things over. After she had decided that she was going to have a talk with Sandy, she felt better. She reached over and turned on the radio. One of her favorite songs was playing, and she began singing along. Yes, she felt better. Mother does know best.

---

[9] **chiropractor:** a doctor who treats illness by pressing on or moving bones
[10] **rebel:** to fight against a person or group in power
[11] **guidance:** help, advice

Reviewing What You've Read

A. Look back at the "Reading Carefully" exercise on page 12. Form groups in which at least one student has answered each of the questions. Discuss the answers and take notes. Work together to construct complete answers. Refer back to the story if necessary.

1. What aspects of the generation gap are Jane and Steve discussing?	2. How do Jane and Steve plan to solve their problems with Sandy?	3. What problems have Jane and Steve had with their son, Bill?

B. What happened in the story? Read these statements. Are they true *(T)* or false *(F)*? Correct the statements that are false.

_____ **1.** Jane is having trouble reading the newspaper today. She is very distracted.

_____

_____ **2.** Jane prepared breakfast for her husband, Steve.

_____

_____ **3.** Steve Finch had apple juice and toast for breakfast.

_____

_____ **4.** Steve is upset this morning. He has knots in his stomach.

_____

_____ **5.** According to Jane, teenagers express their identity in the same way.

_____

_____ **6.** Jane works as a chiropractor in an office far from their home.

_____

_____ **7.** Jane and Steve have not heard from Bill for a while.

_____

_____ **8.** Jane thinks that it's more difficult to raise a daughter than a son.

_____

Reading between the Lines

A. When you read, you usually understand the information on the page. You might also notice additional information that is not on the page. Recognizing this additional information is called **reading between the lines,** or **making inferences.** Look at the paragraph below. Read between the lines to find out the answers to the questions.

> *I looked outside. The sky was gray and the streets were wet. A young man, wearing a heavy coat, was carrying an open umbrella and walking carefully. I noticed a car driving by. The headlights were on and the driver was driving slowly.*

How was the weather? How do you know? Underline the words that give you information about the weather.

B. Read the following true statements about the story. How do you know this additional information is true? Go back to the story and find the information that helps you read between the lines. Write complete answers to these questions.

1. Steve and Jane are not eating breakfast in the kitchen. How do you know?

Steve went to the kitchen to make breakfast. Then he returned to Jane.

_____

2. Jane and Steve have had problems with their son, Bill, since he was fifteen years old. How do you know?

_____

_____

3. Bill wore headphones to bed when he lived at home. How do you know?

_____

_____

4. Chiropractors sometimes have patients who have been in car accidents. How do you know?

_____

_____

5. Jane is proud of her daughter, Sandy. How can you tell?

_____

_____

6. Jane is nervous about talking with Sandy. How can you tell?

_____

_____

7. Steve thinks that Bill might be having problems in college. How do you know?

_____

_____

8. Sandy and Bill have different personalities. How can you tell?

_____

_____

Discussing What You've Read

Work in groups of three or four students. Discuss these questions, and be prepared to share your answers with your classmates.

1. What problems are Jane and Steve having with Sandy? In your opinion, are these problems major or minor? Explain your answer.

2. Do Jane and Steve feel the same way about Sandy's favorite music? How does Jane feel? How does Steve feel?

3. Why does Jane want to talk to Sandy? What is Jane planning to say to Sandy?

4. Jane wants her children to grow up with self-esteem and a sense of values.

    a. What does Jane mean by "self-esteem"?

    b. What does Jane mean by "a sense of values"?

    c. Can Sandy and Bill develop self-esteem and a sense of values on their own? Or do they need their parents' guidance? What is your opinion?

5. How do Jane and Steve think their son is doing in school? Do they share the same opinion?

Writing about What You've Read

A. In Chapter 1, we met Jane Finch, Sandy's mother. In Chapter 2, we learned more about her. Turn back to the "Writing about What You've Read" exercise on page 7 and look at the list you made describing Jane. What new things have you learned about her in this chapter? Complete the list below.

1. *Jane likes to read the newspaper at breakfast time.*

2. _____

3. _____

4. _____

5. _____

Compare your list about Jane with a classmate's list. Add to your list, if necessary, to make it as complete as possible.

_____

B. Write a short paragraph describing Jane Finch. Remember to include information from both Chapter 1 and Chapter 2 in your description.

_____

_____

_____

_____

_____

Connecting the Story to Your Life

A. Compare your life with the Finch family's life.

1. Jane said, "Every generation has a need for self-expression."

    a. How did your parents express themselves when they were young?

    b. How are teenagers expressing themselves in your community today?

    c. How do you think the next generation will express itself?

2. In the Finch home, everybody prepares their own breakfast. Who usually prepares your breakfast?

B. Look at the activities listed below. Use the chart to separate the activities into three lists: activities which cause major generation gap problems in your family or community; activities which cause minor problems; and activities which do not cause problems. Use a dictionary if you need help.

listening to music	dating	eating junk food
watching too much TV	smoking	changing hairstyles
driving a car	going out unchaperoned	going to college
wearing makeup	staying out late with friends	talking on the phone too long
using slang expressions	using technology	getting expelled from school
getting tattoos	choosing friends	marrying a person from a
dropping out of school	drinking alcohol	different background
using offensive language	running away from home	expressing oneself

Major problems between generations	Minor problems between generations	No problems between generations

C. Can you think of other generation gap problems? Add them to your chart in the correct columns.

Building Your Vocabulary

A. Read these sentences. What do the highlighted words and expressions mean? Circle the letter of the correct answer. If you need help, look in the section indicated in parentheses.

1. Steve Finch's stomach **acts up** at breakfast time. (Section 1)
   a. His stomach is upset in the morning.
   b. His stomach is full after breakfast.
   c. His stomach makes funny noises when he eats.

2. Newspapers often have articles about teenagers who **are in trouble.** (Section 3)
   a. The articles talk about teenagers who are having problems.
   b. The articles talk about teenagers who help the community.
   c. The articles talk about teenagers who are excellent students.

3. Jane and Steve want to **have a talk with** Sandy. (Sections 4 & 5)
   a. They often speak with each other about Sandy.
   b. They need to speak with Sandy about serious topics.
   c. They often speak with their friends about Sandy.

4. Jane looked at the clock and then said, "I **have to run.**" (Section 5)
   a. "I'm going to the gym to get some exercise."
   b. "I'm late so I need to hurry up and go."
   c. "Instead of walking, I'll run."

5. Jane is worried that Sandy will **get angry with** her. (Section 6)
   a. Jane thinks that Sandy will be hungry.
   b. Jane thinks that Sandy will worry about her.
   c. Jane thinks that Sandy will be mad at her.

6. Jane wants her children to grow up with **self-esteem.** (Section 6)
   a. She wants them to feel good about themselves.
   b. She wants them to do well in school and work.
   c. She wants them to worry about themselves.

7. Steve and Jane want Sandy to **stay on the right track.** (Section 6)
   a. They want her to be successful and to be involved in school activities.
   b. They want her to take the train instead of the bus to school every day.
   c. They want her to be on the school track team.

8. Jane is happy that she can **talk things over** with Sandy. (Section 7)
   a. Jane and Sandy discuss important issues.
   b. Jane and Sandy talk on the phone over the weekend.
   c. Jane and Sandy often argue over differences of opinion.

B. Complete the sentences with the correct expression.

act up	have a talk with	have to run
be in trouble	get angry with	

1. At the party last night, Sandy ate a lot of potato chips, sandwiches, cookies, candy, and cake. She ate too much. She hopes that her stomach doesn't _____ _____ .

2. I've been very worried about my sister. She isn't sleeping well. She seems unhappy. I need to _____ her. Maybe I can help her.

3. My brother might _____ with my parents. He came home very late last night.

4. Before school, there are a lot of chores to do around the house: I have to make my bed, clean up, make breakfast, and get ready for school. By the time I'm finished, it's usually so late that I say, "I _____. Bye."

5. When you read about the environment, do you _____ corporations that pollute the air, water, and land?

C. The English language has many compound words. **Compound words** use two or more words to express one idea. There are three types of compound words: closed compounds, hyphenated compounds, and open compounds.

   1. A **closed compound** is a combination of two words that are now spelled as one word. An example of a closed compound word is *newspaper*. Look at these closed compounds from Chapters 1 and 2. Separate the two words with a slash.

   Example   *news / paper*

   eyeliner   sweatshirt   earrings   homework
   ponytail   weekday   eyebrows   upstairs
   briefcase   breakfast   makeup   everything
   bathroom

   A **hyphenated compound** is a combination of words joined by one or more hyphens. Examples of hyphenated compounds from Chapters 1 and 2 are:

   old-fashioned   self-expression   self-esteem

   An **open compound** is a combination of words that express one idea, but remain separate words. Examples of open compounds from Chapters 1 and 2 are:

   apple juice   school books

   2. Can you think of other compound words? With a partner, make a list of some compound words that you have used.

   a. _____   **d.** _____

   b. _____   **e.** _____

   c. _____   **f.** _____

Sharing Secrets

Getting Ready to Read

A. Look at the chapter title and the illustration.

   1. Where are Sandy and her friend?

   2. What are they talking about?

   3. What do you think they were doing before they took a break?

B. **Scan** Section 15 of the story.

   1. Who does Sandy meet?

   2. From what you know about Sandy's mother and father, will they be happy about who she has met? Why or why not?

C. You can learn a little more about the chapter by **reading the first sentence** of a few sections. Start with Section 1. Begin by reading the question. Then **scan** the first sentence of the section to find the answer. Write down your answer. Continue to the next section. Remember to work quickly!

1. Section 1: *Where* is Sandy?

_____

2. Section 3: *What* has Sandy noticed lately?

_____

3. Section 5: *What* kind of friend is Autumn?

_____

4. Section 7: *What* don't Sandy and Autumn like to do?

_____

5. Section 9: *What* advice did Autumn give Sandy?

_____

6. Section 11: *Who* are Autumn and Sandy talking about?

_____

7. Section 13: *Who* does Sandy see when she gets to her locker?

_____

D. What do you know about Sandy now that you didn't know before you scanned the chapter?

1. _____

2. _____

3. _____

Reading Carefully

Read the story carefully. As you read, think about the following questions. Underline words, phrases, or sentences in the story that help you answer the questions.

1. In what ways is Autumn similar to Sandy? In what ways is she different?

2. What secrets do Autumn and Sandy share? What secrets don't they share?

3. What kind of a person is Paul?

CHAPTER 3 | *Sharing Secrets*

Section 1   At school, Sandy was usually very busy. She studied hard and enjoyed being with her friends. During lunchtime, she often went to the library with her best friend, Autumn. They sat together and did their homework or worked on research for class projects.

Sandy and Autumn were in the same grade, even though Autumn was a year older than Sandy. Autumn was from Japan. She took ESL[1] classes her first year in the States, so she was a year behind in school. Her real name was Akiko, but when she arrived in the United States and started school, she changed it to Autumn. On her first day of school, Autumn had met Sandy, and they were still the best of friends. They always helped each other with homework and enjoyed talking about their plans together.

Section 2   After school, both girls participated in many activities. They were in the school orchestra; Sandy played the flute and Autumn played the cello. Sandy worked on the school newspaper too. She also played basketball with Autumn and some other friends. Sandy liked school. She was a good student and she had a few good friends. She was not as popular as Samantha. She was not as beautiful either. Samantha was the most beautiful girl in the school. But Sandy was plain and most of the time that was okay.

Section 3   Lately, she had noticed that she was changing. Everything used to be simple. She had always listened to her mother and father. She had never disagreed with them in the past. Yet lately it seemed that everything they said upset her. She wanted to wear makeup, but they didn't like her makeup. She wanted to listen to music, but they didn't like her music. She loved music. *Her* kind of music.

Section 4   Life was growing more **complicated.**[2] Sandy discussed this with Autumn. She explained to Autumn that her parents didn't like her makeup or her music and that they seemed to be getting very **strict.**[3] Autumn's parents sometimes seemed more lenient; Autumn had her own car and could drive anytime. Sandy knew that her parents would never let her drive at night by herself. Yet Autumn's parents made her study on Saturday nights. Sandy didn't tell *her* parents about this. She didn't want to give them any ideas!

Section 5   Autumn and Sandy shared many secrets and trusted each other completely.

---

[1] ESL: English as a Second Language
[2] **complicated:** not easy to understand
[3] **strict:** inflexible about rules

Sandy often confided in Autumn; she told her about the secret telephone conversations she had with Bill. Because Autumn was an only child, she liked hearing about Sandy's brother.

Sandy didn't tell anyone that Autumn had a boyfriend. Autumn's parents would not permit her to date. They also insisted that Autumn attend Japanese school on Saturdays. During lunch breaks, she visited her boyfriend, Jackson, at The Soda Jerk, an ice cream shop nearby. Jackson worked there making sundaes, malts, and ice cream cones. The first time he saw Autumn, he was **hooked.**[4] It was **love at first sight.**[5] Sandy often listened to Autumn describing Jackson. He was a real **comedian,**[6] always making jokes and making Autumn laugh. After seeing Jackson, Autumn usually shared his jokes with Sandy.

Section 6   "What do you find at the end of everything?" Autumn asked Sandy.

"I don't know. What?"

"The letter *g*. Ha, ha," laughed Autumn.

"Autumn, that is the oldest joke. I've heard that joke a million times. Did Jackson tell you that?"

"Yes! I love all the jokes he tells me. I'm always laughing when we're together." Autumn suddenly looked sad.

"What's the matter, Autumn?" asked Sandy.

"I wish I could really go out with Jackson, not just see him secretly. I rarely lie to my parents, but I have to lie about Jackson."

"I understand," said Sandy, "but you're lucky. At least you have a boyfriend."

"I feel lucky. And he is so cute and smart and funny. I really like him. I just wish I didn't have to keep secrets from my parents."

Section 7   "I don't like keeping secrets either. I know what you mean. My brother, Bill, has been calling me, and he doesn't want me to tell my parents that he's called."

"Why not?" asked Autumn.

"Well, he's having a really hard time in school. He's failing one of his classes. It's a really tough class and Bill isn't doing well. I'm worried about him."

"Maybe your parents could help him. He should probably talk to them. What class is it?"

"It's an advanced math class. Math was never his best subject," answered Sandy.

---

[4] **hooked:** intensely interested; to like something a lot
[5] **love at first sight:** instant, immediate love
[6] **comedian:** a person who tells funny stories; a joker

"Isn't he a good student? He always seemed like a really intelligent guy to me," said Autumn.

Section 8   "That's **just an act,**"[7] said Sandy. "Bill has a very difficult time studying. He doesn't know how to sit down and work things out. He has a really hard time concentrating. You know how you and I spend hours at the library? We help each other work things out and solve a lot of homework problems together. Bill can't do that. He won't let anybody know that he isn't perfect. He thinks he has to do everything himself. That's why he doesn't want me to say anything to my mom and dad, but they need to know. I promised him I wouldn't tell them, so I'm telling you. What should I do? His grades are very low, and if he fails this class, he'll be in real trouble. My parents will be so upset."

Section 9   "If you promised him, you can't tell your parents. But he sounds like he needs help."

"You're right, Autumn. He's mentioned dropping out of school, and I'm so worried because my parents would feel terrible. I just don't know what to do."

"I don't get it. Why does he have to drop out? He's only failing one class," said Autumn.

"Well, it's complicated. You see, he feels like he just doesn't **fit in**[8] at college. He's a very quiet guy, a loner who doesn't like to party too much. He likes to sit at home, listen to music, and draw. He's kind of a dreamer."

"Sandy, do you think he's **depressed?**"[9] asked Autumn in a quiet voice.

"I'm not really sure," said Sandy. "When I ask him, sometimes he says no, but sometimes he doesn't really answer me."

"That's brave of you to ask him," said Autumn.

Section 10   "I want to know. He's my brother, and if he's in trouble, I want to help him," Sandy said seriously. "He said that college isn't the right place for him; he doesn't like to study. He sounds so unhappy. But I can't tell my parents because they go crazy when they hear anything is not perfect," said Sandy.

"That's probably why he doesn't **confide**[10] in them," said Autumn. "You know, Sandy, this is a serious problem. Bill is in trouble, and he needs help. Maybe more help than you can give him by yourself."

"Well, maybe we shouldn't have these secret talks, but I'm worried about him. It's so awful when you have to keep secrets. I hate secrets," said Sandy with a sad expression on her face.

---

[7] **just an act:** not real; only pretending
[8] **fit in:** to be accepted by other people in a group
[9] **depressed:** very sad
[10] **confide:** to tell secrets to someone

Section 11   "I do too," smiled Autumn, "but I'm glad you told me about Bill. My problem with Jackson doesn't seem so bad now."

Sandy smiled at her friend. "I'm happy for you, Autumn. Jackson is a great guy. But I hope you can tell me a funnier joke next time. I think you need to stop thinking about Jackson so much because if your parents find out, you're going to have a really big problem."

"You're right. Listen, I'd better get going. I'll talk to you tonight. I'll call you at about eight."

"Okay. And thanks for listening," said Sandy.

"Sure," said Autumn, waving good-bye.

Section 12   Sandy left Autumn and started to walk to her locker. Autumn was lucky to be in love. Sandy hoped that someday she would be in love. Sandy was distracted. She did not want to think about her schoolwork right now. And she didn't want to worry about her brother. She was thinking about music and a boy. A boy named Paul. She didn't even know him, but she had seen him and she knew his name. Paul was older than she was. And he was taller too! He was the tallest player on the basketball team. After seeing him play basketball, she always looked for him on the school yard and in the library. She wanted to meet him. But she didn't tell anyone. It was her secret.

Section 13   When Sandy got to her locker, she looked up and there was Paul. He was walking down the hall with a smile on his face. "He's always smiling," thought Sandy. Then she saw that Samantha was walking right next to him. Sandy did not want to **stare**.[11] Were they really walking together? Sandy's heart was beating so fast. She forced herself to look away. Slowly she picked up her books and closed her locker. She looked down.

Section 14   As Sandy began to walk away from her locker, she was looking down at the floor. She walked right into Paul.

"Oh, excuse me, I'm so sorry," **stammered**[12] Sandy nervously.

"No, it was my fault. I wasn't looking where I was going," answered Paul with a sweet smile.

"Hi, Sandy," said Samantha, who looked as beautiful as ever.

Section 15   They all stood together for a moment. No one spoke, and then, luckily, Samantha saved the day.

"Paul, do you know Sandy?"

"Uh, no, I don't think so, but I've seen her around."

"Well, Paul, this is Sandy Finch. Sandy, this is Paul Good."

"Hi," they both said shyly at the same time.

---

[11] **stare:** to look at someone or something for a long time without moving your eyes

[12] **stammer:** to speak with many pauses or repetitions

"We'd better go, Paul," said Samantha. "We're already late."

"Hey, aren't you the girl who plays the flute in the orchestra?" asked Paul.

"Yes, that's me," Sandy replied.

"Your flute makes a really nice sound," said Paul.

"Thanks," said Sandy.

"Well, see you around."

"Uh-huh, see you around," said Sandy.

Reviewing What You've Read

A. Look back at the "Reading Carefully" exercise on page 24. With a partner, discuss the answers to the questions.

B. What happened in the story? Read the following statements. Are they true *(T)* or false *(F)?* Correct the statements that are false.

_____ **1.** Sandy often goes to the cafeteria at lunchtime with her best friend, Autumn.

_____

_____ **2.** Sandy is involved in a lot of school activities.

_____

_____ **3.** Sandy told Autumn about her secret telephone conversations with Bill.

_____

_____ **4.** Autumn's parents have met her boyfriend, Jackson.

_____

_____ **5.** Autumn studies at a Japanese school on Sunday mornings.

_____

_____ **6.** Autumn's boyfriend is very serious.

_____

_____ **7.** Sandy told Autumn about Bill's problems in college.

_____

_____ **8.** Sandy introduced Paul to Samantha.

_____

Reading between the Lines

Read the following true statements about the story. How do you know this information is true? Go back to the story and find the information that helps you read between the lines. Write complete answers to these questions.

1. Sandy is a serious student. How do you know?

_____

_____

2. Autumn wants to fit in with her American classmates. How do you know?

_____

_____

3. Sandy's relationship with her parents is not as good as it was in the past. How can you tell?

_____

_____

4. Autumn is rebelling against her parents. How can you tell?

_____

_____

5. Bill hasn't told his parents about the problems he's having in college. How do you know?

_____

_____

6. Sandy and Bill have a good relationship. How can you tell?

_____

_____

7. Paul had noticed Sandy at school before actually meeting her. How do you know?

_____

_____

Discussing What You've Read

Work in groups of three or four students. Discuss the following questions and be prepared to share your answers with your classmates.

1. What activities are Sandy, Autumn, and Paul involved in outside of class?

   a. Do you think it is a good idea to get involved in extracurricular activities like these? Why or why not?

   b. Do you think most parents approve of these types of activities? Why or why not?

2. Autumn sees her boyfriend, Jackson, secretly.

   a. Do you think Autumn should see Jackson secretly? Why or why not?

   b. Sandy told Autumn, "You need to stop thinking about Jackson so much, because if your parents find out, you're going to have a really big problem." Do you agree with Sandy? Why or why not?

3. Autumn's parents do not permit her to go out on dates.

   a. Why do you think Autumn's parents made this rule?

   b. Do you agree with her parents' rule? Why or why not?

4. Sandy told Autumn about her secret conversations with Bill.

   a. Do you think Sandy should tell her parents about Bill's problems? Why or why not?

   b. Do you think Bill should call his parents and talk to them directly? Why or why not?

5. What difficulties is Bill having at college?

   a. What do you think he should do?

   b. How can Sandy help Bill with his problems?

6. Why did Sandy seem so nervous before meeting Paul?

   a. Do you think Paul was nervous too? Why or why not?

   b. Do you think Autumn is nervous when she's with her boyfriend? Why or why not?

Writing about What You've Read

A. Look at the following adverbs of frequency.

rarely   always   sometimes   often   never   usually

Place the adverbs of frequency in the correct order on the line below. *Always* has already been placed for you.

always
_____
100%   50%   0%

B. Complete the following sentences about Sandy and Autumn, using the correct adverb of frequency. Notice that adverbs of frequency usually come <u>after</u> the verb *be (am, are, is, was, were)* and <u>before</u> other verbs. Look back at the story to choose the correct word. The section number is listed in parentheses.

  1. Sandy is _____ very busy. (Section 1)

  2. Sandy _____ goes to the library during lunchtime. (Section 1)

  3. Sandy _____ listened to her parents in the past. (Section 3)

  4. In the past Sandy _____ disagreed with her parents. (Section 3)

  5. Autumn's parents _____ seem more lenient than Sandy's parents. (Section 4)

  6. Sandy _____ confides in Autumn. (Section 5)

  7. Jackson is _____ making jokes and making Autumn laugh. (Section 5)

  8. Autumn _____ lies to her parents. (Section 6)

  9. Math has _____ been Bill's best subject. (Section 7)

  10. Sandy _____ looks for Paul on the school yard and in the library. (Section 12)

  11. Sandy has noticed that Paul is _____ smiling. (Section 13)

C. Write five new sentences about the story using adverbs of frequency. Use information from Chapters 1, 2, and 3.

1. _____

2. _____

3. _____

4. _____

5. _____

Connecting the Story to Your Life

Compare your life with the characters' lives.

1. Sandy, Autumn, and Paul all lead very busy lives both at school and outside of school. Jane and Steve, Sandy's parents, have busy lives at work and at home too. Think about your life. Complete the chart with activities from your life. Pay close attention to the adverbs of frequency.

		At school	Outside of school
100%	always	go to English class	
	usually		make my own lunch
50%	often		
	sometimes		
	rarely		
0%	never		

2. On a separate piece of paper, write about your busy life *at* school and *outside of* school. Use the information from the chart to help you organize your ideas. Use adverbs of frequency to make your writing more descriptive and accurate. Remember to indent the first sentence of each paragraph.

Building Your Vocabulary

A. Words that have opposite meanings are called **antonyms**. Look at these antonyms:

big/small   easy/hard   like/dislike   thin/fat

Complete the crossword puzzle by finding the antonyms of the words. The section number in parentheses will help you find the antonym.

Across

2. ugly (2)
7. few (2)
8. agreed (3)
9. before (2)
12. simple (4)
13. worst (1)
16. frown (13)
17. passing (7)
18. slow (13)

Down

1. opened (13)
3. nothing (3)
4. make happy (3)
5. strict (4)
6. younger (12)
10. hated (3)
11. calmly (14)
14. shorter (12)
15. never (1)

B. Match the highlighted words and phrases with the definition or phrase that has a similar meaning.

_____ 1. Sandy didn't want **to stare** at Paul. (Section 13)

_____ 2. Paul said, **"It was my fault."** (Section 14)

_____ 3. Samantha **saved the day.** (Section 15)

_____ 4. **"See you around,"** said Sandy. (Section 15)

_____ 5. Autumn was **an only child.** (Section 5)

a. helped out

b. "See you later."

c. to look at someone or something for a long time, without looking away

d. a person without brothers or sisters

e. "It was my mistake. I was wrong."

Making Music Together

Getting Ready to Read

A. Look at the chapter title and the illustration. What do you think this chapter is about?

B. Prepare to read by **skimming** the first sentence of each section quickly to get the main idea of the chapter. Read only the first sentence of each section.

C. Now that you have previewed the text, review your answer to the first question. Do you have more information now that will make it more complete? If so, revise your answer.

Reading Carefully

Think about what you already know about this chapter. Write down one question of your own that you hope to answer when reading the chapter.

_____

Now read the story carefully. While reading, look for the answer to your question. Underline any words, phrases, or sentences in the story that will help you answer your question.

CHAPTER 4 | *Making Music Together*

Section 1   Sandy sat in her bedroom with the door closed. She was staring into the mirror. She had been staring for a long time. She was trying to see herself. Sandy was thinking and asking herself many questions.

"Who am I? Am I pretty or just plain? What is going to happen to me in life? Will I ever fall in love? Will I ever do anything important in life? What will I do? Will I help the world? Will I ever travel anywhere?" Sandy asked many questions as she continued to stare into the mirror.

Section 2   "I look so serious," she thought. She looked at her face in the mirror. It wasn't an **extraordinary**[1] face. What were the thoughts behind the serious face? Serious thoughts of sadness in the world. She thought of her brother, Bill, and she worried. But there were happy thoughts too. She remembered meeting Paul. Her serious face changed into a smile and she saw her face light up like a flaming candle, warm and bright.

Section 3   "I may not be as pretty as Samantha," she thought, "but when I smile, there is a definite improvement." Sandy laughed and thought about Paul's beautiful smile. She was happy that he knew who she was. He knew that she played the flute. But Sandy also worried that Paul was Samantha's boyfriend. Samantha was so pretty. If Samantha wanted Paul as her boyfriend, did Sandy **stand a chance?**[2]

"Well, maybe if I keep smiling and playing the flute," she thought. She smiled into the mirror and began to do her homework.

Section 4   Sandy didn't see Paul for several days. Then one Thursday morning he walked into her orchestra class. He was wearing a pair of baggy pants and a T-shirt. She was surprised to see him. He was speaking with the teacher, Mr. Gambera. Paul seemed to know Mr. Gambera well.

---

[1] **extraordinary:** unusual, outstanding
[2] **stand a chance:** to have a possibility

Section 5   "Class," said Mr. Gambera, "this is Paul Good. He writes songs and plays the guitar. He wants to sing one of his new songs for you. Maybe you'll be able to accompany him with your instruments."

Sandy was **thrilled.**[3] She thought that Paul was a basketball player. She didn't know that he liked to make music too. She was so happy. She loved to make music. She loved playing her flute and singing. Sandy loved music. Sandy sat very still, waiting to hear Paul play his song. He sang:

> When I see you smile,
> When I see your face,
> When I see you walk,
> When I see your style,
>
> Then I'm happy,
> Yes I'm happy.
> Then I'm happy,
> Oh, so happy.
>
> When the sky is dark,
> When the day is gray,
> When the flowers die
> And love goes away,
>
> Then I need you,
> Yes I need you.
> Then I need you,
> Oh I need you.
>
> You—you're the one I see through the chain-link fence.
> You—you're the essence of innocence.
> You—you can turn my world all right.
> You are a vision of silken light.

Section 6   Sandy was in a dream. The song was so romantic. And Paul sang the song in the same way he smiled: beautifully. Sandy wanted to sing with him and play the flute to accompany his guitar. Everyone in the class applauded. Sandy looked across the room to see if Autumn had also enjoyed Paul's song. Autumn was smiling. Sandy smiled too.

---

[3] **thrilled:** very excited

Section 7   "Paul has a music club that meets after school," said Mr. Gambera. "The club meets twice a week, on Wednesday and Thursday afternoons, right here in the music room. It's a serious **commitment**.[4] If you're interested in joining the music club, sign this list." He gave a sign-up sheet to one of the students to pass around. Sandy waited to write her name on the sign-up sheet. She wanted to join the music club and sing and play with Paul.

"Who was he? Males are so different from females," thought Sandy. "This guy is such a mystery to me. I have no idea how he thinks." Sandy didn't know very much about guys. She knew her dad and her brother, Bill, but Paul was different. Paul was special. Maybe he would be that special new person in her life.

Section 8   After class, Sandy left the classroom singing . . . "Then I need you, make me happy." She was **walking on a cloud**.[5] Suddenly, she saw the clock in the hall. It was late. She started to run. She didn't want to be late. Whenever she was late, her mother got upset. She didn't want her mother to be upset, because she wanted to talk to her about the music club. She ran faster. If her mother was in a good mood, maybe she would be happy about the music club. She wished she could talk to Autumn. Autumn usually had helpful **advice**.[6] She would call Autumn tonight. She ran faster.

Then I'm Happy

words by Nina Rosen
music by Margarita Montes

---

[4] **commitment:** a promise to do something
[5] **walk on a cloud:** to feel light and wonderful
[6] **advice:** a suggestion you give someone to help solve a problem

goes a-way, Then I need you, Yes I need you, Then I need you, Oh I

need you You, you're the one I see through the chain-link fence.

You, you're the es-sence of in-no-cence. You, you can turn my

world all-right. You are a vi-sion of silk - en light.

Reviewing What You've Read

A. Did you find the answer to the question you wrote on page 36? If so, share your question and answer with your classmates. If not, ask your classmates for help.

B. Think about the past few days in Sandy's life. What happened first (1st)? What happened second (2nd); third (3rd); fourth (4th); fifth (5th); sixth (6th); seventh (7th); eighth (8th); ninth (9th)? Put the sentences in order, using the correct word.

_____ Sandy wondered if Samantha was Paul's girlfriend.

_____ Sandy left class humming Paul's song.

_____ Paul came into Sandy's orchestra class.

_____ Mr. Gambera, the music teacher, introduced Paul to the class.

first Sandy was thinking about her future.

_____ Paul sang a song to the class.

_____ Mr. Gambera passed a sign-up sheet for the music club around the class.

_____ Sandy ran home because she didn't want to be late.

_____ Everyone in the music class applauded.

C. What happened in the story? Read these statements. Are they true (*T*) or false (*F*)? Correct the statements that are false.

_____ **1.** Sandy stared into a mirror in the bathroom while thinking about her future.

_____

_____ **2.** Paul is not shy about playing his guitar.

_____

_____ **3.** The music club meets twice a week, on Tuesday and Wednesday afternoons.

_____

_____ **4.** The music club meets in the school auditorium.

_____

_____ **5.** Paul sang a song about the generation gap to Mr. Gambera's music class.

_____

Reading between the Lines

Read the following true statements. Go back to the story and find the information that helps you read between the lines. Write complete answers to these questions.

1. Sandy is signed up for the music club. How do you know?

2. Autumn is a student in Mr. Gambera's orchestra class. How do you know?

3. Mr. Gambera's class liked Paul's song a lot. How do you know?

4. Sandy was worried about her mother's reaction to the music club. How can you tell?

_____

_____

5. Sandy often talks to Autumn about personal problems. How do you know?

_____

_____

6. Sandy usually talks with her mother about new activities that she wants to get involved in. How do you know?

_____

_____

Discussing What You've Read

Work in groups of three or four students. Discuss the following questions and be prepared to share your answers with your classmates.

1. Sandy asked herself questions about her future.

   a. What do you think Sandy is worried about?

   b. Do you think Sandy should be worried? Why or why not?

2. Paul composed a song and sang it to Mr. Gambera's music class.

   a. Do you think the song was romantic? Why or why not?

   b. Do you think Paul wrote his song especially for Sandy? Why or why not?

3. Sandy signed up to join the music club.

   a. What do you think Sandy will learn by joining the music club?

   b. How do you think Sandy's parents will feel about the music club?

4. Sandy ran home after school.

   a. Why did Sandy run home?

   b. What did Sandy want to talk to her mother about?

Writing about What You've Read

A. In Chapter 3, you learned several things about Paul.

✔ Paul is friendly.   ✔ Paul plays basketball.
✔ Paul knows Samantha.   ✔ Paul is taller than Sandy.
✔ Paul is older than Sandy. ✔ Paul has a beautiful smile.

What new information have you learned about Paul in Chapter 4? Complete the list below, and include the section number where you found the answer.

1. _____Paul writes songs._____ (Section _5_)

2. _____ (Section __)

3. _____ (Section __)

4. _____ (Section __)

Compare your list about Paul with a classmate's list. Add to your list to make it as complete as possible.

_____

B. Sandy and Paul are alike in some ways, and different in other ways. Complete the diagram with information about Sandy and Paul. Write their similarities in the middle section, and their differences in the correct side sections.

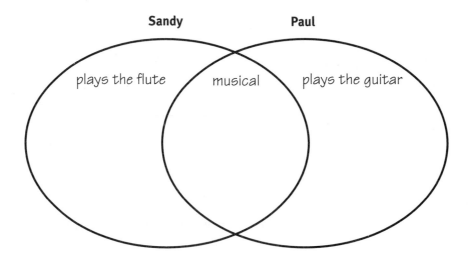

Sandy   Paul

plays the flute   musical   plays the guitar

C. On a separate piece of paper, write about Sandy and Paul. Write about their similarities and differences. Remember to indent the first sentence of each paragraph and to proofread your work.

Connecting the Story to Your Life

Think of someone to whom you would like to dedicate a song. Rewrite Paul's song with this person in mind.

When I see you _____

When I see your _____

When I _____

When I _____

Then I'm _____

Yes I'm _____

Then I'm _____

Oh, so _____

When the _____

When the _____

When the _____

And _____

Then I _____

Yes, I _____

Then I _____

Oh, I _____

You—you're the one I _____

You—you're the _____

You—you _____

You _____

Building Your Vocabulary

A. Verbs in English usually end in *-ed* to form the past tense. These are called **regular verbs**. Look at the examples from Chapter 4.

applaud**ed**	enjoy**ed**	remember**ed**	wait**ed**
ask**ed**	laugh**ed**	seem**ed**	walk**ed**
chang**ed**	look**ed**	smil**ed**	continu**ed**
lov**ed**	start**ed**	wish**ed**	want**ed**

Irregular verbs end in different ways. Write the past tense form of these irregular verbs from Chapter 4. If you need help, look in the section indicated in parentheses.

sit (1)   _____

think (2)   _____

see (2)   _____

know (3)   _____

begin (3)   _____

say (5)   _____

sing (5)   _____

give (7)   _____

have (8)   _____

leave (8)   _____

get (8)   _____

run (8)   _____

B. There are many other irregular verbs. Write the past tense form of these irregular verbs from Chapters 1, 2, and 3. If you need help, look in the section indicated in parentheses.

Chapter 1

hear (1)   _____

wake (1)   _____

come (2)   _____

go (2)   _____

feel (3)   _____

put (3)   _____

eat (4)   _____

Chapter 2

tell (2)   _____

grow (2)   _____

drive (5)   _____

Chapter 3

do (1)   _____

meet (1)   _____

make (4)   _____

speak (15)   _____

C. Circle the 26 irregular past tense verbs that you listed in the above exercises. Verbs are listed both horizontally (from left to right) and vertically (from top to bottom).

```
T  H  O  U  G  H  T  B  E  G  A  N  B
D  R  O  V  E  E  S  P  O  K  E  Y  S
F  E  L  T  C  A  M  E  G  A  V  E  A
K  N  E  W  G  R  E  W  S  A  I  D  T
J  M  F  M  A  D  E  E  A  W  O  K  E
G  O  T  O  L  D  P  N  N  M  E  T  R
S  A  W  J  X  I  U  T  G  E  U  H  A
U  A  C  H  A  D  T  C  E  M  A  S  N
```

Experiencing the Generation Gap

Getting Ready to Read

A. Look at the chapter title and the illustration. What do you think this chapter is about?

B. Prepare to read Chapter 5. **Read only the first and last sections of the story.** Do not read the other sections: Read only Sections 1 and 14. Then answer these questions.

    1. Did Sandy arrive at home on time? Who was waiting for Sandy at the door?

    2. What was Sandy thinking about when she arrived home?

    3. What do you think Sandy and her mother have disagreed about? What did you read in Section 14 that gave you this impression?

Reading Carefully

Read the story carefully now. As you read, think about the generation gap between Sandy and her mother. Underline words, phrases, or sentences that will help you when you discuss the generation gap with your classmates.

CHAPTER 5 | *Experiencing the Generation Gap*

Section 1   Sandy arrived home **out of breath**.[1] But she was on time. Her mother was waiting for her. Her mother was smiling, so hopefully she was in a good mood. Sandy planned to tell her mother that she had signed up for the music club. She wanted to tell her mother how much she loved to sing. And how she wanted to sing with Paul. (But she wasn't going to tell her mother about Paul!) While she was running home from school, Sandy thought about how much she liked Paul's voice, his smile, the words and music he wrote.

Section 2   "Hi, Sandy," said her mother. "Wow! You're out of breath. Have you been running? Sandy? You look so dreamy. Is your head up in the clouds?" Jane was trying to sound **casual**[2] before she spoke to Sandy about her makeup, her music, and Bill. But she was tense. Sometimes she planned to say certain things to Sandy and then she said something different, something that made Sandy upset.

"I'm fine, Mom," Sandy answered. She was still **daydreaming**.[3]

"Sandy?"

"Yes, Mom?"

"Are you sure you're all right?"

Section 3   "Yes, Mom." Sandy waited for a moment. Maybe this was a good time to talk to her mother about the music club. "Oh, I was just thinking about a song I heard at school today." She began to sing, "When the sky is gray . . . " but her mother interrupted her. Why did parents always have to interrupt? Sandy wondered. Didn't her mother want to hear the song Paul wrote? Wasn't she interested in what was important to Sandy?

Section 4   "Sandy, I don't think this is a time for singing. Do you have any homework?"

"Yes, I do. I have a lot of homework and I'm going to do it right now, Mom. But I wanted to talk to you for a minute." Sandy paused. "Guess what? There's

---

[1] **out of breath:** without air, often caused by running
[2] **casual:** relaxed; not formal
[3] **daydream:** to have pleasant thoughts, often about things one wishes would happen

a new club at school and I signed up to join it. It's a music club."

"Don't you think you should have asked your father and me for permission before you joined?"

"Maybe. I didn't think about it. Sorry. I know you're happy about my musical interests, so I thought you'd be happy if I joined a music club."

"I am. I am. But, well, what kind of music club is it? What kind of music do they play?"

"I think it'll be fun, Mom. It's not the kind of music I usually **go crazy for**,[4] but Mr. Gambera recommended it and the guy who played in our class today was really cool."

"A guy? A really cool guy?" Jane said, sounding like Sandy.

Section 5   "Mom, I don't think you need to **make fun of**[5] me. You know, if you were a little more understanding, we might get along better."

"I don't like you talking like that. I also don't like you forgetting to ask for permission. And I don't like you talking about cool guys. You're too young!"

"Mom, I'm fifteen years old. Get serious!"

Jane Finch could feel herself changing from tense to angry.

"Don't talk like that, Sandy Finch!" Jane said in a stern voice. "Your father and I need to talk to you about your behavior. Your father has told you to turn down the weird music, but you continue to argue with him and talk back over and over again."

Sandy interrupted her mother. She knew she shouldn't, but she couldn't help it.

Section 6   "The music I like isn't weird, Mother."

"I know it isn't. It's not the music. It's your **attitude**."[6]

"Oh, now it's my attitude. First it was the music, then it was . . . "

"Sandy, don't interrupt me. And don't correct me either."

"Well, I remember how you were always upset with Bill when he was listening to music and staying out late at night. After a while, Bill stopped coming home at all. You didn't know what he was doing and then he left. Now that he's away at college, are you going to start **picking on**[7] me?"

"Sandy, I don't like the way you're talking to me. You have a bad attitude."

Section 7   "No I don't. I just wanted to tell you about the music club. I was excited. Listen, I have a lot of homework and I'm tired of arguing with you about

---

[4] **go crazy for:** to like a lot
[5] **make fun of:** to laugh at or tease
[6] **attitude:** the way one thinks about something or someone
[7] **pick on:** to treat someone in an unkind way; to hurt someone

music, especially when I love music so much. I'm going to my room."

"I don't think you should talk to me like that, Sandy. I'm your mother. You should be respectful. I have some things to say to you."

"Oh Mom, you just don't understand anything."

Section 8   "Sandy, don't talk to me like that. It's disrespectful. You're beginning to sound exactly like your brother, and I don't like it. Have you been talking to him? We haven't heard from him, but maybe he's been talking to you. Have you spoken with him, Sandy?"

"Mom, why are you asking me all these questions?" said Sandy, looking down at the floor. She did not want to answer her mother. "You just don't understand me. I try to talk to you, but you don't listen. You only want to tell me what to do, just like you did with Bill. But you can't. I'm growing up and I have my own ideas, my own opinions. I'm a person, a person separate from you." Sandy's voice was shaking, but she tried to **control herself.**[8] "Maybe I'm not perfect, Mom, but nobody is perfect. Still, you can trust me. I'm a good student and an honest person."

Section 9   "I'm glad to hear that, Sandy," said Jane, trying not to be angry. She knew that if she wanted to communicate with Sandy, she had to stay calm. "I know that you're growing up, dear, and that you have your own ideas. I'm glad that you have your own ideas and opinions."

"And the makeup I wear is not a **big deal.**[9] Neither is the music."

"Maybe not, but I want to be able to trust you and to trust your decisions. Can I trust you, Sandy? You say that I can."

Section 10   Sandy felt uncomfortable. She had never actually lied to her mother and now her mother had asked about Bill and she was avoiding answering. Jane continued. "It's just that you're changing; you're different now and I don't want to have problems with you like I had with your brother, Bill. I want us to communicate. Remember how he used to listen to music all night long? Soon he stopped studying. Then he failed some of his classes. The situation was terrible. Your father and I had a really hard time with Bill. I don't want that to happen again. I don't want you to stop studying. Your studies are very important."

Section 11   "They're important to me too, Mom. Look Mom, Bill and I are different and I'm a different kind of student. I like studying; I like school. I know a lot about the situation with him, believe me. But I'm not Bill, I'm Sandy. I'm not doing drugs or drinking or anything like that. And neither is Bill."

---

[8] **control (oneself):** to stay calm
[9] **big deal:** something important

"Why did you say that, Sandy? Have you spoken with Bill?" Jane looked worried.

Section 12 "Mom, you have to let us grow up. Both of us. Okay?"

"I don't know, Sandy. I hope everything is okay, but, um, but you're dressing differently, you've been wearing makeup, and I don't know what you and Autumn are talking about on the phone for hours."

"Well, mostly we're talking about our own lives. Mom, stop worrying and everything will be just fine. Relax."

"I'll try. But what about the music?"

"What *about* the music?"

Section 13 "You know, Sandy, I'm so proud of the way you play the flute. You're so talented. The music you play is really nice. But the music you've been listening to lately is too angry. It makes you angry."

"The music I listen to is *beautiful*. I love it. And if I'm angry, it's only because you and Dad don't understand me, don't let me be myself. Forget about the music. I'll put my headphones on so you won't hear it."

"No, Sandy, that would be worse. Then I wouldn't know what you're listening to. I want to know."

"Well, Mom, I think I need to have some **privacy,**[10] don't you?"

Jane stared at her daughter. Privacy? Sandy wanted privacy? She didn't know what to say.

"Well, Sandy," she stammered, "you have your own room and . . . "

"And I play my music and study. Mom, there would not be a problem if you would relax. Aren't you glad I love music? You love music, don't you?"

"That's not the point. I'll discuss this with your father, and then maybe we can all talk it over. In the meantime, no headphones. Is that clear?"

Section 14 "Sure Mom. No problem." Sandy did not want to argue with her mother anymore; she did not want to talk to her either. She was glad that she hadn't told her about Bill. She didn't tell a lie, but she didn't answer her mother either.

"I need to do my homework now, Mom." Sandy weakly tried to smile, then turned and quickly walked to her bedroom, closing the door behind her. She sat down on her bed and quietly began to cry. "My parents do not understand me," she thought. "I'm **sick and tired**[11] of my mother **attacking**[12] me. She wants me to be perfect. And she wants me to tell her what I know about Bill,

---

[10] **privacy:** being able to be alone

[11] **sick and tired:** to be angry and bored with something that has been happening for a long time

[12] **attack:** to speak against or criticize

but I can't. I promised. She never leaves me alone. Parents just don't understand anything. It isn't surprising that so many teenagers run away from home." She was grateful[13] for having her own room and a little privacy. Then her thoughts shifted to the music club and Paul. She wiped away her tears, feeling better, thinking about playing music, about Paul. She opened her school books and began to study.

Reviewing What You've Read

Think about Sandy's conversation with her mother. Choose the correct answer to complete each of the following sentences. Then indicate the section of the story that contains the answer.

1. When Sandy arrived home after school,
   a. she went to her room to do her homework.
   b. she started to play her flute and sing.
   c. she was ready to communicate with her mother.
   Section _____

2. Jane wanted to talk to Sandy about
   a. the need for privacy and respect.
   b. makeup, music, and Bill.
   c. the music club, Paul, and dating.
   Section _____

3. Jane was tense, but she greeted Sandy in a casual way. Later she became angry and annoyed
   a. when Sandy began singing Paul's song.
   b. when Sandy sat down to do her homework.
   c. when Sandy told her mother to "get serious."
   Section _____

4. Sandy did not want to argue with her mother about
   a. Mr. Gambera's recommendation.
   b. the music that she listens to.
   c. staying out late at night.
   Section _____

[13] grateful: thankful

5. Sandy's mother is worried about her. She's worried that
   a. Sandy is changing and will be like her brother.
   b. Sandy's daydreaming will affect her grades.
   c. Sandy is falling in love with Paul.
   Section _____

6. Jane thought that Sandy should have
   a. asked for permission to join the music club.
   b. done her homework immediately.
   c. walked home instead of run home from school.
   Section _____

7. Sandy's mother likes the music that
   a. Sandy plays on the flute.
   b. Sandy listens to on the radio.
   c. Sandy will play in the music club.
   Section _____

8. Jane was surprised when Sandy said she needed some
   a. headphones.
   b. privacy.
   c. relaxation.
   Section _____

9. Sandy thought that her mother wanted her to be
   a. on time.
   b. calm.
   c. perfect.
   Section _____

10. Sandy didn't tell her mother anything about Bill because of
   a. their argument.
   b. a promise.
   c. a secret.
   Section _____

Reading between the Lines

Read the following true statements. Go back to the story and find the information that helps you read between the lines. Write complete answers to these questions.

1. Sandy ran home from school so that she would not be late. How do you know?

_____

_____

_____

2. Sandy wants to be more independent. How can you tell?

_____

_____

_____

3. The problems that Bill is having in college now are not so different from the problems he had in high school. How do you know?

_____

_____

_____

4. Jane does not want Sandy to begin dating. How do you know?

_____

_____

_____

5. Jane thinks Sandy has been talking to Bill. How do you know?

_____

_____

_____

6. Sandy feels uncomfortable when her mother asks her if she has talked to Bill. How do you know?

_____

_____

_____

Discussing What You've Read

Work in groups of three or four students.

1. Think about the conversation between Sandy and her mother. Most of their problems center around generation gap conflicts. Add at least four more examples of their generation gap conflicts to the list below.

   a. _____privacy_____   d. _____   g. _____

   b. _____attitude_____   e. _____   h. _____

   c. _____   f. _____   i. _____

2. Look at the problems that you listed above. Which is the most serious? Which is the least serious? Place all the items from the list, including *privacy* and *attitude,* on the line below, ordering them from <u>least serious</u> to <u>most serious</u>.

_____

least   most
serious   serious

3. How can Sandy and her mother solve their differences of opinion? With your group, discuss the four most serious generation gap problems from above. Suggest two possible solutions for each problem.

Generation gap problems	Possible solutions
1.	a. b.
2.	a. b.
3.	a. b.
4.	a. b.

4. Compare answers with another group. Add ideas to your chart that your group hadn't thought of.

Writing about What You've Read

Imagine that you are a good friend of either Sandy's or Jane's. On a separate piece of paper, write a letter to one of them. Offer advice that she can use to solve her family problems. Use the ideas that you listed in the previous exercise. Follow this format for your letter.

(today's date)

Dear _____ ,

_____

_____

Sincerely,
(your signature)

Connecting the Story to Your Life

Compare your life with the characters' lives.

1. Think of a problem that you've had with a member of your family (such as your mother, father, sister, brother, son, or daughter). What is the problem? Have you solved the problem? If so, how did you solve the problem?

2. Sandy feels lucky to have her own bedroom and some privacy. Do all of the members of your family have enough privacy? Do you? How important is privacy to you?

3. Sandy listens to music during her private time. What do you do during your private time?

4. Sandy signed up for the music club without permission from her parents. In what situations do you think children should ask their parents for permission?

5. Jane said to Sandy, "You should be respectful." In what ways do you show respect to your parents, grandparents, or other older relatives? How do you demonstrate respect for your teachers?

Building Your Vocabulary

A. Read these sentences. What do the highlighted words and expressions mean? Circle the letter of the correct answer. If you need help, look in the section indicated in parentheses.

1. Sandy's mother was **in a good mood.** (Section 1)
   a. perceptive
   b. serious
   c. happy

2. Jane asked Sandy, "Is your **head up in the clouds?**" (Section 2)
   a. Are you daydreaming?
   b. Are you flying?
   c. Are you angry?

3. Sandy began to sing, but her mother **interrupted** her. (Section 3)
   a. Her mother started speaking before Sandy stopped singing.
   b. Her mother asked her a question.
   c. Her mother began to nag her again.

4. Mr. Gambera **recommended** the music club to his students. (Section 4)
   a. reviewed
   b. suggested
   c. introduced

5. Jane could feel herself changing from **tense** to angry. (Section 5)
   a. nervous
   b. distracted
   c. thrilled

6. "Don't talk like that, Sandy Finch!" Jane said in a **stern** voice. (Section 5)
   a. very quiet
   b. very loud
   c. very serious

B. Unscramble these compound words from Chapters 3, 4, and 5. The first letter of each word is provided for you.

   1. ydgameaidrn   <u>daydreaming</u>

   2. hkormewo   h<u>   </u>

   3. bdonyfire   b<u>   </u>

   4. beomrod   b<u>   </u>

   5. ahehdnepos   h<u>   </u>

   6. erapspewn   n<u>   </u>

   7. blslakbeta   b<u>   </u>

   8. oonnerfta   a<u>   </u>

A Telephone Call

Getting Ready to Read

A. Look at the chapter title and the illustration.

   1. Who do you think Sandy is talking to on the telephone?

   2. How do Sandy's parents feel about the phone call?

B. Read the questions on the next page. Then **scan the first three lines** of each section to find the answers. Do not read more than the first three lines in each section. Write down your answers. Remember to work quickly.

1. (Section 1) *Who* is preparing dinner? _____

2. (Section 2) *What* kind of dinner is the Finch family going to have? _____

_____

3. (Section 3) *How* is Sandy getting along with her parents? _____

_____

4. (Section 4) *What* is Sandy upset about? _____

5. (Section 5) *Who* called Sandy? _____

6. (Section 6) *What* does Paul want to do on Friday night? _____

C. Are you ready to read the story? With a partner, check (✔) the topics that you think
you'll read about in this chapter.

____ vegetarian dinners	____ homework	____ meat dinners
____ using slang	____ the generation gap	____ music
____ makeup	____ dating	____ world hunger
____ talking on the phone	____ the music club	____ teenage fads
____ eating habits	____ helping prepare dinner	____ doing the dishes

Reading Carefully

Read the story carefully. As you read, think about your predictions. Did you predict the
contents of the story correctly?

CHAPTER 6 | *A Telephone Call*

Section 1   "Dinnertime!" Sandy's father called. "Come help, Sandy." Sandy went into
the kitchen where her mother and father were preparing dinner.

"Hi, Dad," said Sandy, kissing her father's cheek.

"Hello, sweetheart. Could you make a salad?"

"Sure, Dad. Oh, what's that?" asked Sandy looking at the pot on the stove.
"It looks **yummy.**[1]" Sandy took out a bowl from the cabinet and prepared to
make the salad.

---

[1] **yummy:** delicious

"Your mother and I made a new dish with pasta, garlic, and mushrooms."

"A vegetarian dinner?" asked Sandy.

"Is that okay with you?" asked her dad.

"It's great. Our health teacher told us that being a vegetarian is a thinker's lifestyle."

Section 2   Her mother smiled and nodded her head in agreement. "Vegetarians usually have healthy diets, but it's important to get enough protein too. Vegetarians need to eat . . ."

"Right now! Now let's eat. I'm hungry enough to eat a bear."

"That's an animal, Dad, not a vegetable . . ."

"I hate to interrupt, but let's sit down and eat. I'm very hungry. We can discuss the **pros and cons**[2] of being a vegetarian during dinner or after dessert."

Section 3   Everyone laughed and dinner began. After a moment, Sandy's father declared, "I hope the idea of vegetarianism is not turning into another teenage **fad.**[3] Sometimes teenagers are just imitating other teenagers. Becoming a vegetarian is a big decision. It requires a lot of thought."

"You're right, dear. As a chiropractor, I have many clients, both young and old, who don't eat meat. Planning vegetarian meals is sometimes simple, but it can get complicated. I know vegetarians who often have difficulty ordering at restaurants."

"I don't think it's so difficult to order vegetarian food. Most restaurants usually offer vegetarian meals. If not, there's always the good old reliable grilled cheese sandwich," said Steve.

"And when the grilled cheese sandwich is accompanied by a salad, you have protein and green vegetables, all you need really," added Jane.

Steve and Jane were busy discussing vegetarian lifestyles for a while when they noticed that Sandy had hardly spoken.

Section 4   "You're so quiet, Sandy. What are you daydreaming about?" asked her father.

"I'm not daydreaming, Dad. I'm thinking about how many people in the world are **starving**[4] while we're sitting here talking about food lifestyles. It's simply criminal."

"Now calm down, young lady. You sound like an angry teenager," said Steve.

"Well, maybe I am. But we can't just live our lives ignoring the fact that people are hungry," said Sandy. "Not just in faraway places, but right here."

---

[2] **pros and cons:** the good points and bad points about something
[3] **fad:** an interest that only lasts for a short time
[4] **starve:** to be very hungry; to be without food

"You're right Sandy. This is something for us to **reflect on.**[5] We can't solve all the problems of the world, but we can find solutions to some problems if we work at them. People can make a difference, don't you agree?" asked her father.

Section 5   Sandy didn't have a chance to answer. The telephone rang and she quickly got up to answer it. When she picked up the phone, she could hardly believe her ears. It was Paul!

"Hey, Sandy," said the voice on the telephone. "I hope you don't mind my calling you. I got your phone number from Samantha." Amazing! She didn't know that Samantha even had her number.

"No, that's cool. No problem," Sandy answered, trying to sound relaxed.

"There's a group that's really great and they're singing on TV tonight. I know you'd really like them. They're called Starfish. They've got a super flautist. That's why I thought of you. They're on tonight at nine o'clock on Channel 1."

"That sounds super, Paul, super cool," said Sandy. Her heart was **pounding.**[6] "Thanks for thinking of me. For sure, I'll watch them. Thanks a lot."

Section 6   There was a pause on the telephone. No one spoke. Finally, Paul said **hesitantly,**[7] "I was also wondering if you were free on Friday night. Maybe you and I could go to McBane's. There's a group that's playing there . . . " his voice **trailed off.**[8]

Sandy couldn't believe it. Paul was **asking her out.**[9] Ever since she first saw him, she had hoped for this. And now her dream was becoming a reality. She took a deep breath. Although she was very excited, she pretended to be calm. "Um, hey, that sounds totally *cool*, Paul. I'll have to ask my **folks**[10] and get back to you. Is that okay?"

"Oh, sure. I'll call you tomorrow, okay?"

"Okay, sure, Paul. Cool."

"Well, bye."

"Yeah, bye."

Sandy hung up the telephone very carefully. She loved the telephone. Paul had called her!

"Sandy, who was that? Come back to the table and finish your dinner. I think you said the word *cool* more than twenty times. At least ten!"

"That was a guy named Paul, Dad. He's *very* cool." Sandy laughed, and her dad laughed too.

---

[5] **reflect on:** to think about or consider
[6] **pound:** to beat very hard and fast
[7] **hesitantly:** slowly; with uncertainty
[8] **trail off:** to disappear slowly
[9] **ask (someone) out:** to invite someone to go somewhere, often on a date
[10] **folks:** parents

Reviewing What You've Read

A. Look back at the "Getting Ready to Read" exercise on pages 56 and 57 where you made predictions about the chapter. Did you guess correctly? Which topics were covered? Which were not? Discuss your predictions with a classmate.

B. Scan the section of the story indicated in parentheses to answer these questions.

1. (Section 1) *What* are the Finches having for dinner? _____

2. (Section 1) *Who* made the salad? _____

3. (Section 1) *Who* said that being a vegetarian is "a thinker's lifestyle?" _____

_____

4. (Section 2) *Who* said that vegetarians need to be careful to get enough protein?

_____

5. (Section 2) *When* does Steve want to discuss the pros and cons of being a

vegetarian? _____

6. (Section 3) *How* does Steve describe vegetarianism? _____

_____

7. (Section 3) *What* kinds of difficulties do vegetarians sometimes have? _____

_____

8. (Section 4) *What* was Sandy doing while her parents were discussing vegetarian

lifestyles? _____

9. (Section 4) *Why* does Steve think that Sandy is an angry teenager? _____

_____

10. (Section 5) *Where* did Paul get Sandy's phone number? _____

11. (Section 5) *What* special television show did Paul tell Sandy about? _____

_____

12. (Section 5) *What* is Starfish? _____

13. (Section 6) *Where* does Paul want to take Sandy on Friday night? _____

_____

14. (Section 6) *When* will Sandy tell Paul if she can go out with him? _____

_____

15. (Section 6) *What* one word did Sandy use over and over again in her phone

conversation? _____

Reading between the Lines

Read the following questions about the story. Be prepared to identify the information that helped you answer each question. Write complete answers to these questions.

1. How do you know that Sandy's health teacher thinks that vegetarians are intelligent people?

_____

_____

2. How do you know that Sandy is a thoughtful person?

_____

_____

3. How do you know that Sandy was nervous while talking on the phone with Paul?

_____

_____

4. How do you know that Steve is unhappy with some of the language that Sandy uses?

_____

_____

Discussing What You've Read

Work in groups of three or four students. Discuss these questions and be prepared to share your answers with your classmates.

1. Both Sandy and Paul were nervous on the telephone. Why was Sandy nervous? Why was Paul nervous? Were they nervous for the same reasons?

2. Do you think Sandy's parents will let her go out with Paul on Friday night? Why or why not?

3. Do you think Sandy should go out with Paul on Friday night? Why or why not?

4. Steve said, "People can make a difference." What did he mean? Do you agree or disagree? Why?

Connecting the Story to Your Life

Compare your life with the characters' lives.

1. What are the pros and cons of becoming a vegetarian? Make a list of the advantages and disadvantages.

Advantages of being a vegetarian	Disadvantages of being a vegetarian
1.	1.
2.	2.
3.	3.

2. Overall, do you approve or disapprove of vegetarianism?

3. Can you think of a time when you were nervous on the telephone? Why were you nervous?

4. What words do you use that other members of your family do not use? Why do you think different generations use different words and phrases?

5. Trends and fads among different generations change. Trends—in such things as music, food, technology, and language—are often influenced by the community in which you live. What are some trends or fads among people in your generation that make your generation different from other generations in your community?

Writing about What You've Read

Write a response to one of the topics from the "Connecting the Story to Your Life" exercise above. Before you begin, write down your ideas on a separate piece of paper. After you organize your ideas, you will be ready to write.

After you finish writing, take a few minutes to read over your answer carefully. Check for correct spelling, punctuation, and grammar. Be sure to make all necessary corrections.

Building Your Vocabulary

A. In English, many verbs commonly occur with certain noun phrases. Look at the examples.

Noun phrases *a bath   a paper   a shower   a letter   a difficult test*
                 a note   family photographs

Verb	Noun phrases
take	a bath, a difficult test, a shower, family photographs
write	a paper, a letter, a note
hand in	a paper, a difficult test

Complete the chart. Use the noun phrases listed below that commonly occur with the verbs. You may use the noun phrases with more than one verb.

a painting	advantages and disadvantages	pros and cons
the laundry	lunch	the phone
homework	a coat	a cake
a meal	an assignment	a problem
a child	a speech	some solutions
clothes	different ideas	the bed
a telephone call	a book	a pasta dish

Verb	Noun phrases
prepare	
make	
discuss	
pick up	
hang up	
finish	
do	
have	

B. Complete the following paragraph using verbs from Exercise A on page 63. Remember that the form of some of the verbs may need to be changed.

Sandy is interested in becoming a vegetarian. At school, her health teacher

_____ the pros and cons of vegetarianism during class. Some day, Sandy

would like to _____ a vegetarian dinner for her friends. At the dinner, she

would serve lots of vegetables, rice, and a salad. She would _____ the

salad with a special dressing. When her friends _____ dinner, she'll serve

a special dessert. Maybe the dessert won't be as healthy as the main meal!

C. Read the following sentences. What do the highlighted words and expressions mean? Circle the letter of the correct answer. If you need help, look in the section indicated in parentheses.

1. Sandy's mother and father **made a new dish** with garlic and mushrooms. (Section 1)
   a. They prepared a new recipe.
   b. They used a new set of dishes at the table.
   c. They prepared garlic and mushrooms as usual.

2. Steve thinks that becoming a vegetarian requires a lot of thought. He is worried that vegetarianism might be a teenage fad. He said, "Sometimes teenagers are just **imitating** other teenagers." (Section 3)
   a. watching
   b. copying
   c. arguing with

3. Sandy was thinking about hungry people in faraway places. She said, "It's simply **criminal**." (Section 4)
   a. uncomfortable
   b. illegal
   c. terrible

4. The telephone rang and Sandy quickly got up to answer it. When she picked up the phone, she **could hardly believe her ears**. It was Paul! (Section 5)
   a. She was surprised to hear Paul's voice.
   b. Her ears hurt from listening to the loud voice.
   c. It was hard to hear Paul's voice.

5. Paul called Sandy to tell her about a special TV program. Then there was a **pause** on the telephone. (Section 6)
   a. a short period of silence
   b. a long, loud noise
   c. a long period of silence

chapter

Talking with Friends

Getting Ready to Read

A. Look at the chapter title and the illustration.

   1. Where is Jane Finch?

   2. What is she doing?

   3. What do you know about Jane's friends?

B. Read Section 2 of the story. List four things you learned about Jane and her friends.

   1. _____

   2. _____

   3. _____

   4. _____

C. Compare your list with a classmate's list. Are your lists the same or different?

D. What do you think the women's group will be discussing? With a classmate, make a list of possible topics.

1. _____   4. _____

2. _____   5. _____

3. _____   6. _____

Reading Carefully

Read the story carefully. As you read, identify the topics that the women's group is discussing. Underline words, phrases, or sentences that will help you identify the topics.

CHAPTER 7 | *Talking with Friends*

Section 1   As Jane was getting ready to leave for her monthly meeting, the telephone rang. She went into the kitchen to answer it.

"Hello," she said and waited.

"Is Sandy there?" Jane paused for a moment. The voice was so familiar.

"No, Sandy's not here right now. Who is this, please?" she asked.

Click. The telephone went dead.

"I know that voice," thought Jane. "Oh, no! That was Bill, but he was **disguising**[1] his voice." She thought for a moment and then she felt her stomach knot up. "He doesn't want to speak to me. I'm his mother, yet he doesn't even want to speak a word to me." Jane tried to stop the tears that were filling her eyes. She grabbed her jacket and ran out of the house. She drove to her friend Sun's house, trying not to cry.

Section 2   On the first Thursday of every month, Jane attended a meeting of her women's group. She had been meeting with the same four women for more than six years. They got together regularly and discussed whatever was on their minds. The women had many common concerns, but they also appreciated each other's different approaches to solving problems. Because they came from **diverse**[2] backgrounds, they enjoyed sharing what was similar, what was different, and what was helpful.

---

[1] **disguise:** to change the usual appearance or sound of someone or something to fool others
[2] **diverse:** different, varied

Tonight Jane couldn't wait to get to her meeting. She really needed to talk about Sandy and Bill. She was thinking about how much these women had helped her in the past when Bill had had problems. Now maybe they could give her advice about both Sandy and Bill. She felt as if Bill had something to tell his sister, something that he didn't want his parents to know.

Section 3   Jane was the first woman to arrive at Sun's home, and Sun greeted her with a warm hug. Sun was from Korea and often spoke about her family's customs and traditions. Jane especially enjoyed hearing the sayings that Sun had learned from her grandmother. Her favorite saying was, "Always try your best and you can't go wrong."

"Are you all right, Jane?" asked Sun. "You look a little tearful."

"Well, I've had a big shock. My son, Bill, just called and asked for Sandy, but he hung up without telling me who he was! He even disguised his voice. Can you believe that?"

"Oh Jane, you must feel terrible," said Sun.

"I do. I really do. I'm his mother."

They began to talk and soon Jane felt better. As other members of the group arrived, they caught up on news about mutual friends. When everyone was finally there, they began the meeting. Sun served snacks and tea. Jane was glad to see her good friends again.

Section 4   "Thank goodness for this group," Juana began immediately. "I'm having so many problems at work. I can't complain to my family anymore. My husband and children are tired of hearing about my boss. I complain every night at the dinner table. But you know, my boss never stops thinking of new tasks for me. He never says 'thank you' for anything. I can't imagine him telling me that I've done a good job. And believe me, I'm trying all the time to do things right. I try so hard."

"That's so tough," said one of the women. "We all need to feel like we're doing a good job, no matter how old we are, don't we?"

Section 5   "What do you think might help?" asked Ellen. "What could Juana do to help her boss become more understanding?"

Juana asked, "Has anyone had an experience like mine?"

For a moment, there was silence. Each woman was thinking about her own past and working life. Nearly all of the women worked. Because she worked for herself now, Jane didn't have a boss. In the past, she had worked for a difficult boss. She tried to remember what had helped her.

Section 6   "I don't think it's a gender issue. The problem might be because I'm from Costa Rica. Sometimes he tells me he thinks my accent is cute, but I know he doesn't really think so," Juana said thoughtfully.

"That's ridiculous. You speak English beautifully," said Ellen.

"I agree," said Silvia, who was from Mexico. "I still have a lot of problems with *my* English, but you speak English perfectly. I can't hear any errors at all."

Section 7   Jane spoke quietly. "You know, in the past I worked for a boss who sometimes **treated me like dirt.**[3] It was tough, really difficult. I tried a lot of things: I had a **heart-to-heart**[4] talk with her, I ignored her, I invited her to my home. Nothing helped. Finally, I decided that it was not my problem. That helped. Eventually, I found a way to work for myself. I guess that doesn't sound very **optimistic,**[5] does it? But people can be difficult sometimes and you can't always make things work. Sometimes there's **bad chemistry.**[6] Whatever it is, you try and try and then, if necessary, you move on."

Section 8   The group was silent again for a few minutes. They were thinking about the different solutions that they had heard. At last, Juana said, "You've given me real **food for thought.**[7] I'm going to experiment with your ideas and keep looking for a way to make things work."

"**Keep us posted,**"[8] said Sun. "We all want your problems to work out for you. That's the important thing. Since I'm a stay-at-home mother now, I don't think I'm very helpful with work-related problems."

"That's not true. We all have different ideas to contribute, and we all find different things helpful. But we can find **common ground**[9] too," said Juana.

"Well, what helps me the most is to listen," said Sun.

"Listening is so important, isn't it?" agreed Juana.

"Yes, it is," joined Jane. "And that's what I'm having a hard time doing. Listening."

"But you're such a good listener, Jane. You always listen to us. Even now, when I know you're very upset about what's happening with your kids," said Sun.

Section 9   "I need to listen to you," Jane said. "Your advice is always helpful. And I hope you can help me now. I'm having so much trouble listening to my daughter, Sandy. I know she's trying to talk to me, explain herself to me, but when she talks, I get so upset that I stop listening. She puts up a wall between us; she wants to be totally separate from me, and secretive."

"I know exactly what you mean. That happens to me with my son," said Sun.

---

[3] **treat (someone) like dirt:** to be unkind to someone; to treat someone badly
[4] **heart-to-heart:** personal, honest, intimate
[5] **optimistic:** believing that good things will happen; positive
[6] **bad chemistry:** conflict of feelings between people
[7] **food for thought:** something to think about carefully
[8] **keep (someone) posted:** to continue to tell someone the most recent news
[9] **common ground:** similar interests or beliefs

"I want to **trust**[10] her," Jane said. "I think she's a good person. But maybe I'm wrong. She's talking on the phone to Bill and not telling me about it. I'm worried that something is wrong with Bill. Why don't they want me to know? And she's started wearing a lot of makeup. She's watching dumb TV shows and talking on the phone about nothing. She has her own language with her friends, so I don't know what they're talking about. Some of her friends seem to be so materialistic. They want cars, they want clothes, but there is no struggle, no challenge. As a result, something is missing. I'm sure that some kids at her school are using drugs. Do you think she is too? Am I blind? I want Sandy to continue to be a serious student, to learn about helping others in life, not to hurt her own life."

Section 10   "You know, Jane, I don't think you need to worry about Sandy. I think you need to give her a lot of attention and try not to criticize her too much. Teenagers need some freedom to become adults," said Silvia. "Sandy also needs to be able to have her own relationship with her brother, don't you think?"

"Do you think so? Excuse me, but I see it differently," said Sun. She was speaking quickly. "Jane, I worry about my son. I don't want him to use drugs. I know many of his friends take drugs, and I talk with him all the time. I try to keep my eyes open for any changes in his friends or the way he acts. He's very active on the basketball team, and that helps. But he's also under a lot of stress to get good grades. Teenagers have a lot of energy. They need to use it positively. They also need us to hug them often and to listen to them. I know one thing that helps: to turn off the television. If we turn off the TV for only an hour every day, it gives us a chance to speak to each other."

Section 11   "That's a good point. But my family won't let me turn off the TV. We fight about TV all the time," said Juana.

"Well, sometimes you have to fight because you care. You have to fight to help your children develop strength and to keep the family together. Today there is so much divorce, so many problems, so much materialism. Cars, stereos, computers, VCRs, and expensive clothes that nobody can afford. At our house, we struggle with all these issues during a weekly family meeting. We try to find solutions and make decisions together," said Sun.

"That's a great idea. I might try that," said Juana. "But I don't know if anyone in my family would be willing to turn off the TV."

Section 12   "They would for one hour," said Sun. "You have to keep trying. Make it fun. Make it positive. Don't criticize. Listen to your family. We don't want to

---

[10] **trust**: to believe that someone is honest; to have confidence in someone or something

lose our children, our husbands, or ourselves, do we?"

"I know I don't," said Jane. "The world is a difficult place to live in right now. Thank you all for some great ideas. I'm going to talk to Sandy tonight and make sure everything is okay with her and with Bill."

"Hang in there,[11] Jane. You're a good mom and your children love you. Sandy's having growing pains. Just hang in there. That's what I try to do: Be patient and be a good listener," Juana said.

"I hear you. Thanks to all of you for listening to me," said Jane.

Reviewing What You've Read

A. What topics did the women's group discuss at their meeting? Check (✔) the topics you remember reading about in the story. Compare your answers with a classmate's answers.

_____ independence	_____ worker/boss relationships	_____ chemistry
_____ homework	_____ trust	_____ television
_____ children	_____ benefits of listening	_____ family meetings
_____ the workplace	_____ housework	_____ drugs
_____ need for praise	_____ value of life's experiences	_____ materialism
_____ teenage fads	_____ solutions to problems	_____ communication
_____ Sun's home	_____ language skills	_____ being patient
_____ privacy	_____ paying attention to children	_____ freedom to grow

B. Think about what happened in the story. Choose the correct answer to complete each sentence. Then indicate the section of the story that contains the answer.

1. Bill called to speak with Sandy,
  a. and he left a long message for her.
  b. and he told her about his problems at college.
  c. but he hung up before identifying himself.
  Section _____

2. Jane meets with a group of women
  a. the first Wednesday of each month.
  b. the first Tuesday of each month.
  c. the first Thursday of each month.
  Section _____

---

[11] **hang in there:** to keep trying; to be patient; to refuse to give up

3. Jane has met with the same group of four women for
   a. less than six years.
   b. five years.
   c. more than six years.
   Section _____

4. These women meet to
   a. work on community projects.
   b. discuss problems and issues.
   c. prepare new vegetarian recipes.
   Section _____

5. The meeting was held at
   a. a small church.
   b. a private home.
   c. a local school.
   Section _____

6. Juana is unhappy with her job and
   a. is ready to quit right away.
   b. often complains to her family.
   c. is looking for a new job.
   Section _____

7. Silvia, who is from Mexico,
   a. has problems with her boss too.
   b. has problems with her English.
   c. has problems with her children.
   Section _____

8. After listening to everyone's suggestions and comments, Juana said that she was going to
   a. experiment with the group's ideas.
   b. ask her husband and children for advice.
   c. quit and find another job.
   Section _____

9. Jane and Sun have similar problems with
   a. their children.
   b. their clients.
   c. their husbands.
   Section _____

10. Sun is worried about her son. She doesn't want him

   a. to play professional basketball.

   b. to use drugs.

   c. to be too stressed.

   Section _____

Reading between the Lines

Read the following true statements. Go back to the story and find the information that helps you read between the lines. Write complete answers to these questions.

1. Bill doesn't want to speak with his mother. How do you know?

_____

_____

2. Jane is looking forward to meeting with her women's group. How do you know?

_____

_____

3. Juana appreciated her friends' suggestions. How do you know?

_____

_____

4. The women's group values each person's suggestions and ideas. How do you know?

_____

_____

5. Sun thinks that television limits communication. How do you know?

_____

_____

6. Juana thinks that Jane can work out the problems that she is having with Bill and Sandy. How do you know?

_____

_____

Discussing What You've Read

Work with a partner or in a small group. Discuss the following questions, and be prepared to share your answers with your classmates.

1. What problems did Juana discuss with the women's group?

   _____

   _____

   _____

2. What suggestions did the group make to help Juana? What suggestions do you have for Juana? Complete the chart.

Suggestions from the women's group	Your suggestions
1. have a heart-to-heart talk with the boss	1.
2.	2.
3.	3.
4.	4.

3. What problems did Jane discuss with the women's group?

   _____

   _____

   _____

4. What suggestions did the group make to help Jane? What suggestions do you have for Jane? Complete the chart.

Suggestions from the women's group	Your suggestions
1. give Sandy a lot of attention	1.
2.	2.
3.	3.
4.	4.
5.	5.
6.	6.

5. What should Juana do? What should Jane do? Read over all of the suggestions in the charts. Circle the best suggestion for Juana and the best suggestion for Jane. Then look at the different ways to give advice listed in the box below. Complete one of the sentences for Juana and one for Jane, using the suggestions that you circled in your charts. Share your answers with a classmate.

We think that Juana should . . .	We think that Jane should . . .
We think that Juana ought to . . .	We think that Jane ought to . . .
We think it would be good for Juana to . . .	We think it would be good for Jane to . . .
Perhaps Juana could . . .	Perhaps Jane could . . .

Writing about What You've Read

A. On a separate piece of paper, write a short letter describing a problem at school, at work, at home, or in your community. Explain the details of the problem so that others understand it when they read your letter. Do not sign your letter with your real name. Instead, sign the letter with a name that describes the problem (for example, *Unhappy at Work,* or *Frustrated with English*).

B. After you complete your letter, your teacher will take it and give you one of your classmates' letters. Read the letter and write a helpful response. Follow this format for your letter.

(today's date)

Dear _____,

    I was so sorry to read about your problem. From your letter, I realized that . . .
(describe problem) _____

    Perhaps I can offer you some advice . . . (make suggestions using the expressions
introduced on page 74) _____

                                          Sincerely,

                                     (your signature)

Connecting the Story to Your Life

Compare your life with the characters' lives.

1. Jane Finch is a member of a support group, her women's group. A support group is a group of people with common interests or concerns. They meet on a regular basis to talk and to help each other.

   a. Do you know people who belong to support groups?

   b. What are the benefits of these groups?

   c. What kind of support groups do you think are helpful?

2. Sun thinks that families need to watch television less and communicate more. Would Sun's suggestion work in your family? In your community? Why or why not?

3. Sun thinks that divorce and materialism cause many societal problems. Do you agree? Why or why not?

4. Identify a problem that you are currently having. If you aren't having any problems right now, use a problem that you have had in the past, but pretend that it is happening now.

   a. Ask a classmate for advice by saying the following:

   I'm currently having a problem with . . . What do you think I should do?

   b. Your classmate may offer you advice by using one of these phrases:

   I think that you should . . .   Maybe you need to . . .
   I think that you ought to . . .   Perhaps you could . . .
   I think that it would be a good idea   You might . . .
      for you to . . .

Building Your Vocabulary

A. Read the following sentences. Choose the best synonym for each highlighted word or expression. If you need help, look in the section indicated in parentheses.

1. Jane **couldn't wait** to get to her women's group meeting. (Section 2)
   a. was excited
   b. was worried
   c. was waiting

2. Jane and Sun **caught up on the news** about mutual friends. (Section 3)
   a. read the newspaper to get information about friends
   b. shared current information about friends
   c. listened to the news on the radio and television

3. "That's so **tough**; we all need to feel like we're doing a good job." (Section 4)
   a. easy
   b. difficult
   c. soft

4. Jane **works for herself** now, but she had a boss in the past. (Section 5)
   a. works with her friend
   b. is self-employed
   c. has an office at home

5. Jane had a **heart-to-heart** talk with her boss. (Section 7)
   a. honest
   b. romantic
   c. quiet

6. You can't always **make things work.** (Section 7)
   a. work hard
   b. be successful
   c. try hard

7. Jane said, "If necessary, you **move on.**" (Section 7)
   a. change to something new
   b. walk in a straight line
   c. move back and forth

8. Juana said, "But we can find **common ground** too." (Section 8)
   a. beliefs that a group of people share
   b. a green and beautiful garden
   c. a community vegetable garden

B. Match each expression from Chapter 7 with the correct definition. The expression is in the section indicated in parentheses.

_e_ **1.** can't wait/couldn't wait (2)	**a.** share up-to-date information
___ **2.** be tired of (4)	**b.** do something different
___ **3.** be tough (4)	**c.** not respect someone
___ **4.** work for (oneself) (5)	**d.** be bored with
___ **5.** move on (7)	**e.** be excited
___ **6.** have a heart-to-heart talk (7)	**f.** be patient
___ **7.** be optimistic (7)	**g.** be difficult
___ **8.** treat (someone) like dirt (7)	**h.** be successful
___ **9.** make things work (7/8)	**i.** think positively
___ **10.** find common ground (8)	**j.** be self-employed
___ **11.** keep (someone) posted (8)	**k.** have an honest conversation
___ **12.** hang in there (12)	**l.** find a similar experience

C. Work with a partner. One of you will take the part of Student A. The other will take the part of Student B. Take turns asking each other the following questions. Answer using the highlighted expressions. Be sure to ask and answer all of the questions.

Student A	Student B
1. What subject is **tough** for you at school? Why is it so tough?	1. When is it helpful to have a **heart-to-heart talk**?
2. What are you **tired of**?	2. When was the last time someone or something gave you **food for thought**?
3. Can you think of a difficult situation when you tried to **make things work**?	3. What are the benefits of **working for yourself**?
4. Are you **optimistic** about finding ways to fight world pollution?	4. When you run into old friends, what **news** do you try to **catch up on**?

It's Hard to Be Young

Getting Ready to Read

A. Think about the chapter title. Why is it difficult to be young? List three reasons and then compare your list with a classmate's list.

1. _____

2. _____

3. _____

B. Now look at the illustration. Can you add anything to your list?

_____

C. Preview the story. Read each of the following questions and then **scan** the first two sentences, and only the first two sentences, of each section to find the answer. Choose the correct answer and then move to the next question. Work quickly.

1. (Section 1) *Where* is Sandy?

   a. at school

   b. at home

   c. at the music club

2. (Section 2) *What* is Sandy thinking about?

   a. being a vegetarian

   b. the music club

   c. her date with Paul

3. (Section 3) *What* does Sandy understand?

   a. her school assignment

   b. her parents' rules

   c. her father's jokes

4. (Section 4) *What* is Sandy doing now?

   a. She's thinking about her future.

   b. She's studying her lesson.

   c. She's looking at the chalkboard.

5. (Section 5) *What* is Sandy trying to do?

   a. complete her homework

   b. pay attention to her schoolwork

   c. answer the teacher's question

6. (Section 6) *How* does Sandy feel after school?

   a. excited

   b. confused

   c. worried

7. (Section 7) *Who* do Sandy's parents trust?

   a. Paul

   b. Sandy

   c. Bill

8. (Section 8) *Why* doesn't Sandy eat a big dinner?

   a. She's nervous.

   b. She's daydreaming.

   c. Her head is in the clouds.

9. (Section 9) *What* are Sandy and her parents trying to do?
   a. knock on the door
   b. finish dinner
   c. get along

10. (Section 10) *Who* opens the door for Paul when he arrives to pick up Sandy?
    a. Steve
    b. Jane
    c. Sandy

11. (Section 11) *What* does Paul thank Sandy's parents for?
    a. for inviting him to dinner
    b. for letting him take Sandy out
    c. for lending him a car

12. (Section 12) *What* does Paul do at Sandy's house?
    a. He sings a song.
    b. He reads a poem.
    c. He tells a joke.

13. (Section 13) *What* does Paul do when Sandy's family applauds his singing?
    a. He looks away.
    b. He smiles.
    c. He laughs.

D. Think about the chapter title, the illustration, and what you learned during your preview. What do you think this chapter is about?

Reading Carefully

Read the story carefully. Think about the chapter title while reading. Why is it difficult to be young? Underline words, phrases, or sentences in the story that will help you answer the question when you are finished reading.

CHAPTER 8 | *It's Hard to Be Young*

Section 1   Sandy went to school on Friday with a light feeling in her heart. She had attended the first meeting of the music club the day before. They sang, played their instruments, and talked about music. They were a diverse group with different talents and tastes. Some played piano and guitar, while others sang. One girl played the drums. Some liked rock and heavy metal, others classical, others reggae, others rap. There was one thing they all had in common: They all loved music. They wished they could listen to music all day long.

Section 2   While sitting in class, Sandy thought about her date with Paul. Her parents had said it was okay to go out with him. Of course, she had to follow the rules. She could go out with Paul if he came to the house and they could meet him. And if she promised to be home by eleven o'clock! Rules, rules, rules. Her parents always had so many rules. They were too strict with her. It was probably because of her brother, Bill. Ever since Sandy could remember, Bill had broken the rules. She remembered how he would come home really late when he was a senior in high school. Her parents were awake, waiting and worrying. Once he had come home at 4 A.M., and then, another time, he didn't come home at all! Sandy had been in her room when Bill finally showed up the next day. She heard her parents arguing with Bill, asking him a lot of questions. Later, when Sandy had asked her parents why Bill hadn't come home, why they argued with him, and why they asked him so many questions, her parents had told her that she was too young to know about these things. She had asked her brother too. He had smiled a strange smile, but he didn't give her the answer that she was looking for.

"I'll tell you all about it when you're older, Little Sister," Bill had said.

"Tell me now, Bill. And don't call me Little Sister."

"No, not now. You're still too young, Little Sister," he had said, **teasing**[1] her.

Section 3   Well, now she was old enough—old enough to know how to **play the game,**[2] and she had learned the rules. Sandy didn't want to fight with her parents as her brother had. She wanted everything to go smoothly between her parents and Paul. She wanted her parents to see that she was mature and **trustworthy.**[3] She was different from her brother.

She thought about Bill. She hadn't been able to speak to him lately because her parents were always watching her. They never seemed to give her any privacy. Maybe she needed to talk to her mom and dad about Bill. Sandy knew that school wasn't going well for him. Couldn't her parents help? What could she do?

Section 4   Sandy tried to stop thinking about Bill. She began thinking about the future, about Paul. She was looking forward to being with Paul, talking to him. She tried to pay attention in class and do her schoolwork, but she was distracted. Her thoughts kept wandering. She imagined that she and Paul were

---

[1] **tease:** to annoy; to make fun of
[2] **play the game:** to learn the rules of life
[3] **trustworthy:** honest, dependable

at McBane's listening to music. It was noisy and she was feeling light and free. Paul was smiling at her. . . .

Section 5   Sandy felt the teacher looking at her. She tried to bring her thoughts back to her schoolwork. She also tried to concentrate and listen to the teacher. The teacher was dividing the class into groups. Sandy was glad. She could pay better attention in a group and stop thinking about Paul for a while.

Section 6   After school, Sandy hurried home to get ready for her date. She was excited and happy. Her mom and dad were both at home and she laughed with them for a few minutes, listening to her dad's jokes. Everyone seemed to be enjoying Sandy's good mood. Sandy thought for a moment about talking to her parents about Bill. "Why not? Everyone is relaxed. This might be the perfect time," she thought. And then she changed her mind. "No, I'd better not," she decided. "I'd better not take a chance; I might upset them and I don't want anything to go wrong today. It'll be my first date with Paul, and I hope it won't be my last."

"Sandy seems really happy today," Steve said to his wife.

"Doesn't she?" answered Jane. "I hope her new friend is as nice as she says he is."

Section 7   "Well, I trust Sandy's judgment. She's like you: She has good taste in men." They both laughed. Steve liked to make little jokes.

"It's because she has such a good father to give her inspiration," Jane said with a smile. She walked over to Steve and kissed him on the cheek.

"We're lucky to have a daughter like Sandy, aren't we?"

"I think so," agreed Jane. "She gives us a few surprises, but she's not like the kids I keep reading about in the newspaper, so I'm grateful. Maybe we're doing something right."

"Maybe. Or perhaps it's just luck. Whatever it is, let's **keep our fingers crossed**[4] that Paul is a nice guy and that he and Sandy have a good time."

Section 8   The family had a light dinner together. Sandy wasn't very hungry; she was a bit nervous. After they finished eating, they got up to clear the table. Jane Finch looked at Sandy with **approval**.[5]

"Sandy, you look lovely," said her mother. "Your hair looks so nice." Jane didn't mention the holes in Sandy's jeans. She knew that Sandy wanted to wear jeans with holes in them. It was the style these days.

"You do, Sandy. You look great! I agree with your mother. You're my favorite little girl," said Steve.

"Dad, please don't make jokes now; I am not a little girl. . . ."

---

[4] **keep (one's) fingers crossed:** to hope for good luck
[5] **approval:** the belief that someone or something is good or doing something right

"Oops," said Steve, interrupting his daughter. "Excuse me. I meant, my favorite young lady."

"That's better, Steve," said Jane. "Sandy's growing up and becoming a mature young woman." Jane made an effort to support Sandy; she remembered the advice her women's group had given to her.

Section 9   Everybody was trying to get along tonight. A knock on the door made the family quiet for a moment.

"I wonder who that could be," said Steve with a **wink.**[6]

"Dad, don't be **sarcastic,**[7] please. Not tonight," Sandy said with a pleading look.

"Don't worry. I'll be good. I promise," said her dad.

Section 10   Sandy quickly walked to the door. She could feel her heart beating fast. She opened the door and there was Paul with a beautiful smile on his face.

"Come on in, Paul," said Sandy, returning his smile.

Sandy and Paul walked into the living room, where Steve and Jane were now sitting on the sofa. Sandy introduced Paul to her mom and dad. Steve stood up to shake hands with Paul. Jane shook hands with Paul too. There was silence for a moment, and then everyone began to speak at once. Laughter.

Section 11   Paul spoke. "Thanks for letting me take Sandy out tonight. We're going to hear a really special band at McBane's."

"I understand you play the guitar, Paul," said Jane. "Oh dear," she thought to herself, "I sound so **stuffy.**"[8]

"That's right. I also write songs sometimes, when the inspiration hits me."

"What kinds of songs do you write?" Steve asked.

"Oh, all kinds. I sometimes write songs about world problems, the environment, the homeless, and you know, some political songs. I guess I worry about how the world is changing. There's hardly any green left except for golf courses and stuff like that. Right now I'm working on a song about the **pollution**[9] problem. The environment is really messed up everywhere and people need to do something about it. That's why I'm writing a song, so people will really think about how pollution affects our lives."

"Why don't you sing what you've written for us?" asked Jane.

"Really? Do you want to hear it? It's not finished yet," said Paul.

"Sure, Paul, we'd love to hear what you have," said Jane.

---

[6] **wink:** a quick movement of the eye, often as a message that one is joking or being friendly
[7] **sarcastic:** unkind or critical by saying or writing the opposite of what one means
[8] **stuffy:** formal, boring
[9] **pollution:** air, water, or land that is dangerously dirty

Section 12   Paul began to sing:

> We need a revolution now!
> We need to turn the tide.
> The pain of pollution, now
> Has taken all our pride.
>
> Cars grow old but they don't die!
> **Styrofoam**[10] cups with no place to hide!
> Teenagers **committing suicide!**[11]
> Homeless folks can't go inside!
> I don't know if I can take this ride.
> Something crazy is turning inside.
>
> We need a revolution!
> A green revolution, an evolution revolution,
> What do we need?
> We need a solution.
> We need a revolution, now.

Section 13   The whole family applauded. Paul smiled. He was glad that they liked his new song. He liked it too. He was always thinking about ways to change the world. And he hoped that the songs he wrote could help somehow.

"That song has a powerful message, Paul," said Jane, interrupting Paul's thoughts. "Songs like that help people think about change."

"I liked your song, Paul," said Steve. "I'm not sure we need a revolution, but the song has some interesting ideas."

"I'm glad you liked it. I hope we don't need a revolution, but we certainly need a change. Look around. There are many, many people who don't have enough money to buy food. And there are homeless people in the United States, one of the richest countries in the world. Some people really don't care. They buy much more than they really need, while other people are hungry. They don't do anything to help the environment, and they don't care at all about **global warming**.[12] We've got to do something to protect the world."

"I believe you, Paul," said Steve.

"So do I," said Jane.

---

[10] Styrofoam: a type of lightweight man-made material, often used as insulation or packing material
[11] commit suicide: to end one's own life
[12] global warming: an increase in the world's temperature, caused by an increase in carbon dioxide around the earth

Revolution Now

words by Nina Rosen
music by Andrew Del Monte

Reviewing What You've Read

A. Think about Sandy, Bill, and Paul. They each have different problems, and many are connected to their age. Why is it difficult for them to be young?

   1. Sandy: _____

   2. Bill: _____

   3. Paul: _____

B. Think about the story. Choose the correct answer, and then indicate the section of the story that contains the answer.

   1. Sandy attended the first meeting of the music club. Students in the music club have one thing in common:

     a. They all love rap music.

     b. They all love music.

     c. They all play an instrument.

     Section _____

   2. Sandy's parents said that she could go out with Paul, but they have insisted that

     a. Paul bring Sandy home by 10:45 P.M.

     b. Paul drive carefully and slowly.

     c. Paul come to the house to meet them.

     Section _____

   3. Sandy thinks that her parents are too strict because

     a. they have so many rules.

     b. they let Bill stay out all night.

     c. they ask so many questions.

     Section _____

   4. Sandy hasn't spoken to Bill on the phone lately because her parents

     a. are always on the telephone.

     b. always seem to be watching her.

     c. have a new rule about telephone conversations.

     Section _____

   5. Sandy and her parents were getting along well, but Sandy felt uncomfortable when her father said,

     a. "You're my favorite little girl."

     b. "She has good taste in men."

     c. "I agree with your mother."

     Section _____

6. When Paul arrived to pick Sandy up for their date,
   a. he rang the doorbell.
   b. he called out Sandy's name.
   c. he knocked on the door.
   Section _____

7. Before taking Sandy to McBane's, Paul came in the house to meet Sandy's parents. They met
   a. in the kitchen.
   b. in the dining room.
   c. in the living room.
   Section _____

8. Paul writes songs
   a. for his concerts at McBane's.
   b. when the inspiration hits him.
   c. when Mr. Gambera asks him to.
   Section _____

Reading between the Lines

Read the following true statements. Go back to the story and find the information that helps you read between the lines. Write complete answers to these questions.

1. Sandy's parents did not know Paul before he came to the house. How do you know?

   _____

   _____

2. Sandy thinks about her brother often. She wants to help him but doesn't know how. How do you know?

   _____

   _____

3. Jane did not approve of Sandy's jeans because they had holes in them, but she wanted to support Sandy. How can you tell?

   _____

   _____

4. Paul is a serious person. How can you tell?

   _____

   _____

5. Everyone was nervous when Paul arrived at Sandy's house. How can you tell?

_____

_____

6. Steve did not agree with the entire message of Paul's song. How do you know?

_____

_____

Discussing What You've Read

Work in groups of three or four students. Discuss the following questions and be prepared to share your answers with your classmates.

1. Jane and Steve have given Sandy permission to go out with Paul. Before Sandy and Paul go out, Jane and Steve want to meet Paul. They also expect Sandy to be home by eleven o'clock. Are these rules fair? Why or why not?

2. Sandy was very distracted at school. What was she thinking about?

3. Sandy decided not to talk to her parents about Bill. Why? Do you think that she made the right decision? Why or why not?

4. Steve says that Sandy is like her mother because they both have "good taste in men" (Section 7). What does he mean?

5. We know from Paul's song that he is worried about the environment. He is worried about pollution and concerned about man-made materials, such as Styrofoam cups and old cars. Why is he worried about man-made materials?

Writing about What You've Read

A. Paul believes there are many reasons to worry about the environment. Look at the following scrambled sentences. Unscramble each one to create a sentence with an important fact about the environment. Remember that the first word of each sentence begins with a capital letter. Put a period at the end of each sentence.

> **Example:** *butts down one to Cigarette years break five in*
> _Cigarette butts break down in one to five years._

1. cans 100 to take years disappear 500 to Aluminum

_____

2. break years 1,000,000 bottles Glass after down

_____

3. indefinitely containers last Plastic

_____

4. last to years Steel cans up 100

_____

5. diapers Disposable from last to 100 years 500

_____

6. years bags ten last from Plastic twenty to

_____

B. Paul hasn't finished his song yet. Think about the facts that you unscrambled about the environment in Exercise A. Can you write more verses to the song using this information?

> *We need a revolution now!*
> *We need to turn the tide.*
> *The pain of pollution, now*
> *Has taken all our pride.*
>
> *Cars grow old but they don't die!*
> *Styrofoam cups with no place to hide!*
> *Teenagers committing suicide!*
> *Homeless folks can't go inside!*
> *I don't know if I can take this ride.*
> *Something crazy is turning inside.*
>
> *Glass bottles* _____
>
> *Aluminum cans* _____
> *I don't know if I can take this ride.*
> *Something crazy is turning inside.*
>
> *Cigarette butts* _____
>
> *Plastic containers* _____
> *I don't know if I can take this ride.*
> *Something crazy is turning inside.*
>
> *Plastic bags* _____
>
> *Steel cans* _____
> *I don't know if I can take this ride.*
> *Something crazy is turning inside.*
>
> *We need a revolution!*
> *A green revolution, an evolution revolution,*
> *What do we need?*
> *We need a solution.*
> *We need a revolution, now.*

Connecting the Story to Your Life

Compare your life with the characters' lives.

1. Paul wrote a song about the environment because he is worried about global pollution. He thinks "the environment is really messed up everywhere." Which environmental problems are you concerned about?

_____ noise pollution	_____ recycling	_____ contamination
_____ air pollution	_____ landfills	_____ oil spills
_____ water pollution	_____ toxic waste	_____ pesticides
_____ litter	_____ man-made products	_____ other _____

2. How is your community affected by environmental problems?

3. What is your community doing to fight pollution and other environmental problems?

4. Does your neighborhood have a recycling center? What can be recycled there?

5. What can you and your family do to help the environment?

Building Your Vocabulary

Complete the crossword puzzle by finding common English phrases in the chapter. Look in the section indicated in parentheses to help you find the answer.

Across
1. to pay _____ (4)
4. to be _____ (3)
5. to get _____ (9)
6. to keep one's _____ crossed (7)
7. to have good _____ (7)
10. to have something in _____ (1)
11. all day _____ (1)
12. _____ warming (13)
13. to break the _____ (2)

Down
2. when the _____ hits (11)
3. to be _____ (9)
8. to go _____ (3)
9. to _____ the rules (2)

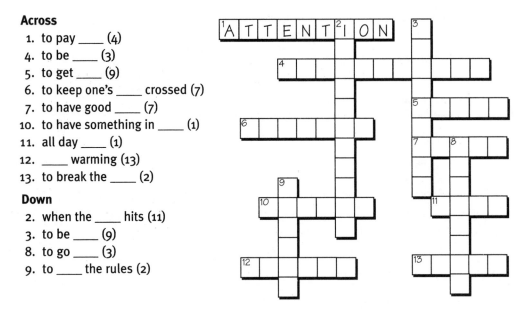

In the Real World

Getting Ready to Read

A. In the story, Sandy and Paul go out on a date. While they are out, they see some real-world problems. Look at the illustration and then read Section 5 of the story. What real-world problems do they see?

B. Homelessness affects all generations. It is a societal problem; it's a real-world problem. Circle the societal problems that your community faces. Does your community face any problems that are not on the list? If so, add them. Compare your answers with a classmate's. Use a dictionary for words you do not understand.

inflation	disease	care of the elderly
unemployment	equal rights	gangs
housing shortages	child care	racism
police brutality	health care	care for the mentally disabled
alcoholism	drug abuse	poor education
homelessness	domestic violence	poverty
pollution	divorce	low salaries
heavy traffic	overpopulation	government corruption
crime	family planning	guns
_____	_____	_____

C. In your opinion, which societal problems are the most serious? Why?

Reading Carefully

Read the story carefully. As you read, think about Sandy's and Paul's reactions to homelessness. Are their reactions similar or different? Underline words, phrases, or sentences that will help you discuss their reactions with your classmates.

CHAPTER 9 | *In the Real World*

Section 1   Sandy and Paul said good-bye to her parents and walked outside. Paul seemed a bit nervous now.

"I hope you don't mind this car, Sandy. It's not mine. My friend Dave let me borrow it. I don't have my own car."

"Neither do I, Paul," smiled Sandy.

"But you're not sixteen yet, are you?"

"Well, no. But I can tell you, I won't have a car for a long time. My parents are worriers. I know they'll worry when I have my own car and I want to drive wherever I want. Anyway, I guess we're lucky that Dave loaned you his car and we're going to McBane's together."

Section 2   "And that you look great tonight. And you smell good too. Mmm, very nice scent." Paul appreciated her taste. She didn't put too much perfume on, just a little. She wasn't sure if Paul would notice, but she didn't want her perfume to smell so strong that Paul was overpowered. She hated when girls wore a lot of perfume in class. Sometimes the perfume gave her a headache when she sat near them.

"Well, thanks. You look pretty good yourself, Paul. I like your shirt." Paul had dressed carefully for Sandy. He wore a long-sleeved green shirt that covered the tattoo on his left arm. He didn't want her to see his tattoo until he knew her better. Sometimes girls **were turned off by**[1] tattoos.

Section 3   Paul and Sandy got into the car. On the way to McBane's, Sandy was thrilled to be sitting in the car next to Paul. "Wow! We're here, together. This is so cool!" thought Sandy. As they drove along, they talked easily about music and the concert that they were going to hear. Sandy could see that Paul was feeling as good as she was.

Section 4   When they got to McBane's, they locked the car and walked toward the entrance. They got in line to pick up their tickets. As they stood there, together, a voice drifted up to them.

---

[1] **be turned off by:** to dislike

"Hey man, can you help me out? I'm **flat broke.**"[2]

Section 5   Sandy looked down and saw a man sitting on the ground. He didn't look too clean. Paul was looking down at the guy who had spoken, but he didn't look away. He spoke to the man on the ground.

"Here's a dollar, buddy. I'm sorry, but that's all I can **spare.**"[3]

"Hey, that's okay. Thanks. Every little bit helps, you know."

"Glad to help you, buddy," said Paul.

"My name's Wes. Wesley North," said the man on the ground, reaching up to shake hands with Paul.

"Good to meet you, Wes," said Paul, shaking hands with him.

"You know, Paul," Sandy whispered, "we don't know what he's going to buy with the money."

Wes heard Sandy and said, "Don't worry. I'm homeless and broke and in a bad way. And I sure can use this money. It's going to a good cause, young lady."

Section 6   Sandy and Paul looked at each other for a moment. Then Paul looked back at Wesley North with a smile. She realized that Paul shared his beautiful smile with the world. He told Wes his name and said they would be back after the show at McBane's. She knew he meant it. The line quickly began to move and soon they were in their seats for the concert. The music was beginning.

Section 7   During the concert, the group was unbelievable. They sang many of Sandy and Paul's favorite songs, and both Sandy and Paul sang and yelled with the crowd in the audience. The group was really **putting on a great show.**[4] Paul took Sandy's hand and she felt they were so close, the two of them, enjoying the wild and wonderful music. For a moment, she was distracted by thoughts of her mother and father: "Why," she thought, "do they think this music is so weird? Oh, I don't want to think about them now." Sandy tried to forget about her parents. She wanted to just listen, sing, be with Paul, and feel the music.

Paul was enjoying the concert and Sandy, but he was also thinking about Wesley North. He couldn't help it. Every time he saw someone on the street, without a home, he felt helpless. How could he do something meaningful?

Section 8   The concert lasted for more than two hours. Sandy and Paul were having a great time together. After a lot of screaming and shouting for the band, they walked with the crowd out of McBane's. Paul had his arm around Sandy's shoulder; she had her arm around his waist. For a moment, they looked at each other and for that moment, everything stopped.

---

[2] **flat broke:** without money
[3] **spare:** to give
[4] **put on a (great) show:** to entertain

Reviewing What You've Read

Think about Sandy and Paul's date. Choose the correct answer, and then indicate the section of the story that contains the answer.

1. Whose car is Paul driving?
   a. his own car
   b. his friend's car
   c. his father's car
   Section _____

2. What did Sandy wear on her first date?
   a. a new perfume
   b. a lot of perfume
   c. a little perfume
   Section _____

3. What does Sandy hate?
   a. getting a headache from classmates who wear too much perfume
   b. sitting next to classmates who complain of headaches
   c. going on a date with someone who has tattoos
   Section _____

4. What did Sandy compliment Paul on?
   a. his shoes
   b. his shirt
   c. his sandals
   Section _____

5. What did Sandy and Paul do when they arrived at McBane's?
   a. They locked the car and went into the concert hall.
   b. They locked the car and stood in line to get their tickets.
   c. They locked the car and showed their tickets at the entrance.
   Section _____

6. Who is Wesley North?
   a. a worker at McBane's
   b. a homeless man
   c. a band musician
   Section _____

7. How much money did Paul give to Wes?
   a. two dollars
   b. a few dollars
   c. one dollar
   Section _____

8. For a moment, Sandy was distracted during the concert. Who was she thinking about?

   a. her brother, Bill

   b. the homeless man

   c. her parents

   Section _____

9. Paul, too, was distracted during the concert. What was he thinking about?

   a. helping the homeless

   b. his next date with Sandy

   c. his musical career

   Section _____

10. How long did the concert last?

   a. for more than two hours

   b. for less than two hours

   c. for exactly two hours

   Section _____

Reading between the Lines

Read the following true statements. Go back to the story and find the information that helps you read between the lines. Write complete answers to these questions.

1. In the place where Sandy and Paul live, teenagers must be at least sixteen years old to get a driver's license. How do you know?

   _____

   _____

2. There were a lot of people at the concert at McBane's. How do you know?

   _____

   _____

3. Sandy felt uncomfortable when Paul began speaking with Wesley North. How can you tell?

   _____

   _____

Discussing What You've Read

Work in groups of three or four students. Discuss the following questions and be prepared to share your answers with your classmates.

1. Paul and Sandy were both looking forward to their first date. They both got ready for their first date carefully. What did Paul do? Why? What did Sandy do? Why?

2. Paul and Sandy met Wesley North while standing in line for their tickets. How would you describe Wes?

3. Paul gave Wes a dollar. Wes told Sandy that the money would go "to a good cause." What did he mean? How do you think Wes will use the money?

4. Do you think Paul and Sandy had a good time on their first date? Why or why not? Do you think they'll go out again? Why or why not?

Writing about What You've Read

A. Paul and Sandy had an interesting first date. What happened? Put the sentences in the order in which the events occured.

- Paul and Sandy walked out of McBane's with a large crowd.

- Paul told Sandy that he had borrowed a car from a friend to go to McBane's.

- They talked easily about music and the concert they were going to hear.

- Sandy wondered what Wes would do with the money that Paul gave him.

- Paul and Sandy complimented each other.

- Paul and Sandy had a great time listening to the music.

- Paul gave Wes a dollar.

- Wes told Paul and Sandy that he was homeless and flat broke.

- Paul and Sandy were outside McBane's when Wesley North asked them for money.

On the way to the car _____

_____

In the car _____

In line for the concert _____

_____

_____

_____

At the concert   _____

After the concert   _____

B. On a separate piece of paper, write a summary of Paul and Sandy's first date. Use information from Exercise A and additional details from the chapter. You should begin with a topic sentence and end with a conclusion. Try to use words like *first, second, then, later,* and *afterwards* to show transitions in time.

Connecting the Story to Your Life

Compare your life with the characters' lives.

1. Paul and Sandy went to a concert on their first date.

    a. What activities might people enjoy on their first dates in your community?

    b. Can young couples go out on dates by themselves? If not, who goes with them?

2. Wes asked Sandy and Paul for some money. Paul gave him a dollar.

    a. Would you have given Wes any money? Why or why not?

3. Homelessness is a problem in the community where Sandy and Paul live.

    a. Is homelessness a problem in your community?

    b. If the problem exists in your community, what is being done about it?

4. Sandy and Paul reacted to Wesley North in different ways.

    a. How did Paul react? What about Sandy?

    b. Which reaction is closer to the reaction you might have?

5. Paul had a tattoo on his arm. He didn't want Sandy to see it on their first date.

    a. What do you think about tattoos?

    b. Would you ever get a tattoo? Why or why not?

6. Paul feels helpless when he sees homeless people. He would like to do something meaningful to help out.

   a. What societal problem makes you feel helpless?

   b. What can you do to help solve the problem?

Building Your Vocabulary

A. Look at the adjectives in the example. They all have the same suffix: *-less*. When we add this suffix to a word, the meaning of the root word changes. With a partner, determine the meaning of the other adjectives listed below. Use a dictionary if you need help. Think about how the suffix changes the meaning of the root words.

   Example:

   homeless   having no permanent home

   countless   too many to be counted; without number

   endless   continuous; without stopping

   1. careless   _____

   2. childless   _____

   3. harmless   _____

   4. helpless   _____

   5. hopeless   _____

   6. jobless   _____

   7. meaningless   _____

   8. painless   _____

   9. restless   _____

   10. speechless   _____

   11. tireless   _____

   12. useless   _____

B. Complete these sentences with one of the adjectives from Exercise A, including the adjectives in the example. Use each adjective once.

   1. Wes lost his job. He didn't have enough money to pay the rent for his apartment. When he became _____, he moved into the community shelter.

2. Mr. and Mrs. Gambera live alone. They don't have any children. They're

_____.

3. If you're _____ with matches, you might start a fire.

4. Steve and Jane went to see a movie that was too long. It went on and on. It seemed _____.

5. The doctor told me the procedure would be _____. I was happy that I wouldn't feel anything.

6. These products are all natural, so they are _____ to the environment.

7. Some people seem to work day and night without getting tired. They are

_____.

8. Jane was shocked when she opened her front door and saw a friend she hadn't seen in twenty-five years. She was so surprised that she couldn't speak. She was

_____.

9. When you have a big family, there are _____ gifts to buy for the holidays.

10. When the local factory closed down, it left many people in the area

_____.

11. There's no obvious solution to the problem. I wish there were, but it seems

_____.

12. This old typewriter is _____; it doesn't work anymore.

13. Steve felt _____ when he saw the car accident. He couldn't do anything for the accident victims.

14. Paul couldn't sit still. He was _____. He was looking for action.

15. The politician's speech was _____. He really didn't say anything.

C. Look at the adjectives *careless* and *careful*. They are **antonyms,** or opposites. Not all adjectives with *-less* have an antonym with *-ful*. For example, you can add *-less* to *end* to make the word *endless*, but you cannot add *-ful* to *end*. Which of the adjectives with *-less* can be changed to create an antonym with *-ful*? Circle *Yes* or *No*. For all *Yes* answers, write the correct word using *-ful*. Check your dictionary if you need help.

Example:

careless	(Yes)	No	___careful___
endless	Yes	(No)	_____

1. homeless	Yes	No	_____
2. harmless	Yes	No	_____
3. speechless	Yes	No	_____
4. tireless	Yes	No	_____
5. hopeless	Yes	No	_____
6. helpless	Yes	No	_____
7. restless	Yes	No	_____
8. painless	Yes	No	_____
9. childless	Yes	No	_____
10. countless	Yes	No	_____
11. jobless	Yes	No	_____
12. useless	Yes	No	_____
13. meaningless	Yes	No	_____

D. Match each expression with the correct meaning. The number in parentheses indicates the section where the expression occurs.

__c__ **1.** I hope you don't mind. (1)

_____ **2.** She was thrilled. (3)

_____ **3.** I'm flat broke. (4)

_____ **4.** That's all I can spare. (5)

_____ **5.** Every little bit helps. (5)

_____ **6.** Wes is in a bad way. (5)

_____ **7.** They were really putting on a great show. (7)

_____ **8.** Paul wanted to do something meaningful. (7)

a. She was excited.

b. His situation is not good.

c. I hope that it is acceptable to you.

d. He wanted to do something important.

e. I don't have more to give.

f. Even a small amount is helpful.

g. The performers did an excellent job.

h. I don't have any money.

Sandy and Paul Together

Getting Ready to Read

A. Think about Sandy and Paul. What do you remember about them? Read these
statements. Are they true (*T*) or false (*F*)? Correct the statements that are false. Go
back to the chapter and section indicated to check your answers.

_____ **1.** Paul plays basketball. **(Chapter 3, Section 12)**

_____

_____ **2.** Sandy had seen Paul before meeting him. **(Chapter 3, Section 12)**

_____

_____ **3.** Autumn introduced Paul to Sandy. **(Chapter 3, Section 15)**

_____

_____ **4.** Paul invited Sandy's class to join the cooking club. **(Chapter 4, Section 7)**

_____

_____ **5.** Paul sang a romantic song to Sandy's music class. **(Chapter 4, Section 5)**

_____

_____ **6.** Sandy called Paul on the phone to tell him about a concert on television. **(Chapter 6, Section 5)**

_____

_____ **7.** Paul met Sandy's parents on the evening of their first date. **(Chapter 8, Section 10)**

_____

_____ **8.** Paul drove Sandy to McBane's in his own car. **(Chapter 9, Section 1)**

_____

B. Look at the chapter title and the illustration. In small groups, predict the future by discussing these questions.

  1. What do you think is going to happen to Sandy and Paul in this chapter?

  2. Do you think they'll see Wes after the concert? Why or why not?

  3. Do you think they'll continue to be friends after their first date? Why or why not?

  4. Do you think they have a future together? Why or why not?

Reading Carefully

Read the story carefully. As you read, consider your predictions about Sandy and Paul.

CHAPTER 10 | *Sandy and Paul Together*

Section 1   Sandy had forgotten the **incident**[1] with Wesley North, but when they got outside McBane's, who was waiting for them? Wesley North.

"Hey, Paul. How was the concert?" asked Wes.

---

[1] **incident:** an event, often an unusual or serious one

"Oh, hey Wes. It was incredible! It was great, wasn't it, Sandy?"

"Uh-huh," said Sandy quietly. "Why is this guy here now?" she wondered to herself.

"Listen, Paul, maybe you want to come with me to meet a few of my friends."

"No, I don't think so," said Paul. "Not tonight. Sandy and I have to be somewhere. Maybe another time."

"Oh, yeah, sure. Well, they aren't far away. You see, we've got a couple of **tents**[2] by the freeway over there. If you want to come over, there's a **campfire**[3] going and . . ."

"Not tonight, Wes. Sorry. Maybe another time."

"It's not far. Just across that street over there," Wes said. "See that bright glow? That's the campfire. Can you see it?"

Sandy and Paul looked at where Wes was pointing and saw something shining brightly.

Section 2   "You *live* there?" asked Sandy in a surprised whisper. She was sorry she had spoken. Paul looked at her.

"Hey, it's not so bad, sleepin' under the stars. I don't live there all the time. Sometimes I go to the downtown **shelter**[4] and sometimes I sleep here and sometimes . . ." Wes didn't finish his sentence; instead he just waved his hand in the air. Sandy saw that he didn't really have a place to call home. "I like it by the freeway," Wes continued. "There are a lot of noisy cars going by though, so I pretend that I'm listening to the ocean **roar.**"[5]

Sandy and Paul laughed with Wes. He was a funny guy.

"Hey, we'll see you another time, Wes," said Paul.

"Right," said Wes.

"See you," said Sandy.

Sandy and Paul waved good-bye and walked to the parking lot. The crowd had thinned and they were practically alone.

Section 3   "You know, Sandy," Paul said, "I really feel like we're having our own **adventure**[6] here, a special night."

"You help me see things differently, Paul. I don't usually talk to people I don't know. Wes scared me at first. But being with you and seeing you talking to him, I saw that he was just a regular guy. I don't know, I guess I just don't

---

[2] **tent:** a shelter that you can easily move, often made of cloth or plastic
[3] **campfire:** outdoor fire, used for warmth or cooking
[4] **shelter:** temporary housing or building that protects people
[5] **roar:** to make a deep, loud sound
[6] **adventure:** an event that is unusual, exciting, or dangerous

have enough faith or trust in people. You have **ideals.**[7] I haven't been out in the world, to learn and understand. I want to see more, do more, learn more."

Section 4   "So do I, Sandy," said Paul. "There's so much to see and do. And you're right; there's a lot to learn. People don't feel safe in the world anymore. Nobody trusts anybody, it seems. Everything you read in the newspaper or watch on TV makes you afraid. And yet you have to talk to people. I don't think the world is really like what they show on TV. TV makes life look too **superficial,**[8] too materialistic. Life has to be better than what you see on TV. Is a person with a home better than a homeless person? I don't think so. Think about the concert tonight; there were lots of different people having a wonderful time. Everyone was great. It was like a beautiful party. You never see good news like that on TV."

Section 5   Sandy looked at Paul. He was definitely different. He made her ask herself questions. Questions that she had never thought about. Paul was a thinker, and he was very **perceptive.**[9]

"You know, Paul," said Sandy, "I feel like you're the first person, except for my friend Autumn, who I can really talk to. My parents and I don't always communicate, if you know what I mean. They don't understand that I'm changing, and they worry about me. But I can talk to you about my ideas, all kinds of ideas."

Section 6   "Let's go for a walk, Sandy," said Paul, taking her hand. "I want to tell you about my plans to change the world." He smiled at her with his beautiful smile.

"Oh, Paul. I'd really like to, but I'd better go home. I'm sure that my parents are sitting on the sofa waiting for me. They won't like you if I come home late. They'll blame both of us."

"But I need to talk to you. I have so much on my mind."

"I do too. I'd like to talk to you about so many things, Paul."

"Like what?" he said, still holding her hand and walking slowly.

Section 7   "Well, one thing I'd like to talk to you about is my brother, Bill," Sandy **blurted**[10] out, and before she knew what was happening, she was crying. "I'm sorry, Paul. I don't know why I'm crying. It's just that my brother is having a lot of trouble at school. I think he's failing and he doesn't want me to tell my parents. I feel terrible about keeping this a secret from them."

"Wow, Sandy, I can see why you're crying," said Paul. He thought for a

---

[7] **ideals:** standards that you would like to see achieved
[8] **superficial:** based only on the first things noticed; not deep
[9] **perceptive:** quick to understand
[10] **blurt:** to say quickly

moment, and then slowly and carefully said, "But there's only one thing to do. Tell the truth. Explain the situation to your parents. They're good people, and they'll help you and your brother. Things always work out, once the truth is told."

Section 8   "Do you think so?" asked Sandy. She listened to Paul's words.

"Telling the truth helps everyone," smiled Paul.

"You're so right," said Sandy, wiping her tears.

Sandy looked at Paul. He looked sad and sweet and funny.

"I hope we can see a lot of each other, Sandy," Paul said seriously.

"I hope so," said Sandy. He turned to look at her and their eyes met. Sandy could feel her heart beating as she looked into Paul's eyes.

"We'd better **get going**,"[11] she said softly. They got into the car. "Thanks for helping me with my problem, Paul. I feel better knowing that I'm going to tell my parents the truth," said Sandy, taking a deep breath as Paul started the car.

"And you'll feel even better when Bill gets some help from them," said Paul. "He needs them."

"I hope you're right."

Section 9   They drove in silence for a while, and then Sandy spoke.

"You know what, Paul? I used to think you were Samantha's boyfriend," laughed Sandy.

"Well, I was Samantha's boyfriend for a little while. I really liked her, but she's had a problem with alcohol. She was drinking a lot. I tried to help her by taking her to a self-help program, but she told me not to bother. I really like Samantha. Don't be **jealous**,[12] Sandy. I'm only interested in you. I want to spend a lot of time with you. You're so special, so understanding. And so musical.

"Really? I didn't know I was so valuable."

"Well, you are. I have plans for this world, and I want you to be a part of them. I know you have dreams too, and I hope we can share our dreams."

"I do have dreams and big plans too. It would be wonderful to share our dreams."

They arrived at Sandy's house and Paul parked the car.

Section 10   "I hate to leave you. We have so much to talk about," said Paul. "But now you need to go in and talk to your parents. They're probably waiting up for you."

"Good idea."

---

[11] **get going:** to leave
[12] **jealous:** angry or unhappy because someone you care about is paying attention to another person

"I'll call you tomorrow morning. But don't worry. I'm sure it'll be okay."

"Thank you, Paul. And thanks for a special night."

Paul walked her to her front door and they parted.

Reviewing What You've Read

Think about Sandy and Paul's date. Choose the correct answer, and then indicate the section of the story that contains the answer.

1. Who did Paul and Sandy meet immediately after the concert?

   a. Autumn

   b. Wes

   c. Samantha

   Section _____

2. Where did Wes invite Paul and Sandy to go?

   a. to another concert at McBane's

   b. to meet his friends by the campfire

   c. to the downtown shelter

   Section _____

3. Why did Paul want to go for a walk with Sandy after the concert?

   a. He wanted to talk to her about homeless people.

   b. He wanted to tell her about his future plans.

   c. He wanted to give her advice about Bill.

   Section _____

4. What does Paul think Sandy should do about her brother, Bill?

   a. talk to her parents and tell them the truth

   b. continue talking to Bill while keeping his secret

   c. tell Bill to come home and be with the family

   Section _____

5. What kind of relationship did Paul have with Samantha?

   a. He was her boyfriend for a while.

   b. He talked with her at a self-help program.

   c. He used to drink alcohol with her.

   Section _____

6. What does Paul want?
   a. He wants to spend a lot of time with Sandy.
   b. He wants to ask Sandy out to another concert.
   c. He wants to build a homeless shelter.
   Section _____

7. What does Sandy think about Paul?
   a. She thinks that he is a deep thinker.
   b. She thinks that he is a worrier.
   c. She thinks that he is a jealous person.
   Section _____

Reading between the Lines

Read the following true statements. Go back to the story and find the information that helps you read between the lines. Write complete answers to these questions.

1. Sandy feels comfortable with Paul. How do you know?

   _____

   _____

2. Sandy thinks her parents are worried about her and Paul. How do you know?

   _____

   _____

3. Paul thinks that Sandy's parents can help Bill. How do you know?

   _____

   _____

Discussing What You've Read

Work in groups of three or four students. Discuss the following questions and be prepared to share your answers with your classmates.

1. Sandy felt uncomfortable speaking with Wes. Why?

2. Wes spoke with Sandy and Paul in Chapters 9 and 10. What do you know about Wes's life?

3. Paul and Sandy discussed many serious topics on their first date. Write down two topics that they discussed.

Topic 1: _____

Topic 2: _____

  a. What were their opinions?

  b. Did they agree with each other?

4. Paul advised Sandy to tell her parents the truth about Bill. Do you agree with Paul's advice? Explain your answer.

5. What kind of person is Paul? How would you describe him to someone who doesn't know him? Complete the chart with information about Paul.

a. What does he look like?	
b. What's he like?	
c. What are his talents and interests?	

Writing about What You've Read

Before you read the story carefully, you made predictions about Sandy and Paul. Look back at your predictions. Were you correct?

Now that you know more about Sandy and Paul, what do you think will happen to them in the future? On a separate piece of paper, write your predictions about their future. Give reasons to support your predictions.

After you finish writing, take a few minutes to read over your work carefully. Check for correct spelling, punctuation, and grammar. Be sure to make all necessary corrections.

Connecting the Story to Your Life

Compare your life with the characters' lives.

  1. Sandy doesn't usually talk to strangers. Do you think that it's okay to talk to strangers? If so, when and why? If not, why not?

2. Paul thinks that TV makes life look too superficial. What do you think about TV programs? In general, do you think they are realistic or superficial? Why?

3. Paul likes to help people. He tried to help Samantha when she was having a problem. Have you ever helped a friend or family member who was in trouble? If so, how did you help?

4. Sandy and Paul spoke to Wes before and after the concert. Would you talk to a homeless person? Why or why not?

5. Paul and Sandy spoke about Samantha. Samantha was Paul's girlfriend in the past. Paul told Sandy, "Don't be jealous." Have you ever been jealous of another person? If so, why?

Building Your Vocabulary

A. Complete these sentences with the correct words from the list. If you need help, look in the section indicated in parentheses.

secret	trust	beating	truth
place	safe	dreams	perceptive

1. Wes didn't really have a _____ to call home. (Section 2)

2. Sandy said that she didn't have enough faith or _____ in people. (Section 3)

3. Paul said, "People don't feel _____ in the world anymore." (Section 4)

4. Sandy thought that Paul was a thinker. She felt that he was very _____. (Section 5)

5. Paul told Sandy to tell the _____. (Section 7)

6. Sandy said, "I feel terrible about keeping this a _____ from them." (Section 7)

7. Sandy could feel her heart _____ as she looked into Paul's eyes. (Section 8)

8. Paul said, "I hope we can share our _____." (Section 9)

B. Now write your own sentences using words from the list in Exercise A. Use as many different words as you can.

   1. Write a sentence about a world problem using two words from the list.

   _____

   _____

   2. Write a sentence about your best friend using two words from the list.

   _____

   _____

   3. Write a sentence about yourself using two words from the list.

   _____

   _____

Sharing Problems

Getting Ready to Read

Look at the chapter title and the illustration. Then read Section 1 of the story.

1. Do you think Sandy will tell her parents the truth about Bill? Why or why not?

2. How do you think Sandy's parents will react to the truth about Bill? Circle the words that describe how you think they'll feel.

happy	hopeful	unhappy	relieved
upset	surprised	frustrated	glad
shocked	excited	disappointed	tense

Reading Carefully

Read the story carefully. As you read, think about Steve's and Jane's reactions to the news about Bill. Underline words, phrases, and sentences that describe their feelings.

CHAPTER 11 | *Sharing Problems*

Section 1   Sandy put her key in the lock and turned it. Very slowly and quietly, she opened the door. She was hoping that her parents were asleep and that she could sneak[1] into her room without disturbing them. Unfortunately, her parents were sitting in the living room, waiting up for her. Sandy collected herself. Perhaps this was the best time to talk to them. She was still **on cloud nine.**[2]

Section 2   "Sandy, we've been waiting up for you. Did you have a good time on your date, honey?" asked her mother.

Sandy smiled. "Oh Mom, Paul is a really nice guy."

"He seemed like a nice guy to your mother and me," said her father. "He was genuinely friendly, and I think he likes you. I like your taste, honey. And how was the concert?"

"Oh, you know, that group is always amazing. They rocked."

"They rocked?" laughed her dad. "Well, I guess that's very cool."

Section 3   Everybody laughed. Sandy took a deep breath and thought, "Well, this is it. It's now or never. I've got to tell them the truth about Bill."

"Listen, Mom, Dad," she began bravely, "there's something I want to talk to you about. It's about Bill."

"Well, Sandy, we just got off the phone with Bill. He called about an hour ago and we had a long talk. You know, I think he really called to talk to you, but since you weren't here, your dad started talking to him and told him not to hang up on us. We knew there was something wrong, but we didn't know what it was. Did you know he called here last week and hung up on me? His own mother?" Jane said. She looked sad and upset.

Sandy nodded her head. "I know, Mom. But he asked me not to tell you what was going on, so I couldn't say anything," explained Sandy. "I felt so bad, so torn between my parents and my brother. I want to be loyal to all of you."

Section 4   "Well, we had a long talk with Bill and finally found out that he's failing a class."

---

[1] **sneak:** to move quietly; to try not to be noticed
[2] **on cloud nine:** very happy

"I know," said Sandy sadly. "He doesn't have any confidence in himself as a student."

"I could hear that when he was talking," said Jane. "I found out that he's having a very hard time in several of his classes, and I know he feels just terrible."

Section 5   "You know, Mom, college isn't for everybody. Maybe college isn't the right place for Bill. He has lots of other talents. He can build anything; he can grow anything. I think he feels like a fish out of water in college," said Sandy.

"You might be right. Bill's talents and interests are a little unusual. Remember when he grew all those different kinds of tomatoes and made his own special sauces? I know he'll be successful once he decides what he wants to do. You both know that I've always wanted the best for our two children," said Jane. "But maybe I've been too **rigid**[3] in my ideas. Maybe I haven't listened to Bill carefully enough. I always thought he was a capable student, but as I was listening to him tonight, I heard him say that he doesn't feel comfortable in a college classroom. I was so surprised, but he said it, and we listened, didn't we Steve?" said Jane, looking at her husband.

"We did. Your mom and I have suggested to Bill that he take next semester off and do some thinking. He's going to speak to his counselor and ask if he can do that. He's going to fail one of his courses, and it will be on his record."

Section 6   "Oh Dad, I feel so bad for him. Is he upset?"

"Of course he is. We all are. But it's not the end of the world, is it? Some people are meant for college, but others aren't. He's hardworking and capable, but his interests aren't really academic. You know, Sandy, you're the real student in this family, aren't you?"

Sandy looked down and nodded. "I do love school," she said quietly.

Section 7   "People are different. Even though you and Bill are sister and brother, that doesn't mean you're the same," said her dad. "I'm just glad he was finally able to tell us what was going on. He's been so unhappy for the last few years, and I could never get him to communicate with us. I told him that he could live at home next semester and we can help him figure out what he's going to do. It might be hard for all of us, but we'll learn a lot from each other; we always do."

"You're great parents," said Sandy.

Section 8   "We try," laughed her mom. Her dad laughed too. Sandy hugged them and said good night. She went to her room, feeling much lighter. Although Bill still

[3] **rigid:** very stiff; not flexible

had big problems at school, at least he was facing them. And he wasn't facing them alone; his whole family was behind him.

"Good night, Mom and Dad. Good night, Bill. And good night, Paul. I'll dream about what happened tonight," said Sandy to herself as she got into bed.

Reviewing What You've Read

A. How did Sandy's parents react to the news about Bill? Look back at what you predicted in the "Getting Ready to Read" exercise on page 111. Were your predictions right? Why or why not?

B. What happened in the story? Read these statements. Are they true (*T*) or false (*F*)? Correct the statements that are false.

_____ **1.** Steve and Jane were asleep when Sandy got home from her date with Paul.

_____

_____ **2.** Sandy's parents liked Paul when they met him.

_____

_____ **3.** Sandy told her parents about Bill's problems at college.

_____

_____ **4.** Bill called home and told his parents that he was failing two of his classes.

_____

_____ **5.** Jane and Steve want Bill to stay in college until he graduates.

_____

_____ **6.** Bill is going to speak with a counselor about next semester.

_____

_____ **7.** Bill doesn't have any special interests or skills.

_____

_____ **8.** Sandy went to bed feeling unhappy.

_____

Reading between the Lines

Read the following true statements. Go back to the story and find the information that helps you read between the lines. Write complete answers to these questions.

1. Bill had a heart-to-heart talk with his parents. How do you know?

   _____

   _____

2. Sandy agreed with Paul about telling the truth. How can you tell?

   _____

   _____

3. Sandy thinks things over before she goes to sleep. How can you tell?

   _____

   _____

Discussing What You've Read

Work in groups of three or four students. Discuss the following questions and be prepared to share your answers with your classmates.

1. Bill hadn't communicated with his parents for a long time.

   a. Why do you think he finally decided to be truthful with his parents?

   b. Do you think that Bill did the right thing? Why or why not?

2. Jane and Steve suggested that Bill return home and "do some thinking."

   a. Do you think Bill will come home at the end of the semester? Why or why not?

   b. Do you think Bill should come home? Why or why not?

   c. Do you think Bill can solve his problems at home? Why or why not?

3. Steve told Sandy, "Some people are meant for college, but others aren't."

   a. What did Steve mean?

   b. Do you agree or disagree with Steve? Why?

4. When Bill comes home from college, life will change for the Finch family. Some of the changes will be easy, and others will be more difficult. Complete the chart with examples of the changes that the Finch family might experience.

	For Bill	For Sandy	For Jane and Steve
Changes that might be easy	1. 2. 3.	1. 2. 3.	1. 2. 3.
Changes that might be difficult	1. His parents may wait up for him when he goes out. 2. 3.	1. 2. 3.	1. 2. 3.

Writing about What You've Read

On a separate sheet of paper, write a letter to a member of the Finch family about Bill's homecoming. Give advice about how to deal with some of the changes the family will experience. Use some of these expressions in your letter.

I think that you should . . .
I think that you ought to . . .
I think that it would be a good idea for you to . . .
Maybe you need to . . .
Perhaps you could . . .
You might . . .

Follow this format for your letter. Remember to indent the first sentence.

```
                                                    (today's date)

Dear _____,

_____

_____

_____

                              Sincerely,

                              (your signature)
```

Connecting the Story to Your Life

Compare your life with the characters' lives.

1. Steve told Sandy, "You're the real student in this family." Is there a *real* student in your family?

2. Sandy's parents stayed up until she came home from her date. If you had children, would you stay up until they came home from a date? Why or why not?

3. Bill chose to leave home and live near his college. What do teenagers in your community do when they go to college? Do they live at home with their families or live near campus? Which do you think is better for the students? For the families?

Building Your Vocabulary

A. Read the sentences. What do the highlighted words and expressions mean? Circle the letter of the correct answer. If you need help, look in the section indicated in parentheses.

1. Sandy **collected** herself. (Section 1)
   a. She got control of herself so that she could talk to her parents calmly.
   b. She organized her books and homework for the next school day.
   c. She called her brother collect, because she couldn't pay for the telephone call herself.

2. Sandy said, "**It's now or never.**" (Section 3)
   a. She never wanted to think about the past. She only wanted to think about the present.
   b. She thought, "If I don't talk to them now, I probably won't talk to them in the future."
   c. She wished that she had told her parents the truth about Bill in the past.

3. Sandy felt bad because she was **torn between** her parents and her brother. (Section 3)
   a. She found it painful to choose between her parents and Bill.
   b. She felt unhappy about her parents and Bill.
   c. She wasn't truthful with her parents or Bill.

4. Bill doesn't **have confidence in himself.** (Section 4)
   a. He doesn't confide in anybody.
   b. He isn't always perceptive.
   c. He doesn't have much self-esteem.

5. Sandy thinks that Bill **feels like a fish out of water** in college. (Section 5)
   a. Bill would rather be fishing than studying.
   b. Bill doesn't feel comfortable in college.
   c. Bill wants to be a strict vegetarian.

6. Jane **wants the best for** her two children. (Section 5)
   a. She wants things to go well for them.
   b. She wants them to be the best students in school.
   c. She wants her best friend to talk to Sandy and Bill.

7. Steve thinks that Bill should **do some thinking.** (Section 5)
   a. He thinks Bill should be more thoughtful and considerate.
   b. He thinks Bill needs to think carefully about his future.
   c. He thinks Bill should stop complaining so loudly.

8. Steve said, **"It's not the end of the world."** (Section 6)
   a. Life is just beginning.
   b. Things could be worse.
   c. The world is in trouble.

9. The Finch family wants to help Bill **figure out** his future. (Section 7)
   a. They want Bill to take art classes because of his artistic talents.
   b. They want to help Bill finish his math class successfully.
   c. They want Bill to understand his problems so that he can solve them.

10. Bill is lucky because his whole family **is behind** him. (Section 8)
   a. His family is supportive.
   b. His family is perceptive.
   c. His family is hiding from him.

B. Work with a partner. One of you will take the part of Student A. The other will take the part of Student B. Take turns asking each other these questions. Be prepared to report one of your partner's answers to your classmates.

Student A	Student B
1. Can you think of a situation when you felt **like a fish out of water**? Please describe the situation to me.	1. Can you think of a time in your life when you needed **to do some thinking**? Please describe it to me.
2. Can you think of a time when you wished that your family **was behind** you? Please describe it to me.	2. Can you think of a situation when you thought **it was "now or never"**? Please describe the situation to me.
3. Can you think of a situation when you felt **torn between** two people? Please describe the situation to me.	3. Can you think of a difficult moment when you thought, **"It's not the end of the world"**? Please describe that moment to me.
4. Can you think of a time when you **had a lot of confidence in yourself**? Please describe it to me.	4. What problem do you want to **figure out** in the next few months? Please describe it to me.

A Family Man

Getting Ready to Read

A. Look at the chapter title and the illustration. Who do you think Chapter 12 is about?

B. What do you remember about Steve from previous chapters?

C. Read Sections 1 and 7. What did you learn about Steve that you didn't know before?

D. What else do you think you'll learn about him in this chapter?

Reading Carefully

Read the story carefully. As you read, underline new information about Steve.

CHAPTER 12 | *A Family Man*

Section 1   Steve Finch was forty-one. He was **attractive,**[1] and he had dark hair and a big, bushy mustache. He worked out at a gym regularly and maintained a healthy diet, so his body was strong and **trim.**[2] Steve worked as an administrator in the Palace Forum, a popular theater downtown.

Section 2   The Palace Forum was an old Victorian building with wood floors and high ceilings. It was very elegant but often needed repairs because it was so old. Steve's job was to manage the theater—to make sure everything was working, including the electricity and the plumbing. Steve also **booked**[3] the performances that were presented at the Palace.

Section 3   The Palace Forum presented an annual Shakespeare Festival during the summer. There were three Shakespearean plays performed by actors and actresses who came from all over the United States. During the winter months, local actors, poets, musicians, and artists used the Palace to present their work.

Section 4   Steve Finch **wore many hats**[4] at work. He was the handyman, so he was responsible for fixing what was broken. Because he was also the administrator, he was responsible for booking winter performances and setting up **auditions**[5] for local performers too. With the artistic director, he sometimes sat in on auditions. Steve had trained for his job. He had gone to graduate school and earned a Ph.D. in the history of theater. He was always busy at the theater and he loved his work.

Section 5   Lately Steve had been especially busy. There was a problem with the ceiling in the theater, and a section of it had fallen down onto the stage. Steve had needed to hire a construction crew to repair it because he couldn't fix the damage alone. For five days, Steve had worked with the crew repairing the ceiling. He was very tired when he left work on Friday afternoon.

Section 6   "I'm really looking forward to this weekend," thought Steve. "I'm going to play tennis, go to the gym, and try to relax. Maybe I'll take Jane and Sandy out.

---

[1] **attractive:** nice looking
[2] **trim:** thin and healthy looking
[3] **book:** to arrange or reserve something
[4] **wear many hats:** to have many jobs or responsibilities
[5] **audition:** a trial performance

They'd like to go to dinner and maybe see a play." Then Steve remembered that Sandy might have a date with Paul. Sandy had gone out with Paul twice since their first date two weeks ago. "Or maybe I'll just take my bride out for a date," he thought with a smile.

Section 7   Steve and Jane met when he was twenty-three and she was twenty-four. They had met as students in graduate school. They didn't have a lot in common at the time, because Steve was so involved in being an actor, director, and **stage technician**[6] in the theater department. Time had changed their lives a lot. He still worked in the theater, but he was also a **devoted**[7] husband and father. Jane and Steve had been married for almost twenty years. He treasured his wife and considered her his love and his friend. Steve was a family man.

Section 8   When he arrived home that night, Steve was glad, as always, to see Jane and Sandy. They both greeted him at the door with hugs all around. Jane and Sandy were busy preparing a **care package**[8] to send to Bill at school. Bill had called and explained that he had spoken with his counselor, who had helped him make arrangements to finish the semester.

Sandy and Jane thought it would help Bill feel better if they sent him a package with his favorite cookies and a new sweatshirt. They also added some recent photographs, one including Paul.

"How was work, honey? Is the ceiling at the theater fixed yet?" asked Jane.

"Oh, there's too much to do, and too little time. And that theater is so old. Of course, there's never enough money. I'm tired. But something in this house smells good."

Section 9   "I'm baking something. It's a surprise," said Jane with a smile. "Why don't you go into the kitchen, get a drink, and relax? Sandy and I will join you in a minute."

Steve went into the kitchen and got some drinks for everyone while Sandy and her mom continued preparing Bill's care package.

"Do you think Dad will guess what's in the oven, Sandy?" asked her mother.

"Of course he will. He always knows, by the smell, what's cooking. He's a perceptive guy."

They heard Steve in the kitchen. Without opening the oven door, he said, "Oh boy! Chocolate chip cookies. They're Bill's favorites, but they're mine too."

---

[6] **stage technician:** a person who works in a theater helping with the shows
[7] **devoted:** loving, caring, dedicated
[8] **care package:** a package of special gifts sent to someone who is living away from home

"They're not done yet," said Sandy.

Jane added, "You can't eat too many. They're for Bill. He needs his favorite cookies to cheer him up."

Section 10   After Sandy and Jane had finished preparing the package for Bill, they all sat down together in the living room to relax and talk. Steve discussed his problems at work with his wife and daughter.

"Sometimes I wish we could build a new theater," he said. "The ceiling is falling apart, and the plumbing is so old-fashioned; everything in that theater is ancient! It seems that every week something needs repairing."

Section 11   "That theater is an antique, Dad. Maybe someday it will be a historic **landmark.**[9] It's such a beautiful theater," said Sandy. "I think it's wonderful that you maintain it and keep it functioning."

"So do I," said Jane. "Nobody else could do that job. You and that theater are like an old married couple." Jane paused; she was thinking. "You know, I just had a thought."

"What's that, honey?" asked Steve.

"Maybe Bill could work with you for a while, helping you fix up the theater," said Jane.

Steve's face brightened. "Hmm," he said. "That sounds like a neat idea. We'll have to think about that." Steve thought for a moment and added, "Maybe Bill *could* help with the theater. He'd make some money and we could work together. He's always been a good carpenter."

"Maybe," said Jane. "But we don't want to push him into anything right now. And you work so hard at the theater. I'm not sure if that would be the best thing for Bill. He's having a hard time."

"You take your job so seriously, Dad," said Sandy. "I don't know if Bill could **handle the pressure.**"[10]

Section 12   "Well, maybe you're right, but you know, Sandy, it's important to do work that **inspires**[11] you, to have a job that you love and care about. And sometimes I worry, but a little stress helps get the job done. You can't live without a little stress and worry. It's human nature. I feel fortunate that your mother and I both have work we enjoy and take seriously. I hope you and your brother find meaningful work in your lives as adults. Your mother helps people, and by working in the theater, I help people too—in a different way. Going to the theater helps people laugh and cry and forget about their own lives for a while.

---

[9] **landmark:** special building or point of interest
[10] **handle the pressure:** to face difficulties
[11] **inspire:** to encourage someone to do well or produce something good

But I'm talking too much. Hey, could we think about food for a minute? Is anybody hungry?" Steve asked.

Section 13   "I am," said Jane. "I'm starving." Jane, Steve, and Sandy sat down at the table for dinner.

"You know, I think if I didn't love the theater so much, I would have been a chef. I love to cook, and I love to eat," said Steve as he began to eat. "Maybe tomorrow night I'll take you two out for dinner. After all, it's Saturday night."

"That sounds great, honey," said Jane with a smile.

Sandy said, "Well, actually, I need to talk to you both about tomorrow night."

"What is it, Sandy?" asked Jane. "Is everything okay?"

"Yes, everything's okay with me. But you know, things are not okay with the world. Paul and I have been talking and we've decided to do something about it."

Jane and Steve exchanged looks.

Section 14   "Are you and Paul a **couple**[12] now?" asked her father.

"Well, we're sort of a couple. We want to, um, we're going to play for a group of homeless people," Sandy stammered. "We're organizing a benefit concert for a homeless shelter, and we have to **rehearse**[13] tomorrow night. We met a guy from the shelter named Wes, and he inspired us to do something to help. So we're going to try to raise some money with our music."

"Sandy, you always surprise me. That sounds like a really interesting idea. Tell us more. As I told your brother, all you need to do is talk to us, dear. We always like to know your plans, and we just want you to be safe. Will the concert be at the shelter? Is it safe there?" asked Jane.

Section 15   "I think it's safe Mom, but you know, life isn't always safe. Sometimes we need to take chances. I think we can help with our music."

"Is this your idea or Paul's?" asked her mother.

"We thought of it together. We have a lot in common. We both love music and we both want to help the world. This is a way to make music, share music, and help the world a little."

Steve looked at his daughter. "I think it's very **generous**[14] of you and Paul. Such big ideas. Why don't I go with you and help out? My theater experience might be helpful. You never know."

"That's a generous offer, Dad, but everything is already **arranged**.[15] Paul

---

[12] **couple:** two people who have a special relationship, usually a romantic one
[13] **rehearse:** to practice for a performance
[14] **generous:** willing to give kindness, help, or money
[15] **arranged:** organized

and I have worked it all out. For this concert, he's planning on singing a few of his songs with the guitar; I'm going to play the flute and join him in some singing too. Maybe you and Mom could come and see the show."

Section 16 "And then we'll **treat**[16] you two to dinner."

"Oh, Dad," said Sandy, "you don't need to do that. We need to raise as much money as we can for the people at the shelter. I'm glad you both want to come."

"Sandy, we're interested in everything you do. And we feel the same way about Bill. Now that we're all talking again, I'm sure things are going to be better, much better. We've always been on Bill's side, and we're on your side too, Sandy."

"Absolutely!" said Jane in agreement.

Reviewing What You've Read

A. What happened in the story? Read the following statements. Are they true (*T*) or false (*F*)? Correct the statements that are false.

_____ **1.** Steve Finch is in good shape at forty-two years old.

_____

_____ **2.** Steve has many responsibilities at work, including fixing the plumbing, repairing ceilings, and setting up auditions for local performers.

_____

_____ **3.** Steve met Jane when he was twenty-one years old.

_____

_____ **4.** Steve and Jane have been married for more than twenty years.

_____

_____ **5.** When Steve arrived home from work, Jane and Sandy were busy preparing a care package for Bill.

_____

_____ **6.** Steve complained about the condition of the old theater.

_____

[16] treat: to pay for someone else

_____ **7.** Sandy compared the theater to a beautiful antique.

_____

_____ **8.** Jane suggested that Bill work at the Palace Forum theater with Steve.

_____

_____ **9.** Sandy turned down an invitation to have lunch with her parents.

_____

_____ **10.** Sandy would like her mother and father to attend the benefit concert.

_____

B. Think about what happened in the story. Match each <u>cause</u> statement with the most appropriate <u>effect</u> statement.

   Example:

   Steve works out at a gym regularly, so he is in good shape.
   <u>Cause</u>   <u>Effect</u>

___c___ **1.** Steve works out at a gym regularly,

2. The Palace Forum is an old theater,

3. Steve did most of the work on the electricity, the plumbing, and carpentry jobs,

4. Steve couldn't fix the ceiling by himself,

5. Steve worked hard all week,

6. Jane and Sandy were baking chocolate chip cookies,

7. Paul and Sandy have been practicing their new songs,

8. Bill has skills in carpentry,

9. Jane and Steve are talking with Bill again,

a. so the Palace Forum rarely had to call in other repairmen.

b. so he was tired on Friday afternoon.

c. so he is in good shape.

d. so it often needs repairs.

e. so he hired a construction crew to help him.

f. so Steve might be able to hire him to work at the Palace Forum.

g. so things are going to be better.

h. so the house smelled good when Steve got home.

i. so they are ready to play at the shelter.

Reading between the Lines

Read the following true statements. Go back to the story and find the information that helps you read between the lines. Write complete answers to these questions.

1. The owners of the Palace Forum value the old theater. How do you know?

   _____

   _____

2. Steve didn't learn everything that he needed to know about his job in college. How do you know?

   _____

   _____

3. The Finch family really wants to help Bill when he returns home from college. How do you know?

   _____

   _____

4. Sandy and Paul have had many serious conversations since their first date. How do you know?

   _____

   _____

5. Steve offered to go to the homeless shelter with Paul and Sandy to help out. He probably offered to help for other reasons. How do you know?

   _____

   _____

Discussing What You've Read

Work in groups of three or four students. Discuss these questions and be prepared to share your answers with your classmates.

1. Steve is considered **a family man.** What does that mean to you?

2. Sandy was planning to go to a rehearsal with Paul on Saturday night but didn't tell her parents. Why did she **wait until the last minute** to tell them?

3. Why do you think Sandy and Paul are **organizing** a benefit concert at a local homeless shelter?

4. If Bill wants to work at the Palace Forum when he returns home, his father will hire him. Do you think a job in the theater will help Bill? Why or why not?

Writing about What You've Read

A. Circle the adjectives that describe Steve Finch.

tall	careless	weak	loving	attractive	trim
inconsiderate	strong	considerate	childless	generous	thoughtful
mean	careful	short	helpful	speechless	homeless

B. Circle the adjectives that describe the Palace Forum theater.

new	plain	beautiful	true	modern	historic	run-down
old	Victorian	contemporary	ordinary	unique	ancient	elegant

C. On a separate piece of paper, write about Steve Finch and the theater where he works. Remember to include information about Steve from other chapters. Use the adjectives that you circled to "paint a picture with your words." Remember to indent the first line of each paragraph. Be sure to check spelling, grammar, and punctuation.

Connecting the Story to Your Life

Compare your life with the characters' lives.

1. Jane and Sandy were busy preparing a **care package** for Bill. We know that they included homemade chocolate chip cookies, a sweatshirt, and some photographs. They might have also included a CD or cassette of his favorite music, new socks, or a computer game.

   If you were to prepare a care package for a member of your family who is away from home, what would you include?

   _____   _____

   _____   _____

   _____   _____

2. Steve spends some of his free time **working out** at the gym.

   a. Do you think that working out is a good way to spend your free time? Why or why not?

   b. What is your favorite free-time activity? Why do you enjoy it?

c. Interview three classmates. Complete the chart with information about their favorite free-time activities. Include information on what the activities are, how often they do them, and how much time they spend on them.

Classmate's name	Favorite free-time activity	How often?	How much time?

3. Jane and Steve worry about Sandy's safety. What concerns do parents in your community have?

4. Steve told Sandy, "It is important to do work that inspires you, to have a job that you love and care about." What did he mean? Is it always possible to have such a job? Why or why not?

5. On a separate piece of paper, write a short description of your ideal job. Include information about schedule, salary, location, growth opportunities, benefits, and job security. Remember to check your spelling, punctuation, and grammar. Share your work with a classmate when you are finished.

Building Your Vocabulary

1. Steve **wears many hats** at work. Scan the chapter and make a list of at least five of his responsibilities.

a. _____

b. _____

c. _____

d. _____

e. _____

2. Write down the name of a person you know who **wears many hats.** Describe the job and some responsibilities this person has. If you wear many hats, write about yourself.

Name: _____

Job: _____

Responsibilities: _____

_____

_____

3. Jane and Steve want to **treat** Paul and Sandy to dinner after the benefit concert. Who is going to pay for the dinner?

    a. Steve

    b. Jane

    c. Jane and Steve

    d. Paul and Sandy

4. Have you ever **treated** anyone to dinner?

    a. Who? _____

    b. Why? _____

    c. When? _____

    d. Where? _____

5. In addition to being the Palace Forum administrator, Steve is also the **handyman.** What does that mean?

    a. He does everything at the theater with his hands.

    b. He does many odd jobs around the theater.

    c. He is available to work twenty-four hours a day.

6. After a busy work week, Steve **looks forward to** playing tennis, going to the gym, and relaxing with his family over the weekend. Write down three things that you **look forward to** after a busy week.

    a. _____

    b. _____

    c. _____

7. Sandy and Jane wanted to **cheer** Bill **up,** so they sent him a care package with some of his favorite things. Write down three things that cheer you up on a difficult day.

a. _____

b. _____

c. _____

8. Steve told Sandy, **"We've always been on Bill's side,** and **we're on your side** too." What did he mean?

a. Jane and Steve are helpful parents who support their children.

b. Jane and Steve always sit next to their children when they can.

c. Jane and Steve are always very upset with Bill and Sandy.

9. Complete the crossword puzzle by finding descriptive adjectives in the chapter. Look in the section in parentheses to help you find the answer.

Across

1. a _____ diet (1)

5. _____ hair (1)

7. _____ landmark (11)

10. a _____ theater (11)

11. a _____ husband and father (7)

12. a _____ mustache (1)

13. _____ ceilings (2)

14. _____ experience (15)

16. _____ performances (4)

17. _____ performers (4)

Down

2. _____ director (4)

3. an old _____ couple (11)

4. _____ school (7)

6. a _____ shelter (14)

8. _____ package (8)

9. a _____ technician (7)

10. a _____ concert (14)

15. _____ Shakespeare Festival (3)

How Can We Help?

Getting Ready to Read

Look at the chapter title and the illustration.

1. *What* do you see in the illustration?

2. *What* are Sandy and Paul talking about so seriously?

3. *Who* do they want to help?

4. *Why* do they want to help?

Reading Carefully

Read the story carefully. As you read, think about the different ways that Sandy and Paul can help the homeless.

CHAPTER 13 | *How Can We Help?*

Section 1   Paul and Sandy had a rehearsal for the benefit concert. They rehearsed for several hours. They prepared ten songs for the performance. Paul had invited two of his friends to join them. One of them was Samantha, who played the drums. The other, Keith, played the bass guitar. Sandy was tense. They were performing some of Paul's new songs and she wanted them to sound good. It was fun to **harmonize**[1] with the flute. Sometimes Sandy and Paul sang together too. Paul had a strong voice and he sang on pitch. Sandy could harmonize with her voice and together she and Paul made a strong **duo**.[2] After they finished rehearsing, Samantha and Keith left.

"I'm tense because I feel like I don't know the music well enough," said Sandy. "I get so worried before I perform, and I haven't had much experience. It's great to have Samantha and Keith as a backup team. They're really supportive. They both play well too."

Section 2   "You don't mind that Samantha is playing with us, do you?" asked Paul.

"No. Why should I mind? Because she's beautiful?" They both laughed.

"You're beautiful to me," said Paul.

"Thank you, Paul," said Sandy with a smile. They both laughed again.

"Samantha seems to be doing better with her drinking problem, and I thought that playing some music with her friends might be positive for her," said Paul.

Section 3   "You're always so busy helping people, Paul. You helped me when you told me to talk to my parents about my brother. It really helped all of us. We've all spoken with Bill, and we even sent him a care package. I hope he's feeling better."

"He has to feel better knowing his family is on his side. And I'm sure he knows that now," said Paul.

"I hope so," said Sandy. "Well, it was your idea and you really helped. By the way, I heard a **rumor**[3] that you have a tattoo. Actually, Samantha told me. Does your tattoo say *May I help you?*"

[1] **harmonize:** to combine two parts, as in music
[2] **duo:** two people who do something together, especially play music or sing
[3] **rumor:** information that is passed from one person to another and which may not be true; gossip

"No. Anyway, I don't really help people, Sandy; they help themselves," said Paul, feeling embarrassed for a moment. "Don't be a tease." Paul rolled up his sleeve, and on the inside of his upper arm, Sandy could see his tattoo. It had a vertical line with a diagonal line balanced on top of it. There were two horizontal lines to the right of the vertical line. The top horizontal line was shorter than the bottom horizontal line.

"Well, what does it mean? I've never seen anything like it."

"It's a Japanese character," said Paul.

"A Japanese character?" asked Sandy.

"That's right. It means *compassion* or *benevolence*. My Japanese friend Isamu helped me **design**[4] it."

"That's a very interesting tattoo, Paul," said Sandy. "I know that *compassion* means when you share another person's pain. Does *benevolence* mean the same thing?"

"*Benevolence* means an act of kindness. I want to remember to be kind, and the tattoo might help me remember. I guess it's a private tattoo between me and myself," said Paul with a smile. Sandy returned his smile. They shared a moment of quiet understanding.

Section 4   "It's a cool tattoo, Paul. Some people like tattoos and others hate them. I like your tattoo; it fits you. Hey, did I tell you that my parents are going to come to the performance?"

"That's great. At least someone in the audience will think we're good," Paul laughed. "You know," continued Paul, "Wes has been on my mind lately; I've really been thinking about him a lot. I'm glad we're going to have this special event for the homeless shelter. I know Wes is glad too. But I wonder if we could help in an ongoing way, in a real, long-term way."

"What do you mean, Paul? Don't you think we're helping in a real way?"

"I guess so. But wouldn't it be incredible if everybody at the shelter had more than just one night of music? It would be a shame if we had just one night of fun and then everything went back to normal."

Section 5   "This event we're putting together for Wes and his friends will really help them, Paul. They'll get some money, and I'm sure they'll all enjoy hearing our group and having a night of music," said Sandy.

"I hope so. I just wish there were something more we could do. Something ongoing, something **enduring**,"[5] said Paul. He was still thinking.

"Like what?" asked Sandy.

---

[4] **design:** to draw up a plan for making something
[5] **enduring:** lasting; continuing to exist

"Well, everybody needs work. Everybody needs to have a **skill**[6] of some kind. My skill, my gift, is music, but not everybody has that. I feel really lucky to be musical."

"You *are* lucky, Paul. Music is a special gift. But you've also worked at it for a long time. You're always working at it. You know, it's not enough to have talent. You also have to work hard."

"I agree. You're lucky, Sandy, because you have a musical gift too. But every person needs to express himself or herself in some way—through a skill, a trade, a hobby, or something. I'm not sure how that happens."

Section 6   "Well," said Sandy thoughtfully, "I'm not sure either. I know that we're always learning a lot at school. Learning about different ideas in different subjects helps us to see what we like, what is interesting to us. Activities outside of school help too. I know for me taking music classes and then music lessons has changed my life."

"And our parents, our friends, and our life experiences have given us so many opportunities to learn," Paul interrupted her.

"I guess you can learn from anything if you're open to it, if you have an open mind."

"People teach each other in a lot of ways. How could we do that for Wes and his friends? How can we help them? I'm sure they teach each other and take care of each other too. But maybe we should start some kind of school or club at the shelter." Paul was getting ideas. He was feeling inspired.

Section 7   "Why don't we think about the long-term possibilities after the performance? Right now, I'm worried about the performance, and I'm afraid of being distracted. We have to perform in front of all these people who I don't know, so I really need to focus my attention. You're used to it, but for me it's a new experience."

"That's true. It will be a new experience, but don't worry, you'll be fine, and you'll love performing, Sandy. It'll be great to perform together." He smiled at her. "And aren't you glad that your mom and dad will be there? I know they'll have a good time."

Section 8   "You like my mom and dad, don't you? You make me feel better about them. In fact, we all seem to get along better since you've been around. You have big dreams, Paul. I think that's one of the things my parents like about you. Hey, maybe my dad could help you with some ideas for the homeless shelter."

"Maybe he could," said Paul. He was quiet again. He was deep in thought. Sandy felt very close to him.

---

[6] **skill:** an ability to do something well, especially when it results from training and practice

Reviewing What You've Read

Think about Sandy and Paul's conversation. Choose the correct answer, and then indicate the section of the story that contains the answer.

1. Paul and Sandy rehearsed for the benefit concert
   a. for seven hours.
   b. for several hours.
   c. for the whole afternoon.
   Section _____

2. Paul invited two friends, Samantha and Keith,
   a. to perform at the homeless shelter.
   b. to join the music club at school.
   c. to start a school or a club at the shelter.
   Section _____

3. Paul showed Sandy his tattoo. It was
   a. a peace symbol.
   b. a Japanese character.
   c. a map of Japan.
   Section _____

4. Paul was worried about
   a. having dinner with Sandy's parents after the concert.
   b. helping Wes and other homeless people in a long-term way.
   c. the music performance at the homeless shelter.
   Section _____

5. Sandy was nervous about the performance because
   a. she has had little experience performing in front of people.
   b. she didn't want to perform with Samantha.
   c. she was embarrassed about her musical talents.
   Section _____

6. Sandy thinks that
   a. Paul is daydreaming about the shelter too much.
   b. her father can help Paul with his dream for the shelter.
   c. her mother won't come to the concert at the shelter.
   Section _____

Reading between the Lines

Read the following true statements. Go back to the story and find the information that helps you read between the lines. Write complete answers to these questions.

1. Sandy planned to sing, rather than play the flute, during part of the concert. How do you know?

   _____

   _____

2. Paul wanted to help the homeless in more than one way. How can you tell?

   _____

   _____

3. Paul has spent time developing his musical talents. How do you know?

   _____

   _____

4. Paul thinks that Sandy did the right thing by talking to her parents about Bill. How do you know?

   _____

   _____

5. Paul is interested in solving serious societal problems. How can you tell?

   _____

   _____

6. Samantha might have gone to a self-help program for support. How do you know?

   _____

   _____

Discussing What You've Read

Work in pairs. Discuss the following questions and be prepared to share your answers with your classmates.

1. Paul has a special tattoo on the inside of his upper arm.

   a. What does his tattoo look like? Work with your partner to draw the tattoo here.

   b. What does the tattoo mean?

   c. Do you think that the tattoo fits Paul's personality? Why or why not?

2. Paul said, "We've been given so many opportunities to learn." Sandy and Paul agreed that they had learned from different people (parents, friends, and teachers) and in different situations (in and outside of school).

   a. Is this true for everyone? Why or why not?

   b. How do you learn best? By listening? observing? practicing? experimenting? writing? reading? talking? drawing? Explain your answer.

   c. In what situations do you learn the best? Why?

3. In what ways has Paul helped Sandy?

   a. _____

   b. _____

   c. _____

4. Paul wonders if the concert at the shelter will help the homeless. In what ways might the concert help?

   a. _____

   b. _____

   c. _____

5. Paul is interested in finding long-term solutions to problems; he worries that short-term solutions are not enough. Complete the chart with the pros and cons of short-term and long-term solutions.

	Pros	Cons
Short-term solutions	They make people happy for a short time.	
Long-term solutions		

Writing about What You've Read

Sandy and Paul want to help homeless people in their community. What can they do to help? On a separate piece of paper, write a letter offering suggestions to them. Follow this format for your letter. Remember to indent the first sentence.

(today's date)

Dear Sandy and Paul,

_____

_____

_____

Sincerely,

(your signature)

Connecting the Story to Your Life

Compare your life with the characters' lives.

1. In Sandy and Paul's community, homelessness is a big problem. Write down a major problem in your community. Describe why it is a problem. What are some short-term solutions that might help? Can you think of solutions that might have an ongoing, long-term effect? Complete the chart with your ideas. Be creative!

Major problem in my community: _____

_____

_____

_____

_____

Short-term solutions	Long-term solutions
1.	1.
2.	2.
3.	3.

2. Compare your problem and answers to Question 1 with a partner's. Are you able to add any solutions to your partner's lists? Can you add anything new to your lists?

3. Paul thinks that his musical ability is his *special gift*. He works at improving his musical skills all the time. Sandy works at improving her musical skills too. What is your special gift? Is there a special gift that you would like to have?

Building Your Vocabulary

A. Complete the crossword puzzle by finding common English phrases in the story. Look in the section indicated in parentheses to help you find the answer.

Across

1. to be on one's _____ (4)
5. to be _____ (1)
6. to have a special _____ (5)
8. to feel _____ (3)
9. to focus one's _____ (7)
11. to be on someone's _____ (3)
13. to sing on _____ (1)
14. to take _____ of (6)

Down

2. to be afraid of being _____ (7)
3. to _____ at it (5)
4. to have an _____ mind (6)
7. to _____ open to something (6)
10. to feel _____ (6)
12. to be deep in _____ (8)

B. Read the following sentences. What do the highlighted words and expressions mean? Circle the letter of the correct answer.

1. Paul is an excellent singer. He always **sings on pitch.**
   a. He sings in a loud voice.
   b. He likes to sing in a group.
   c. He sings in the right key.

2. Wes **was on Paul's mind.**
   a. Wes was thinking about Paul.
   b. Paul was thinking about Wes.
   c. Wes was waiting for Paul.

3. Paul and many students in the music club **worked at** becoming good musicians.
   a. They talked about music and listened to the radio.
   b. They earned money at a fast-food restaurant after school.
   c. They practiced and studied music to improve their musical abilities.

4. In most situations, Paul **has an open mind.**
   a. He is willing to consider new ideas.
   b. He likes to be outside in the open air.
   c. He often thinks about his friends.

5. Jane and Steve **were open to** Sandy's new musical activities.
    a. They wanted Sandy to open a music school.
    b. They allowed Sandy to perform at the homeless shelter.
    c. They opened the door to listen to Sandy practice the flute.

6. When Paul was **inspired,** he had lots of good ideas.
    a. Paul had positive and creative feelings.
    b. Paul liked to be with his friends.
    c. Paul felt rested and calm.

7. When Paul **was deep in thought,** he had trouble paying attention to others.
    a. Paul was worried about himself.
    b. Paul was concentrating on his ideas.
    c. Paul was listening carefully to Sandy.

8. Samantha and Keith were very **supportive**.
    a. They were serious.
    b. They were helpful.
    c. They were distracted.

C. Work with a partner. One of you will take the part of Student A. The other will take the part of Student B. Take turns asking each other the following questions.

Student A	Student B
1. When you sing, do you **sing on pitch** or **off pitch**?	1. Do you **have an open mind** toward new fads? Which ones?
2. Who **is** currently **on your mind**?	2. **Are** you **open to** new types of music? What kinds of new music do you like?
3. Are you **working hard at** improving your language skills? In what way(s)?	3. When was the last time you **felt inspired**? What did you do?
4. What do you **have on your mind** besides schoolwork?	4. Do you ever find yourself **deep in thought** while you are in class? What are you thinking about?

14

Making Our World a Better Place

Getting Ready to Read

A. Look at the chapter title and the illustration.

   1. *Who* do you see in the illustration?

   2. *Who* do you think is going to make the world a better place?

   3. *How* are they going to do it?

B. Think about the characters you've met in *Changing Generations*. What do you think will happen to them in this chapter?

   1. Sandy Finch _____

   _____

   _____

2. Paul Good _____

_____

_____

3. Jane Finch _____

_____

_____

4. Steve Finch _____

_____

_____

5. Wesley North _____

_____

_____

6. Bill Finch _____

_____

_____

Reading Carefully

Read the story carefully. Think about the predictions you just made in the "Getting Read to Read" exercise on pages 143–144. Consider the following questions:

   1. Are the predictions you made correct?

   2. How are Sandy and Paul making the world a better place?

   3. Who benefited from the concert? How did each person benefit?

CHAPTER 14 | *Making Our World a Better Place*

Section 1   On the afternoon of the performance, Paul and the other musicians went over to Sandy's house for their last rehearsal. They played for Jane and Steve, who thought that they sounded very **lyrical**.[1] The group packed up their musical instruments and went over to the homeless shelter to set up. Wes was

[1] lyrical: expressing emotions in a beautiful way

there to meet them and was glad to see them.

The homeless shelter was a **modest**[2] one-room building. There was a big industrial kitchen used to prepare food for the many people who ate there. There was also an area with **cots**[3] where some of the homeless people slept.

Section 2 "This time you have time to look around," said Wes. "It's **cozy**[4] here. We've made it really nice."

"You have. You've made this into a great space. It looks like you've done a lot of work on it," said Sandy.

"You're right. It was a small, empty warehouse, but Lyle and Jim, my buddies, are pretty good with a hammer and nails and they helped to make it more comfortable. It's a friendlier place now."

"Your friends, Lyle and Jim, should meet Steve, Sandy's dad. He runs the Palace Forum. Do you know the place?"

Section 3 "You mean that beautiful old theater downtown? That building must be at least 100 years old," said Wes.

"It is. It's 101, actually. I think it's a city landmark. It's Victorian, and because it's so old, it always needs work. Steve manages the theater," explained Paul.

"No kidding. Maybe you could introduce him to Lyle and Jim. They're two good guys who know a lot about carpentry. Maybe Steve could find them some work."

"Maybe," agreed Paul. "It never hurts to ask."

"I'll introduce Lyle and Jim to my dad," said Sandy. "He's always looking for skilled workers."

Section 4 "Thanks," said Wes. He smiled at her. Sandy and Paul continued talking to Wes for a few minutes. Sandy was relaxing and beginning to enjoy herself.

"Since this is a benefit concert, we're going to put a box for **donations**[5] by the door, so people can donate a few dollars to the shelter," said Wes.

"That's a great idea," Sandy said. As the afternoon wore on, other people began to **drift in**.[6] There was a special feeling in the air. People were excited about an evening of music, a live performance.

Sandy wandered over to the kitchen area, where volunteers were making a **hearty**[7] meal. She put on an apron and **pitched in**[8] to help prepare a big pot of

---

[2] **modest:** small in size, quantity, or value; simple
[3] **cot:** a simple, narrow bed that folds up
[4] **cozy:** comfortable, pleasant
[5] **donation:** a gift or conribution given to help a person or organization
[6] **drift in:** to come in slowly
[7] **hearty:** large
[8] **pitch in:** to join others helping on an activity

chili. Soon the food was cooking on the stove and it was time for Sandy to change hats. She left the kitchen and went to the stage to make sure her music was all in order.

As the day wore on, many more people appeared at the shelter: homeless friends, volunteers, and others who simply wanted to hear some live music. Then Sandy saw her mom and dad walking in. She was happy they had come and walked over to greet them.

Section 5   "Hi, Mom, hi Dad. You guys look great! You got all dressed up."

"And guess what? We have a surprise for you," said Jane.

"What's up?" asked Sandy.

"It's a surprise, so I'll tell you later," said Jane.

"Oh Mom, you always like surprises. Anyway, it's cool that you two are here."

"Yeah, cool," winked her dad. "We wouldn't miss it. Hey, this is a neat space." He was looking around, noticing everything about the shelter. Steve always liked to inspect buildings. "Where's Paul?" he asked.

"He's over there setting up. There isn't a real stage here, so we're trying to make a space for the band," explained Sandy.

Section 6   Soon the shelter was filled with people. All kinds of people. Sandy saw lots of people whom she didn't know and some whom she did. There were Autumn and Jackson. Sandy walked up to them.

"Do your parents know you're out with Jackson? Is it okay?" asked Sandy.

"Well, I told them we were working on a school project. That's kind of true, isn't it?"

Sandy and Autumn laughed.

"Hi, Sandy. It looks like it's going to be a good concert," said Jackson.

"Look," said Sandy, taking Autumn's arm, "there's Mr. Gambera! He's here with his wife, and they're talking to Paul." Sandy knew that Mr. Gambera was proud of his students. Everyone was talking, laughing, and having a good time. The energy was building in the room. Sandy could see that it was a special night, a real concert. It was time to begin making music.

"I'll see you guys after the show. Thanks for coming," said Sandy to Autumn and Jackson. She walked over to Paul.

Section 7   "I'm going to turn off the lights for a few seconds," Paul told her. When I turn off the lights, you, Samantha, and Keith walk up to the stage we've set up. Get your instruments ready, and then I'll turn the lights back on, okay?" asked Paul.

"Okay," said Sandy. She was excited now, but she wasn't tense.

Paul went to the corner of the room. People were **milling about.**[9] He turned off the lights and it grew silent in the shelter. Sandy, Samantha, and Keith walked onto the stage to get their instruments. Paul quickly turned the lights back on and ran up to join them. Sandy's heart was beating so fast. She was so excited. The audience cheered.

Section 8   Then the group began to sing. Their first song was a big hit. The audience shouted for more. Sandy looked into the audience and smiled. For a moment, she couldn't believe her eyes. There was her brother, Bill! So that was the surprise her parents had mentioned. Bill waved at her, and Sandy walked up to the microphone.

"This song is for my brother, Bill," said Sandy. "He's here tonight and we're so glad." The crowd welcomed Bill with applause. And then the band sang a quiet ballad for Bill.

> Things may not always go the way we plan them.
> Hey, but that's okay.
> People tell us truths and we can't stand them.
> Hey, but that's okay.
>
> I look out at the road ahead,
> It's staring back at me.
> Tomorrow I might be dead.
> But for now I can see . . . that
> Hey, it's okay.
>
> This life is what's unfolding.
> This life is what I'm holding.
> And hey, hear what I say.
> It's okay.
> Yes it's okay.
> Hey, it's okay.

For more than two hours, the band sang and played music while people in the audience listened, sometimes joining them by clapping or singing along. Looking at the audience, they saw a group of friendly faces. Bill was sitting in the front row. Sandy was happy that he had come home. The concert was a big

---

[9] **mill about:** to move around without a particular plan

success, and people stayed for a long time, enjoying the music, enjoying being together.

Section 9   Finally, it was time to leave. The group had said their good-byes and put away their instruments. Wes walked up to the group with a big smile on his face.

"Well, almost everyone has left," he said. "I really want to thank all of you for what you did. Did you see all the money we collected? We made a pile of money. I haven't counted it yet, but it looks like a lot more than we expected. I hope we can all do this again soon. It was great!" he said. "This money will really help the shelter." Wes shook hands with everybody.

"I think we should plan to do it often," said Paul. "We raise some money, we get to practice our music, and everyone has a good time."

"I agree," said Steve, joining the group. "Anyway it's getting late, and I think we'd better get going. I hope to be seeing you and your friends again, Wes. It was good to meet you."

Section 10   Sandy and Paul loaded their instruments and equipment into Steve's car. Steve, Jane, and Bill helped them. They all went back to the Finches' house. Autumn and Jackson came too, so everyone had a chance to talk with Bill and welcome him home. Everyone was very hungry after a long night of making music, so Steve brought in some pizza. They all sat around the kitchen table eating pizza and talking about the concert and the future. Life seemed a little lighter tonight. Paul and Bill were **getting acquainted**[10] and talking about Bill's plans. Under the table, Paul and Sandy held hands.

"It's been a wonderful evening, full of promise, promise for each person here, promise for those at the homeless shelter, and promise for the future," said Steve. "It would be great if tonight never ended."

"Somebody turn on the music," said Sandy and Bill at the same time. Everybody laughed.

THE END

---

[10] **get acquainted:** get to know

Bill's Song

words by Nina Rosen
music by Nina Rosen
and Andrew Del Monte

Things may not al-ways go the way we plan them. Hey, but that's o-kay.

Peo-ple tell us truths and we can't stand them. Hey, but that's o-kay.

I look out at the road a-head, it's star-ing back at me. To-mor-row I

might be dead But for now I can see... that hey, it's o-kay.

This life is what's un-fold-ing. This life is what I'm hold-ing. And hey, hear what I say. It's o-

kay. Yes it's o - kay. Hey, it's o - kay.

Reviewing What You've Read

What happened before, during, and after the concert? Choose the correct answer, and then indicate the section of the story that contains the answer.

1. Paul, Sandy, and their friends rehearsed for the concert
   a. at Paul's house.
   b. at Sandy's house.
   c. at the homeless shelter.

   Section _____

2. The homeless shelter was a one-room building
   a. with an industrial kitchen and a sleeping area.
   b. with an industrial kitchen and a stage.
   c. with a sleeping area and a modest library.
   Section _____

3. Wes's friends, Lyle and Jim, know a lot about
   a. plumbing.
   b. music.
   c. carpentry.
   Section _____

4. Wes put a box by the door to the shelter so that people could
   a. donate money to the shelter.
   b. drop their concert tickets in the box.
   c. leave written suggestions for future concerts.
   Section _____

5. Before the concert, volunteers at the shelter were
   a. putting books on the library shelves.
   b. preparing a big meal for the homeless.
   c. selling concert tickets at the door.
   Section _____

6. Jane told Sandy that she and Steve
   a. donated money to the shelter.
   b. wanted to meet Lyle and Jim.
   c. had a big surprise for her.
   Section _____

7. At the very beginning of the concert, Paul got everyone's attention by
   a. turning the lights off and then on.
   b. screaming into the microphone.
   c. beginning to play music.
   Section _____

8. The group played music
   a. for the whole evening.
   b. for more than two hours.
   c. until morning.
   Section _____

9. The audience donated _____ to the shelter than Wes expected.
   a. more clothing
   b. more food
   c. more money
   Section _____

10. Instead of going out to dinner after the concert, Sandy, her friends, and her family _____ at home.
   a. made sandwiches
   b. had a pizza party
   c. listened to music
   Section _____

Reading between the Lines

Read the following true statements. Go back to the story and identify the information that helps you read between the lines. Write complete answers to these questions.

1. Sandy and Paul had visited the shelter before the day of the concert. How do you know?

_____

_____

2. Autumn's parents knew that she was with her boyfriend, Jackson. How do you know?

_____

_____

3. Paul is a very organized and resourceful person. How do you know?

_____

_____

4. Steve is interested in Wes and his friends. How do you know?

_____

_____

5. Bill's relationship with his family was improving. How do you know?

_____

_____

Discussing What You've Read

Work in groups of three or four students. Discuss these questions and be prepared to share your answers with your classmates.

1. Why did Paul want Lyle and Jim to meet Sandy's father?

2. What was the surprise that Jane talked about with Sandy?

3. The concert for the shelter was a success. Think about the people who were at the concert. Everyone probably enjoyed the concert for different reasons. Why was the concert successful for each of these people? List as many reasons as you can. Then compare your answers with another group's.

People who attended the concert	Reasons why the concert was successful for them
Paul and Sandy	They had a chance to perform.
Wes and the other homeless people	
Jane and Steve Finch	
Bill Finch	
Autumn	
Samantha	
Mr. Gambera	
People from the community	

Writing about What You've Read

What do you think the future holds for the characters of *Changing Generations*? Write an additional chapter, Chapter 15, for this book. Focus on one or more of the characters. Remember to be creative and to do the following:
- include a title for your chapter;
- indent the first sentence of each paragraph;
- check your spelling, punctuation, grammar, and paragraph development.

Connecting the Story to Your Life

Compare your life with the characters' lives.

1. Paul and Sandy want to make the world a better place. They thought that they could help by putting on a concert at a local homeless shelter. How can you help? How can you make a difference?

2. Sandy's relationship with her parents has improved in many ways. What can you do to improve your relationship with someone special (for example, your parents, children, teachers, friends, partner, spouse, coworker, boss)?

Building Your Vocabulary

A. What do the highlighted phrasal verbs mean? Match each expression with the correct meaning. The number in parentheses indicates the section where the phrasal verb occurs.

_____ **1.** The group **packed up** their musical instruments. (1)

_____ **2.** The group went over to the homeless shelter to **set up.** (1)

_____ **3.** As the afternoon wore on, other people began to **drift in.** (4)

_____ **4.** Everybody **pitched in** to prepare a big pot of chili. (4)

_____ **5.** Wes **walked up** with a big smile on his face. (9)

a. come in slowly

b. put away

c. approached

d. prepare

e. helped at a time of need

B. Read these sentences. What do the highlighted words and expressions mean? Circle the letter of the correct answer. If you need help, look in the section indicated in parentheses.

1. Steve **runs** the Palace Forum downtown. (Section 2)
 a. He is the carpenter.
 b. He is the manager.
 c. He is an athlete.

2. The Palace Forum always **needs work.** (Section 3)
 a. The Palace Forum is looking for workers.
 b. The Palace Forum lost two workers.
 c. The Palace Forum has to be fixed.

3. Paul said, "It **never hurts** to ask." (Section 3)
 a. He said, "It's not a good idea to ask questions."
 b. He said, "You should ask questions because it might help."
 c. He said, "If you ask questions, you will be sorry."

4. Sandy left the kitchen to see if her music was **in order.** (Section 4)
 a. She wanted to see if her music was organized properly before the concert.
 b. She wanted to order new music from a catalog for a future concert.
 c. She wanted to practice her songs with the music in front of her.

C. Work with a partner. One of you will play the part of Student A. The other will play the part of Student B. Take turns asking each other these questions.

Student A	Student B
1. Does your house or apartment **need work**? What kind?	1. Would you like to **run** a business someday? If so, what kind? If not, why not?
2. Do you ever **drift in** to class? How does your teacher react?	2. Do you keep your bedroom **in order** or not?
3. Do you **pack up** your books at the end of the school day or leave them in your locker?	3. On a regular weekday, do you ever have to **change hats**? What are your various responsibilities?

Word Recognition Exercises

One way to become a better reader is by learning to identify English words quickly and accurately. The exercises in this section will help you develop the ability to recognize key words from each chapter in the book. Before you begin, practice by following these steps:

1. Look at the **key word** at the beginning of each line.

2. Read the other five words on the same line as quickly as you can. When you see the *same* word, cross it out and continue to the next line.

3. Work as quickly as you can; time yourself, or your teacher will time you. Remember that it is faster to put a line through the word than to put a circle around the word.

4. Look at the sample exercise below. The first line is completed for you. Try lines 2, 3, and 4 on your own. Work quickly!

KEY WORD

1. **read**	lead	red	reed	read	need
2. **five**	hive	fire	five	fine	hire
3. **one**	own	on	none	owe	one
4. **quick**	quiet	quickly	quick	quite	quietly

5. Practice again on the next group of words. After you finish,
   ○ record your time at the end of the exercise.
   ○ check your work. When you find a mistake, put a circle around the correct word.
   ○ write the number of correct answers at the end of the exercise.

KEY WORD

1. **play**	pay	pray	play	quay	clay
2. **sing**	song	sang	sung	sting	sing
3. **fun**	fin	fun	bun	fan	pun
4. **walk**	walks	walked	woke	walk	weak
5. **book**	took	cook	book	look	hook

6. **teach**	teach	beach	track	peach	team
7. **house**	mouse	home	house	honey	haste
8. **pencil**	peasant	pepper	pendant	pencil	penny
9. **desk**	dime	deck	duck	dust	desk
10. **chalk**	child	chalk	talk	cheek	choke

Record your time here. → Time: _____ seconds

Record the number correct here. → Number correct: _____ /10

6. Now practice charting your word recognition progress. Here is an example of two completed columns, where there were seven correct answers, and the time was forty seconds:

How many words did you get correct on the practice recognition exercise?

How much time did you need to finish the practice recognition exercise?

How many words did you get correct on the practice recognition exercise?

How much time did you need to finish the practice recognition exercise?

7. As you do the word recognition exercises, try to
   ○ increase your speed. (Go faster!)
   ○ increase your accuracy. (Get more correct answers!)

Remember . . .
   ○ If you don't make any mistakes, try to go faster.
   ○ It is okay to make a mistake if you are trying to improve your speed.
   ○ Have fun improving your recognition skills. Good luck!

Word Recognition Exercise 1A

KEY WORD

1. **radio**	radish	radio	rather	rodeo	radios
2. **clicked**	checked	crooked	chicken	clicked	slicked
3. **music**	museum	moose	mucous	musty	music
4. **loud**	load	look	love	loud	hood
5. **heard**	beard	hound	feared	proud	heard
6. **bullet**	bullet	pallet	ballad	ballet	buffet
7. **clock**	shock	clock	block	flock	crock
8. **sang**	sing	rang	sang	hang	fang
9. **along**	aloud	along	alone	ahead	alias
10. **words**	woods	wards	weak	weeks	words
11. **listening**	listless	largely	lantern	landlord	listening
12. **favorite**	fictitious	faithful	facility	favorite	fairground
13. **station**	storage	station	stallion	standard	stammer
14. **shouted**	cheated	stationed	shouted	shipyard	shelter
15. **weird**	wired	winded	wider	weird	warned
16. **green**	groan	gowns	grown	train	green
17. **jeans**	jewels	jeans	jokes	gears	games
18. **minute**	minute	waitress	minstrel	mishap	nitrate
19. **offensive**	opposites	attentive	offensive	offering	officials
20. **ready**	steady	really	cloudy	lately	ready

Time: _____ seconds

Number correct: _____ /20

Record results in Column 1A of the Word Recognition Progress Chart on page 199.

Word Recognition Exercise 1B

KEY WORD

1. **walked**	talked	rocked	packed	walked	nailed
2. **bathroom**	bathtubs	bathtub	bathroom	pathway	bedroom
3. **washed**	mashed	packed	wished	washed	wailed
4. **wrapped**	warped	swamped	wrapping	wrapped	strapped
5. **shower**	shoulder	shampoo	shower	shaver	sample
6. **water**	matter	later	cater	heater	water
7. **hotter**	totter	fatter	better	batter	hotter
8. **grabbed**	greater	trapped	strapped	grabbed	sadder
9. **soap**	soup	soap	coat	boat	seep
10. **towel**	tunnel	rower	power	lower	towel
11. **dried**	drape	breed	drain	pride	dried
12. **brushed**	crushed	brushed	fished	bleached	bruised
13. **hair**	hour	hear	hair	hail	heat
14. **shirt**	sheet	shout	short	shirt	shade
15. **earrings**	eagles	eating	earrings	easily	earnings
16. **toast**	taste	toast	roast	waste	treats
17. **standing**	steadily	stairway	stadium	standing	string
18. **sink**	rink	pink	wink	link	sink
19. **poured**	passed	poured	ground	garage	pounds
20. **already**	already	allows	almond	around	albums

Time: _____ seconds

Number correct: _____ /20

Record results in Column 1B of the Word Recognition Progress Chart on page 199.

Word Recognition Exercise 1C

KEY WORD

1. **kitchen**	chicken	ketchup	kitchen	kittens	kitchens
2. **healthy**	hearty	healthy	heated	healing	height
3. **breakfast**	bedroom	dreaded	benefit	breakfast	basketball
4. **homework**	husband	homework	housework	homeless	holiday
5. **banged**	banged	hanged	ranged	boarded	bandage
6. **flute**	salute	flood	slave	shout	flute
7. **brush**	crush	proud	broad	brunch	brush
8. **teeth**	tooth	treat	teeth	booth	truth
9. **finish**	finite	honest	forward	finish	figure
10. **blouses**	bushes	blades	bikinis	bibles	blouses
11. **closet**	closest	cables	cutlet	closet	clowns
12. **wearing**	sewing	naming	meaning	tearing	wearing
13. **months**	mouths	moths	months	nothing	moons
14. **stop**	step	stop	strip	tops	pots
15. **pretend**	pilots	payment	pretend	pertain	patent
16. **pierced**	pieced	pierced	priced	pleased	private
17. **notice**	nuisance	motion	waters	notice	nothing
18. **annoyed**	antonym	anxiety	annoyed	apology	appetite
19. **young**	ground	yellow	tongue	young	wound
20. **upstairs**	upsets	uptown	upside	upward	upstairs

Time: _____ seconds

Number correct: _____ /20

Record results in Column 1C of the Word Recognition Progress Chart on page 199.

Word Recognition Exercise 2A

KEY WORD

1. **after**	around	often	alter	after	altars
2. **gone**	game	gone	gown	zone	jeans
3. **down**	dawn	bone	pawn	down	drown
4. **coffee**	coffee	toffee	raffle	waffle	baffle
5. **guidance**	guarantee	gruesome	grotesque	guidance	guideline
6. **quiet**	quite	polite	queen	quiet	quilt
7. **table**	tennis	table	tales	tremble	tablet
8. **sipped**	slipped	skipped	clipped	sipped	staple
9. **slowly**	slower	slowed	slowly	spoiled	stately
10. **began**	begin	bottom	begging	began	pagan
11. **read**	bead	dead	reed	read	seed
12. **newspaper**	newsroom	newscaster	newspaper	nuisance	snowstorm
13. **husband**	heather	hunters	panther	heaven	husband
14. **join**	gain	jail	join	jump	gone
15. **would**	wooded	could	should	would	mound
16. **dear**	bear	tear	dear	pear	dare
17. **asked**	asked	again	ailed	acted	added
18. **some**	come	same	soon	some	cone
19. **thanks**	thinks	shanks	thanks	shawls	changes
20. **stomach**	should	started	streets	stomach	stewed

Time: _____ seconds

Number correct: _____ /20

Record results in Column 2A of the Word Recognition Progress Chart on page 199.

Word Recognition Exercise 2B

KEY WORD

1. **acting**	reacting	acting	eating	seeing	sewing
2. **apple**	apple	eagle	ripple	temple	pepper
3. **juice**	judge	queen	price	prince	juice
4. **toast**	taste	boast	roast	toast	toads
5. **today**	table	today	total	heyday	relay
6. **starting**	trailing	stories	starting	creating	reacting
7. **okay**	aloe	oily	okay	early	akin
8. **reading**	reeling	calling	weeding	reading	leading
9. **kitchen**	chicken	cabinet	kittens	kitchen	kindling
10. **prepare**	protest	privilege	prepare	prolong	garage
11. **returned**	realized	reprinted	realistic	returned	created
12. **down**	round	sewn	brown	drown	down
13. **wife**	wise	wipe	weep	wife	wind
14. **section**	seaside	sector	section	reason	creation
15. **silence**	syllable	sickness	nuisance	silence	reasons
16. **moments**	minutes	moments	mountain	nutrients	enforces
17. **looked**	hooked	booked	looked	leaked	docked
18. **tattoos**	tailors	tokens	tripped	tattoos	voodoo
19. **fifteen**	fifteen	fireman	filters	fiftieth	firefly
20. **morning**	meeting	warning	warming	morning	mounting

Time: _____ seconds

Number correct: _____ /20

Record results in Column 2B of the Word Recognition Progress Chart on page 199.

Word Recognition Exercise 2C

KEY WORD

1. **eyeliner**	elephant	evening	eyesight	eyeliner	enlighten
2. **rebel**	retail	rebel	retell	navel	radar
3. **knots**	knife	knows	know	knot	knots
4. **worried**	married	varied	carried	worried	curried
5. **terrible**	trouble	terrible	scrabble	scribble	waffles
6. **teenager**	teenager	teenagers	tentative	taxation	relaxation
7. **briefcase**	basketball	baseball	basement	briefcase	boulder
8. **honey**	honey	heaven	beauty	heavy	funny
9. **office**	often	office	coffee	suffice	police
10. **kissed**	fished	hashed	kissed	leased	bashed
11. **distracted**	diseases	distance	doubtful	distracted	subtracted
12. **injury**	instead	injury	import	insult	inquiry
13. **daughter**	dangerous	delightful	beautiful	daughter	drought
14. **dating**	rating	leaking	seating	waiting	dating
15. **musical**	magical	musical	radical	natural	satirical
16. **phone**	ghost	phase	phone	groan	plane
17. **opinion**	optional	onions	opinion	oriented	ownership
18. **mother**	neither	nature	mother	another	bother
19. **angry**	angry	gray	weary	really	many
20. **capable**	coupled	contrary	countries	capable	critical

Time: _____ seconds

Number correct: _____ /20

Record results in Column 2C of the Word Recognition Progress Chart on page 199.

Word Recognition Exercise 3A

KEY WORD

1. **usually**	musically	unusual	utility	useful	usually
2. **studied**	stayed	studied	carried	started	streaked
3. **enjoyed**	annoyed	engaged	enraged	enjoyed	employed
4. **concentrate**	container	countryside	comfortable	concentrate	capability
5. **friends**	frantic	friends	flowers	hurried	franks
6. **during**	during	daring	boring	pouring	herring
7. **library**	lounge	lantern	library	lightning	hairy
8. **best**	dust	beet	best	dash	hash
9. **behind**	below	behind	bearded	detour	behead
10. **together**	tonight	touchdown	together	torches	tailgate
11. **projects**	perfect	promote	rejects	projects	program
12. **research**	rotates	reaches	related	reasoned	research
13. **worked**	marked	nailed	worked	walked	wounded
14. **participate**	paperweight	participate	pictorial	pigtails	philosophy
15. **cello**	cellar	cells	cello	celery	caller
16. **activities**	activates	captivates	navigates	activities	accidents
17. **orchestra**	orchards	originals	orchestra	octagonal	orchestras
18. **played**	gladly	played	paged	quietly	prayed
19. **popular**	popcorn	garbage	playful	popular	pulpits
20. **plain**	plane	please	phone	ghost	plain

Time: _____ seconds

Number correct: _____ /20

Record results in Column 3A of the Word Recognition Progress Chart on page 199.

Word Recognition Exercise 3B

KEY WORD

1. **lately**	lately	lastly	Italy	leaky	lonely
2. **noticed**	national	motioned	noticed	maturity	captured
3. **simple**	simply	simple	symbol	sandal	salmon
4. **seriously**	sustained	something	curiously	sweetened	seriously
5. **either**	evenly	center	either	easier	neither
6. **listen**	fasten	loosen	hasten	listen	lastly
7. **never**	river	woven	mover	waken	never
8. **disagree**	business	disagree	distance	dissect	disturb
9. **brave**	please	broad	brood	bread	brave
10. **mother**	motors	mother	neither	neighbor	motions
11. **father**	fatter	heater	bother	father	brother
12. **upset**	uptown	option	upset	ugliest	uproar
13. **wanted**	mounted	weeded	waded	wanted	needed
14. **lenient**	leather	leaders	lenient	lantern	latest
15. **kind**	land	hand	hind	kind	lost
16. **growing**	gaining	pointing	growing	quality	grooming
17. **complicate**	congratulate	complicate	compliment	contrary	considers
18. **older**	colder	other	lonely	alarm	older
19. **taller**	rather	taller	caller	holler	volley
20. **secrets**	certain	seaside	secrets	secures	curtains

Time: _____ seconds

Number correct: _____ /20

Record results in Column 3B of the Word Recognition Progress Chart on page 199.

Word Recognition Exercise 3C

KEY WORD

1. **yard**	guard	bored	yard	gold	jade
2. **always**	around	always	airport	alcove	airline
3. **locker**	locker	halter	rocker	walker	latter
4. **shyly**	short	shyly	shortly	slight	shady
5. **smile**	smart	smoke	smile	snore	snail
6. **dropping**	dripping	dropping	tripping	limping	dreaming
7. **dreamer**	dreamer	streamer	plumber	slumber	trimmer
8. **stare**	store	stain	steal	star	stare
9. **heart**	haste	heart	heats	learn	hear
10. **beating**	boating	dating	beating	dealing	bowling
11. **confide**	contrast	complete	confide	surprise	callous
12. **forced**	family	horses	fasted	placed	forced
13. **away**	only	about	await	away	array
14. **floor**	broom	proud	flour	float	floor
15. **right**	night	might	sight	right	tight
16. **excuse**	extra	extreme	excuse	extend	evicts
17. **sorry**	sorry	curry	carry	sunny	money
18. **comedian**	comments	commentary	complete	comedian	comfortable
19. **sweet**	sweat	steak	smoke	snore	sweet
20. **fault**	fault	horse	flesh	flavor	fatal

Time: _____ seconds

Number correct: _____ /20

Record results in Column 3C of the Word Recognition Progress Chart on page 199.

Word Recognition Exercise 4A

KEY WORD

1. **happen**	happier	holiday	hopping	happen	hunted
2. **thought**	though	thought	through	thorough	drought
3. **player**	planet	platter	player	played	planter
4. **making**	making	molding	waking	needing	major
5. **boyfriend**	backyard	bothered	breakfast	boyfriend	friendly
6. **pretty**	pretty	greatly	really	proudly	quietly
7. **chance**	shower	choose	channel	chance	shouts
8. **class**	chase	close	class	choose	chess
9. **surprised**	surprise	sunrise	sandwich	surprised	shortened
10. **worried**	warmed	married	mourned	wanted	worried
11. **several**	suggest	several	covered	sanded	seventy
12. **morning**	mourning	nothing	morning	counting	something
13. **meeting**	morning	something	meeting	mourning	mailing
14. **beautiful**	beautiful	bountiful	doubtful	daughter	beneficial
15. **thrilled**	tailored	teammate	throats	thrilled	tricked
16. **orchestra**	ordinary	organize	official	orchestra	ornament
17. **teacher**	tailors	teacher	creator	traitor	transfer
18. **writes**	strikes	mounts	writes	wrote	waiters
19. **mirror**	minor	sorrow	warrior	mirror	winter
20. **maybe**	negate	majors	minors	mayors	maybe

Time: _____ seconds

Number correct: _____ /20

Record results in Column 4A of the Word Recognition Progress Chart on page 199.

Word Recognition Exercise 4B

KEY WORD

1. **accompany**	accountable	accompany	articulate	anything	anyway
2. **instrument**	implement	instructs	instrument	intolerant	insight
3. **sadness**	sandals	sadness	seedless	candles	serious
4. **basketball**	baskets	baseball	breakfast	beautiful	basketball
5. **loved**	lived	lonely	dived	layer	loved
6. **happy**	happy	tabby	healthy	hoping	husky
7. **flute**	flake	flour	flute	slate	float
8. **advice**	admire	advise	avoid	advice	advance
9. **still**	style	while	shrill	until	still
10. **hear**	horn	hear	hair	lore	lame
11. **smile**	smoke	snail	stone	steak	smile
12. **staring**	stealing	staring	sailing	speaking	crossing
13. **dark**	bark	lark	hark	park	dark
14. **travel**	token	taken	teaspoon	travel	trails
15. **gray**	grip	gray	grey	grow	guys
16. **flaming**	playing	glaring	flaming	flamingo	flowery
17. **flowers**	fountain	football	flower	flowers	fixtures
18. **baggy**	buggy	doggy	baggy	daddy	sandy
19. **guys**	gays	gaps	goes	pays	guys
20. **chain**	crane	shame	chair	chain	cheese

Time: _____ seconds

Number correct: _____ /20

Record results in Column 4B of the Word Recognition Progress Chart on page 199.

Word Recognition Exercise 4C

KEY WORD

1. **link**	sink	rink	link	hand	hind
2. **fence**	fancy	lance	faint	fence	hence
3. **essence**	entertain	emblems	essence	elephant	earring
4. **innocence**	intellect	innocent	important	innocence	identical
5. **turn**	burn	pain	turn	fern	worm
6. **world**	waters	molded	wailed	world	could
7. **right**	might	right	sight	light	plight
8. **silken**	sudden	colder	silken	sighted	silky
9. **vision**	notion	motion	fission	vision	cushion
10. **dream**	dream	broom	scream	cream	learns
11. **romantic**	realistic	nomadic	romantic	rounded	romance
12. **guitar**	garage	guitar	guilty	quality	garbage
13. **applaud**	approach	opposed	applause	applaud	oppressed
14. **club**	shop	bulb	club	crowd	shout
15. **joining**	growing	joining	jointly	jockey	gaining
16. **list**	last	mist	best	list	lost
17. **males**	meals	moles	males	nails	tales
18. **sheet**	shout	throat	sleet	skate	sheet
19. **extraordinary**	excellence	especially	extraordinary	extravagantly	exuberantly
20. **bright**	brought	delight	plight	bright	slight

Time: _____ seconds

Number correct: _____ /20

Record results in Column 4C of the Word Recognition Progress Chart on page 199.

Word Recognition Exercise 5A

KEY WORD

1. **signed**	signal	sighed	signed	snored	shared
2. **club**	stub	slap	clap	club	stab
3. **home**	bone	hair	foam	lone	home
4. **breath**	bathe	bread	depth	breath	breathe
5. **words**	worms	words	warms	walks	world
6. **hopefully**	hopefully	usefully	carefully	helpfully	painfully
7. **over**	oven	even	over	cover	entry
8. **exactly**	entirely	exactly	innately	evenly	expertly
9. **waiting**	making	writing	waiting	tailing	painting
10. **wrote**	write	wrote	house	mouse	crowd
11. **school**	stool	shame	school	straight	smooth
12. **casual**	careful	casual	natural	quiet	cautious
13. **sound**	found	hound	mound	sound	pound
14. **control**	center	central	control	counter	compile
15. **terrible**	trouble	terrible	horrible	double	tumble
16. **perfect**	portrait	perform	portray	perfect	perfume
17. **asked**	oiled	asked	nailed	about	around
18. **answered**	ownership	announced	answered	armchair	alienate
19. **daydream**	breakfast	blackened	daylight	daydream	dateline
20. **permission**	punishment	permission	pleasantly	painfully	permanence

Time: _____ seconds

Number correct: _____ /20

Record results in Column 5A of the Word Recognition Progress Chart on page 199.

Word Recognition Exercise 5B

KEY WORD

1. **moment**	motions	waters	moment	minute	mention
2. **waited**	watered	waited	wasted	written	wrapped
3. **today**	rodeos	toenail	today	really	reality
4. **began**	detain	begin	bacon	beyond	began
5. **interrupt**	interfere	introduce	interrupt	entertain	incident
6. **homework**	hometown	honesty	lonesome	homework	husbands
7. **guess**	guest	guess	quiet	queen	quite
8. **tense**	tight	rinse	sense	tense	meant
9. **sounds**	crowns	drowns	sounds	pounds	mounds
10. **shaking**	shouting	shaping	striking	shaking	changing
11. **relax**	repay	relay	latex	relax	relics
12. **remember**	reminder	remember	romance	romantic	restates
13. **angry**	hungry	lonely	money	angry	ample
14. **staying**	saying	standing	praying	staying	trying
15. **always**	allows	please	always	analyze	closed
16. **attitude**	altitude	aptitude	arranged	attitude	alternate
17. **picking**	packing	picking	kicking	licking	skating
18. **college**	collage	carriage	college	courage	cartons
19. **argue**	allow	argue	alone	crown	atomic
20. **grateful**	gracious	gateway	grateful	grapefruit	grandpa

Time: _____ seconds

Number correct: _____ /20

Record results in Column 5B of the Word Recognition Progress Chart on page 199.

Word Recognition Exercise 5C

KEY WORD

1. **little**	rattle	latter	little	litter	platter
2. **serious**	silent	social	curious	serious	cereals
3. **either**	neither	either	enough	another	mother
4. **weakly**	weekly	meekly	neatly	weakly	wisely
5. **different**	dissident	different	distance	difficult	doorway
6. **problems**	grounds	pleased	probably	problems	phonics
7. **brother**	mother	bothers	brother	fathers	mothers
8. **privacy**	powerful	publicly	privacy	greatly	private
9. **crazy**	crazy	cozy	cranky	crafty	creamy
10. **meantime**	mountain	meantime	maintain	mundane	mentions
11. **talented**	tortured	trained	talented	treatment	teenager
12. **shifted**	shouted	shielded	shifted	shadow	showers
13. **listen**	loosen	listen	lesson	lunches	lessons
14. **headphones**	headphone	earphones	telephones	headphones	headlines
15. **discuss**	distrust	disgust	beaches	discuss	disease
16. **quickly**	quietly	gladly	quickly	pleased	quarter
17. **attacking**	attempting	attending	attaching	attracting	attacking
18. **behind**	between	beehive	behind	brunch	death
19. **opened**	painted	opened	churned	opinion	applied
20. **worse**	nurse	mouse	wears	worse	mounts

Time: _____ seconds

Number correct: _____ /20

Record results in Column 5C of the Word Recognition Progress Chart on page 199.

Word Recognition Exercise 6A

KEY WORD

1. **called**	culled	rolled	killed	caller	called
2. **animal**	animate	antelope	animal	autumns	annotate
3. **where**	whale	where	while	when	wheel
4. **telephone**	telephone	telegraph	touchdown	television	microphone
5. **prepare**	postpone	politics	postman	prepare	prepays
6. **cheek**	check	creek	cheek	sheet	sleet
7. **kissing**	listing	kissing	wishing	sipping	hosting
8. **imitating**	imitation	intimating	imitating	initiating	initially
9. **salad**	salad	solid	sorbet	seals	soiled
10. **stove**	grove	prove	drove	stove	loose
11. **garlic**	garage	garlic	jargon	pardon	quick
12. **mushroom**	bedroom	newsroom	mushroom	mention	maintain
13. **pasta**	paste	pasta	gates	quake	pizza
14. **dinner**	winner	sinner	diner	dinner	banner
15. **declared**	decided	deliberate	designed	decorated	declared
16. **decision**	determine	develops	declining	decisive	decision
17. **nodded**	molded	needle	seated	nodded	needed
18. **head**	bead	feed	heed	lead	head
19. **agreement**	agreement	apartment	opponent	appointed	another
20. **healthy**	beautify	reality	wealthy	healthy	healthier

Time: _____ seconds

Number correct: _____ /20

Record results in Column 6A of the Word Recognition Progress Chart on page 199.

Word Recognition Exercise 6B

KEY WORD

1. **protein**	protein	posture	question	portion	promote
2. **interrupt**	interfere	interface	interrupt	insertion	insight
3. **vegetable**	verbalize	maturity	vegetable	volatile	volcano
4. **hungry**	handle	hasten	hurried	hungry	handsome
5. **discuss**	destroy	because	discuss	biscuit	distill
6. **dessert**	desert	dessert	busted	business	delight
7. **laughed**	launched	happened	lightning	laughed	laundry
8. **moment**	notice	moment	message	massage	comment
9. **trailed**	traveled	teenage	trailed	streamed	trailer
10. **teenage**	tennis	morning	teamwork	teenage	toilet
11. **tomorrow**	tomorrow	mountains	sorrowful	tomatoes	romance
12. **clients**	silence	clowns	clients	closet	crises
13. **young**	yarrow	pound	yellow	young	yearly
14. **awhile**	await	whale	evolve	awhile	amend
15. **hardly**	neatly	coldly	holly	glory	hardly
16. **chance**	choice	cheese	chance	choose	should
17. **flautist**	flounder	founder	plumber	flautist	follower
18. **picked**	gifted	pickled	picked	poked	kicked
19. **believe**	deliver	believe	relief	delight	behind
20. **reliable**	realistic	routines	rotated	relapse	reliable

Time: _____ seconds

Number correct: _____ /20

Record results in Column 6B of the Word Recognition Progress Chart on page 199.

Word Recognition Exercise 6C

KEY WORD

1. **meals**	seals	meets	meals	limbs	lambs
2. **mind**	wind	rind	mink	mind	wink
3. **calling**	sailing	calling	mailing	dialing	kindly
4. **number**	member	ember	sender	number	kinder
5. **lifestyle**	lifeguard	librarian	likelihood	lightning	lifestyle
6. **criminal**	counters	criminals	criminal	animals	seasonal
7. **super**	sender	supper	super	cater	opener
8. **tonight**	tailgate	threads	neighbor	tailors	tonight
9. **channel**	tunnel	channel	shudder	charter	school
10. **sounds**	around	sands	crowns	sounds	crowds
11. **group**	group	grape	proud	queen	prune
12. **cabinet**	cabin	combine	cabinet	candidate	clarinet
13. **starving**	stealing	streaming	smiling	starving	swimming
14. **folks**	yolks	fakes	lakes	folks	forks
15. **careful**	careless	cautious	careful	curtains	company
16. **finish**	kitchen	focused	focuses	finish	furnish
17. **sandwich**	sometime	sandbags	sandwich	sentenced	sailboat
18. **reflect**	reflect	reference	retract	refrain	rainfall
19. **faraway**	farther	feather	fabulous	fearfully	faraway
20. **table**	table	handle	cable	rabbit	label

Time: _____ seconds

Number correct: _____ /20

Record results in Column 6C of the Word Recognition Progress Chart on page 199.

Word Recognition Exercise 7A

KEY WORD

1. **talking**	walking	talking	packing	sulking	reading
2. **blind**	bland	blond	blink	blind	black
3. **friends**	fried	French	frail	friends	friendly
4. **familiar**	fountains	familiar	fabulous	females	famously
5. **women**	woman	moment	women	waist	water
6. **group**	troop	proud	grape	group	pride
7. **disguising**	disgusted	digesting	deliberating	disguising	deciding
8. **every**	enough	every	energy	entire	eager
9. **month**	mouth	route	which	month	wound
10. **meeting**	wedding	meeting	reading	weeding	needing
11. **criticize**	critical	capital	contracted	criticize	citation
12. **trying**	prying	crying	trying	paying	laying
13. **years**	gears	wears	pears	years	pores
14. **discuss**	digest	discuss	process	progress	digress
15. **problems**	problem	programs	problems	progress	protests
16. **issues**	items	invent	ensure	issues	italics
17. **appreciate**	apprehend	appearance	amputate	approach	appreciate
18. **difference**	dominates	different	diligent	diffuses	difference
19. **helped**	hunted	heaped	helped	horses	honored
20. **whatever**	whenever	whether	whatever	weather	wherever

Time: _____ seconds

Number correct: _____ /20

Record results in Column 7A of the Word Recognition Progress Chart on page 199.

Word Recognition Exercise 7B

KEY WORD

1. **night**	sight	might	night	right	light
2. **maybe**	maybe	needy	mounts	misled	money
3. **advice**	advance	advise	advice	adjust	alters
4. **struggle**	strangle	struggle	straggle	stranger	stubble
5. **related**	retrained	railroad	related	roasted	reality
6. **minds**	winds	rinds	sends	minds	mints
7. **arrived**	survived	arrived	assumed	annoyed	carved
8. **chemistry**	chemicals	cremates	criminals	chemistry	cheapest
9. **members**	numbers	wonders	wanders	mentors	members
10. **especially**	easygoing	externally	extensively	especially	explosively
11. **treated**	tailored	treated	trailed	started	treaded
12. **grabbed**	greeted	rubbed	grabbed	grated	graded
13. **mutual**	notate	mutual	mouse	maintain	ritual
14. **sayings**	sighing	signing	sayings	sightings	paying
15. **gender**	gender	tender	render	lender	sender
16. **eventually**	entertainment	enchantment	eventfully	eventually	evenhanded
17. **goodness**	gradual	weakness	goodness	goddess	address
18. **complain**	compete	complete	comforts	complain	candid
19. **anymore**	anyone	around	anymore	assists	ordinary
20. **posted**	painted	roasted	pasted	posted	postage

Time: _____ seconds

Number correct: _____ /20

Record results in Column 7B of the Word Recognition Progress Chart on page 199.

Word Recognition Exercise 7C

KEY WORD

1. **immediate**	irregular	indicate	immediate	innovate	encounter
2. **afford**	effort	affect	allured	afford	allowed
3. **expensive**	expansive	elaborate	exaggerate	expensive	entrances
4. **snacks**	stream	sneaks	snakes	snacks	pranks
5. **hearing**	fearing	hearing	learning	earning	hiring
6. **shock**	shook	clock	shock	shake	shack
7. **tasks**	tacks	masks	sacks	lasts	tasks
8. **solutions**	solutions	salutations	straighten	sweetens	salvation
9. **matter**	better	meters	neater	matter	mother
10. **believe**	relieve	deceive	perceive	behaves	believe
11. **tough**	rough	bough	tough	tight	weigh
12. **silence**	silent	silence	patience	gracious	license
13. **working**	walking	making	working	caring	wearing
14. **positively**	positioning	negatively	politely	positively	protective
15. **herself**	handsome	himself	herself	hurried	harden
16. **relate**	rotate	respond	relate	detain	radiate
17. **divorce**	detracts	dividend	divisive	divorce	decorate
18. **strength**	straight	streaked	slightly	strength	staggered
19. **stress**	strike	stones	sweets	stress	skills
20. **computer**	complete	complaint	computer	comfortable	container

Time: _____ seconds

Number correct: _____ /20

Record results in Column 7C of the Word Recognition Progress Chart on page 199.

Word Recognition Exercise 8A

KEY WORD

1. **hard**	ward	road	hired	hard	heard
2. **young**	round	yellow	yours	yucca	young
3. **feeling**	failing	hailing	feeling	fishing	dealing
4. **future**	feather	feature	nurture	mature	future
5. **attend**	attend	alright	around	cotton	trend
6. **diverse**	divides	deadens	distinct	diverse	beavers
7. **reggae**	really	regal	reggae	rapper	arrange
8. **smoothly**	smoothly	swimming	standard	something	smother
9. **played**	pilots	played	gladly	plowed	plumber
10. **people**	purple	playful	people	garage	geology
11. **talents**	tastes	wastes	pilots	talents	traits
12. **tastes**	wastes	latest	pastes	treats	tastes
13. **piano**	piano	peace	piece	pasta	peons
14. **guitar**	garage	quotes	guitar	queens	quieter
15. **others**	other	others	covers	mothers	caters
16. **drums**	trees	dreams	drops	drowns	drums
17. **rock**	rake	rock	real	room	rule
18. **metal**	needle	neater	maker	metal	motel
19. **classical**	chosen	classes	classical	cleaner	climber
20. **teasing**	toasting	roasting	teaching	teasing	tasting

Time: _____ seconds

Number correct: _____ /20

Record results in Column 8A of the Word Recognition Progress Chart on page 199.

Word Recognition Exercise 8B

KEY WORD

1. **common**	summon	bottom	summer	common	swimmer
2. **loved**	liked	loved	lived	leaked	moved
3. **perfect**	perfect	project	parade	positive	pervade
4. **distracted**	displaced	distasteful	disdainful	distracted	deadline
5. **parents**	patient	parents	patents	prevents	warrants
6. **follow**	flower	flesh	follow	fellow	feather
7. **rules**	roles	soles	poles	tools	rules
8. **house**	horse	mouse	lounge	house	towns
9. **promise**	practice	granted	pounded	picture	promise
10. **broken**	bottom	dropped	crowded	broken	blacken
11. **senior**	sailor	seaside	senior	junior	center
12. **awake**	awoke	await	about	awake	around
13. **inspiration**	installment	inspiration	inspecting	incalculable	inspirational
14. **arguing**	around	applying	earring	crying	arguing
15. **question**	question	quarrel	garages	general	geometry
16. **strange**	stronger	stranger	strange	streaks	streams
17. **fingers**	figures	follows	feathers	fingers	features
18. **little**	light	bitter	letter	little	litter
19. **enough**	coughs	elephant	alcohol	enough	explode
20. **mature**	matter	measure	mature	nature	creature

Time: _____ seconds

Number correct: _____ /20

Record results in Column 8B of the Word Recognition Progress Chart on page 199.

Word Recognition Exercise 8C

KEY WORD

1. **game**	pane	grow	gone	game	pain
2. **learned**	leaned	learned	cleaned	hounded	worried
3. **fight**	flight	float	fight	right	light
4. **laughter**	daughter	laughter	laundry	lighter	haughty
5. **smooth**	tooth	month	smother	smoke	smooth
6. **wink**	woke	weak	wink	wean	mink
7. **approval**	automatic	appraise	appropriate	aggravate	approval
8. **forward**	failure	faithful	forward	fortune	flower
9. **attention**	attraction	attention	attitude	attentive	attractive
10. **wander**	wonder	wander	winter	waiter	weather
11. **imagine**	illustrate	entertain	imagine	magazine	mountain
12. **silence**	silence	callous	sentence	sailors	subjects
13. **powerful**	pondered	wonderful	provision	powerful	popular
14. **pollution**	protection	practices	portions	pollution	proteins
15. **sarcastic**	searched	sarcastic	secrets	statistic	statistics
16. **concentrate**	condition	concerts	concentrate	concerned	conference
17. **finished**	famished	fountain	flounder	finished	flourish
18. **judgment**	gentleman	jellyfish	judgment	contentment	apartment
19. **grateful**	garages	grateful	grapefruit	grounded	grandfather
20. **message**	massage	message	passage	sewage	rummage

Time: _____ seconds

Number correct: _____ /20

Record results in Column 8C of the Word Recognition Progress Chart on page 199.

Word Recognition Exercise 9A

KEY WORD

1. **real**	role	reel	real	seal	meal
2. **outside**	courts	orders	ornate	outside	output
3. **nervous**	motions	nations	nervous	mermaids	notions
4. **borrow**	burrow	bottom	sorrow	button	borrow
5. **neither**	noontime	neighbor	ignites	neither	energize
6. **sixteen**	sinister	sixteen	cisterns	socialize	simmers
7. **during**	dining	during	boring	building	doubly
8. **loaned**	leaned	loaned	learned	lighter	leased
9. **tonight**	toenail	tailored	tonight	together	teaspoon
10. **favorite**	fantasy	flavored	fabulous	favorite	famous
11. **appreciated**	appropriate	appreciate	appreciated	accountant	accelerate
12. **unbelievable**	uncomfortable	unpleasant	unmentionable	unbelievable	immeasurable
13. **perfume**	perform	perfume	practice	powers	prefers
14. **carefully**	cautiously	centrally	carefully	certainly	quietly
15. **shirt**	short	shoot	shirt	shout	sheet
16. **easily**	eagerly	earlier	early	curly	easily
17. **headache**	homework	heighten	headache	harmonica	harmful
18. **heard**	hoard	board	loaned	heard	hateful
19. **overpower**	opinions	orchestra	overpower	oversight	overseas
20. **smell**	small	smell	shell	stall	swell

Time: _____ seconds

Number correct: _____ /20

Record results in Column 9A of the Word Recognition Progress Chart on page 199.

Word Recognition Exercise 9B

KEY WORD

1. **thrilled**	threatened	treated	thrilled	skilled	trailed
2. **sitting**	setting	sitting	cutting	getting	meeting
3. **group**	great	greet	ghost	proud	group
4. **whispered**	weathered	whitened	whispered	warehouse	whether
5. **show**	shin	show	shed	chow	shoe
6. **putting**	getting	panting	putting	quitting	sitting
7. **great**	group	grate	grain	treat	great
8. **concert**	concert	conceit	concept	contract	conceal
9. **band**	bind	bend	hand	band	land
10. **locked**	looked	loosen	locked	blocked	talked
11. **tickets**	traffic	tokens	targets	tickets	rockets
12. **entrance**	entertain	entrance	elegant	mentions	weather
13. **flat**	flow	late	flat	flirt	flute
14. **broke**	break	plowed	broken	broke	stroke
15. **street**	stream	cream	strain	street	treats
16. **ground**	found	pound	proud	ground	grind
17. **clean**	grain	clone	clean	scream	clams
18. **drifted**	dreamed	drafted	dropped	drifted	sifted
19. **seats**	soaks	coats	notes	meats	seats
20. **dollar**	dealer	dollar	hollow	holler	caller

Time: _____ seconds

Number correct: _____ /20

Record results in Column 9B of the Word Recognition Progress Chart on page 199.

Word Recognition Exercise 9C

KEY WORD

1. **spare**	spoke	spoon	steam	spark	spare
2. **thanks**	themes	throw	tanks	thanks	thimble
3. **shake**	share	shale	shake	cheer	cheek
4. **realized**	realized	realistic	returned	reported	related
5. **beginning**	between	banquets	beginnings	beginning	budgeting
6. **worry**	sorry	carry	penny	money	worry
7. **homeless**	careless	homeless	childless	reckless	pickles
8. **moment**	mention	mounts	notices	moment	wonder
9. **cause**	counts	pause	mouse	cause	rouse
10. **meaningful**	meaningless	meanwhile	maintenance	meaningful	meadowlark
11. **enjoying**	annoying	crying	enjoying	trying	drying
12. **stopped**	stooped	scooped	stripped	stopped	stagger
13. **hours**	heals	leads	hours	honors	flour
14. **helpless**	helpful	holdings	helpless	hopeless	handles
15. **shoulder**	showers	boulders	shadows	shoulder	shudder
16. **crowd**	crown	cloud	clear	cared	crowd
17. **weird**	waist	waste	wired	wield	weird
18. **screaming**	streaming	sketching	stretching	screaming	something
19. **waist**	moist	waste	waist	raises	weight
20. **audience**	auditions	applause	around	audience	automatic

Time: _____ seconds

Number correct: _____ /20

Record results in Column 9C of the Word Recognition Progress Chart on page 199.

Word Recognition Exercise 10A

KEY WORD

1. **forgotten**	fountains	forgotten	flashlight	failures	fingernail
2. **incident**	instance	insights	identical	indicated	incident
3. **outside**	online	outlined	outside	counted	owners
4. **waiting**	winters	wearing	willing	waiting	mailing
5. **concert**	cousins	curtain	concert	candle	concern
6. **incredible**	inconsiderate	uncovered	entertained	incredible	inconsistent
7. **herself**	himself	herself	hindered	kindred	hounded
8. **maybe**	might	nobody	wonder	maybe	mount
9. **quietly**	quietly	quickly	smoothly	gaily	politely
10. **couple**	supper	ripple	capable	couple	triple
11. **tents**	rents	dents	tints	tents	cents
12. **freeway**	failure	freeway	freedom	causeway	yesterday
13. **campfire**	compound	comfortable	candidate	calculate	campfire
14. **bright**	plight	light	straight	bright	right
15. **glow**	blow	grow	plow	plea	glow
16. **across**	about	acorns	across	around	alarms
17. **shining**	shaving	climbing	shouting	shining	slipping
18. **pointing**	painting	pointing	playing	grinding	pointer
19. **surprised**	shouted	comprised	appraised	surprised	supplied
20. **whisper**	shiver	splinter	whether	whither	whisper

Time: _____ seconds

Number correct: _____ /20

Record results in Column 10A of the Word Recognition Progress Chart on page 199.

Word Recognition Exercise 10B

KEY WORD

1. **stars**	stairs	steps	stares	stars	stirs
2. **downtown**	downstairs	duplicate	dreadful	downtown	donations
3. **shelter**	shouted	children	shelters	shoulder	shelter
4. **sentence**	centimeter	cemetery	singular	sentence	censured
5. **instead**	indeed	instead	entrance	unstable	unsteady
6. **waved**	woven	moved	needed	waved	wanted
7. **noisy**	nailed	money	needy	nasty	noisy
8. **ocean**	online	outline	outside	ocean	union
9. **practically**	punctually	punctuation	practically	gratefully	gleefully
10. **thinned**	rimmed	tanned	thinned	shined	trimmed
11. **adventure**	abstract	adventure	accepted	accompany	additional
12. **scared**	screamed	scared	scooped	soiled	sailed
13. **regular**	routine	revolving	regular	regulate	respected
14. **faith**	health	fault	traits	threads	faith
15. **trusts**	treats	trusts	trades	trails	trains
16. **superficial**	southwest	sensitive	souvenir	superficial	supervisor
17. **homeless**	breathless	careless	homeless	priceless	fruitless
18. **wonderful**	whenever	whirlpool	wondering	wonderful	wonderland
19. **interested**	instantly	indirectly	immediate	interested	illuminated
20. **definitely**	distinctly	directly	definitely	detergent	distinguished

Time: _____ seconds

Number correct: _____ /20

Record results in Column 10B of the Word Recognition Progress Chart on page 199.

Word Recognition Exercise 10C

KEY WORD

1. **thinker**	tinker	tanker	thinker	thanks	teacher
2. **perceptive**	provocative	proactive	principled	perceptive	persuasive
3. **except**	accept	expect	except	receipt	excited
4. **communicate**	contradict	connection	communicate	contagious	combination
5. **blame**	banned	bland	plane	blame	shame
6. **holding**	healing	welding	laughing	hiding	holding
7. **blurted**	bleached	spurted	planned	blurted	boiled
8. **crying**	drying	caring	crying	saying	paying
9. **trouble**	thirty	through	tremble	trouble	trigger
10. **secret**	savage	secret	harvest	crescent	secrete
11. **failing**	failing	falling	feeling	keeping	features
12. **truth**	tooth	fruit	truth	wrath	stretch
13. **sweet**	sweat	smell	sneak	snail	sweet
14. **softly**	sweetly	surely	mostly	lastly	softly
15. **breath**	breathe	breath	preach	proudly	bread
16. **alcohol**	argued	athlete	alcohol	apricot	altitude
17. **seriously**	surprising	cautiously	secretly	seriously	quietly
18. **jealous**	previous	precious	jealous	jewelry	jasmine
19. **bother**	brother	bother	panther	lather	holder
20. **understanding**	understated	underlying	entertainment	unnecessary	understanding

Time: _____ seconds

Number correct: _____ /20

Record results in Column 10C of the Word Recognition Progress Chart on page 199.

Word Recognition Exercise 11A

KEY WORD

1. **lock**	lack	lake	lock	leak	load
2. **turned**	tamed	turned	tuned	trained	trimmed
3. **opened**	sprained	opener	outweigh	opened	orphaned
4. **asleep**	aspirin	autumn	asterisk	ascend	asleep
5. **sneak**	snake	smoke	sneak	snail	snore
6. **disturbing**	distanced	dangerous	disappoint	disturbing	destroying
7. **collected**	collected	connected	collated	created	colored
8. **perhaps**	patience	patents	parents	perhaps	pictures
9. **cloud**	crowd	clown	cloud	slowed	plowed
10. **honey**	honey	hijack	homely	honestly	horses
11. **concert**	concept	concert	connect	carpet	campus
12. **genuinely**	generously	graciously	genuinely	gorgeous	generally
13. **friendly**	fastened	freedom	fantastic	friendly	family
14. **taste**	waste	paste	taste	toast	roast
15. **amazing**	analyze	amnesty	amusing	amazing	among
16. **rocked**	racked	mocked	docked	rocked	locked
17. **laughed**	laughter	launched	laundry	landmark	laughed
18. **thought**	through	thought	throughout	though	trough
19. **bravely**	gravely	bounty	between	bravely	blindly
20. **phone**	shone	proud	prince	pounce	phone

Time: _____ seconds

Number correct: _____ /20

Record results in Column 11A of the Word Recognition Progress Chart on page 199.

Word Recognition Exercise 11B

KEY WORD

1. **wrong**	wring	cringe	wreak	wrong	wound
2. **upset**	until	upset	under	unless	untie
3. **nodded**	needed	padded	rotted	nodded	nailed
4. **explained**	extremely	entertained	explained	experiment	expended
5. **between**	beneath	bottom	bracelet	behaved	between
6. **loyal**	royal	legal	loyal	mayor	lawyer
7. **confidence**	confession	contemplate	conference	confidence	comfortable
8. **sauces**	saints	sources	sauces	scarce	saucer
9. **terrible**	trouble	terrible	tremble	horrible	fictional
10. **college**	collage	collect	contrive	collapse	college
11. **talents**	patents	patients	tables	talents	torrents
12. **build**	guild	built	bolded	build	soiled
13. **water**	weather	waiter	matter	wader	water
14. **successful**	successful	subjective	substantive	substitute	sufficiency
15. **decides**	denies	decides	believes	beliefs	decided
16. **remember**	retainer	reminder	remember	relocate	returned
17. **rigid**	regal	rained	right	remind	rigid
18. **carefully**	cautiously	carelessly	calculus	canyon	carefully
19. **capable**	canceled	carbonated	caramel	capable	captured
20. **tonight**	romantic	toenail	together	tornado	tonight

Time: _____ seconds

Number correct: _____ /20

Record results in Column 11B of the Word Recognition Progress Chart on page 199.

Word Recognition Exercise 11C

KEY WORD

1. **suggested**	surprised	suggested	costumed	snuggled	succeeded
2. **semester**	seminar	spacious	semester	staggered	standard
3. **counselor**	corridor	counters	commerce	counselor	commander
4. **world**	mauled	whirled	curled	world	worried
5. **meant**	wound	meant	would	number	meaning
6. **interests**	interests	interest	interface	intellect	itemized
7. **academic**	astronaut	atomic	arithmetic	academic	artistic
8. **family**	famine	family	funny	hurriedly	framing
9. **unhappy**	unstable	unseemly	unselfish	unhappy	unfasten
10. **figure**	finally	linger	picture	finger	figure
11. **hugged**	bugged	mugged	lugged	luggage	hugged
12. **lighter**	fighter	writer	latter	lighter	laughter
13. **facing**	facing	lacing	dicing	fixing	feeling
14. **alone**	along	agreed	alley	alike	alone
15. **whole**	while	whale	wheel	whole	white
16. **behind**	behold	behalf	bother	between	behind
17. **dream**	broom	dream	cream	learn	drama
18. **tonight**	toenail	tongue	tomato	tonight	tolerate
19. **problems**	possibly	probable	potential	probably	problems
20. **facing**	racing	fading	waxing	fixing	facing

Time: _____ seconds

Number correct: _____ /20

Record results in Column 11C of the Word Recognition Progress Chart on page 199.

Word Recognition Exercise 12A

KEY WORD

1. **attractive**	attested	attentive	attractive	traction	attraction
2. **bushy**	busily	bushy	banker	buyer	beeper
3. **mustache**	mistletoe	mushroom	mountain	mustache	mustards
4. **regularly**	registrar	regulate	regularly	requisite	reproduce
5. **maintain**	mountain	maintain	muscles	married	mounted
6. **healthy**	healing	horses	healthy	hearth	heated
7. **trim**	team	time	trip	trim	thin
8. **downtown**	downhill	dangerous	downtown	download	dateline
9. **forum**	found	forum	fairy	hound	bored
10. **palace**	police	parade	garage	graces	palace
11. **floors**	floods	flows	flower	floors	fleas
12. **ceilings**	ceiling	railings	ceilings	earrings	mailing
13. **repair**	require	repaint	repeat	repair	repeal
14. **manage**	marriage	mirage	manage	narrate	carriage
15. **electricity**	electrify	electronic	elephants	electricity	elasticity
16. **plumbing**	pounding	plumbing	grounding	plumber	praying
17. **present**	preface	greatest	pretense	presents	present
18. **booked**	hooked	looked	docked	booked	beaded
19. **annual**	account	anoint	annual	canals	animal
20. **summer**	manner	winner	sinner	summer	somber

Time: _____ seconds

Number correct: _____ /20

Record results in Column 12A of the Word Recognition Progress Chart on page 199.

Word Recognition Exercise 12B

KEY WORD

1. **perform**	preface	prefer	perform	palace	prepare
2. **actresses**	actions	accounts	actresses	addresses	arguments
3. **winter**	wander	weather	wonder	winter	waiter
4. **local**	legal	later	labor	latter	local
5. **artists**	actress	actions	artists	acquaint	waitress
6. **poets**	piles	poets	pairs	posts	paints
7. **technician**	telephone	television	technology	technician	technique
8. **fixing**	faxing	filing	liking	fixing	waxing
9. **broken**	beacon	golden	dragon	button	broken
10. **auditions**	audience	conditions	renditions	auditions	auditorium
11. **director**	dictator	director	direction	directed	delegate
12. **especially**	carefully	gracefully	entirely	especially	tirelessly
13. **popular**	postage	popular	pampered	puncture	populate
14. **section**	suction	section	sanction	solution	sentence
15. **fallen**	broken	failure	feature	fallen	golden
16. **damage**	rampage	baggage	bandage	danger	damage
17. **crew**	brew	drew	true	crew	screw
18. **forward**	failure	fountain	frequent	fortune	forward
19. **tennis**	tables	tennis	tenants	toenail	tailors
20. **musicians**	mountains	nuisance	musicians	numerous	musician

Time: _____ seconds

Number correct: _____ /20

Record results in Column 12B of the Word Recognition Progress Chart on page 199.

Word Recognition Exercise 12C

KEY WORD

1. **chances**	choices	chances	showers	chooses	glances
2. **loving**	lonely	playing	flowing	loving	leaving
3. **package**	garage	pickles	parking	passage	package
4. **surprise**	carriage	superior	seamless	surprise	comprise
5. **earned**	aimed	creamed	earned	meant	weaned
6. **relax**	repair	relax	velour	waxes	relapse
7. **ancient**	answer	nature	mansion	antique	ancient
8. **meaningful**	meanwhile	mentioned	maintained	meaningful	mentoring
9. **landmark**	bandstand	bookmark	landmark	landlord	downsize
10. **function**	fountain	landmark	feature	function	handsome
11. **twice**	twice	twins	swine	crime	tease
12. **inspires**	installs	ensures	inspires	inspects	instead
13. **inspire**	inspire	instant	insults	instead	inspect
14. **hungry**	angry	handy	hunter	hungry	fancy
15. **historic**	homesick	homonym	historic	historian	scientific
16. **honey**	lonely	humbly	solely	honey	money
17. **arranged**	managed	marriage	arrange	oranges	arranged
18. **history**	husband	mystery	library	history	rivalry
19. **treat**	treat	trout	create	meant	wheat
20. **shelter**	shower	shoulder	shelter	cheater	children

Time: _____ seconds

Number correct: _____ /20

Record results in Column 12C of the Word Recognition Progress Chart on page 199.

Word Recognition Exercise 13A

KEY WORD

1. **rehearse**	retires	reheats	rehearse	retails	relates
2. **several**	southern	shallow	seventeen	several	seabed
3. **positive**	positive	potential	purpose	proteins	position
4. **backup**	butcher	backup	butler	banter	beater
5. **performance**	playhouse	performer	pronounce	performance	performed
6. **invited**	entered	enticed	immature	invited	invaded
7. **private**	primate	private	pirates	pleasure	placate
8. **drums**	dreams	beans	beams	domes	drums
9. **laughed**	lounged	laughed	ploughed	lengthen	longitude
10. **drinking**	drilling	draining	drinking	driving	drowning
11. **sound**	sound	round	wound	could	mound
12. **enduring**	during	endurance	enduring	engaging	endearing
13. **harmonize**	marmalade	helplessly	harmony	harmonize	hospitalize
14. **together**	tighten	feather	tonight	together	rotation
15. **even**	oven	even	event	upon	into
16. **vertical**	critical	vegetable	vertical	visual	variety
17. **tease**	tense	terse	raise	tease	lease
18. **diagonal**	diamonds	diagonal	debated	dominant	diameter
19. **horizontal**	horticulture	handsome	happening	horizontal	happiness
20. **laughing**	lounging	laughter	laughing	daughter	leading

Time: _____ seconds

Number correct: _____ /20

Record results in Column 13A of the Word Recognition Progress Chart on page 199.

Word Recognition Exercise 13B

KEY WORD

1. **pitch**	glitch	print	pitch	patch	touch
2. **character**	childhood	challenge	chartered	character	cheated
3. **special**	spoken	speaker	special	spatial	selfish
4. **event**	entail	every	error	event	enters
5. **wonder**	wander	winter	wonder	meander	ponder
6. **ongoing**	outward	opening	counting	ongoing	oneself
7. **design**	details	design	drawn	distant	degree
8. **package**	package	garage	guarantee	pleasing	pleasant
9. **normal**	nature	morals	nurture	normal	neater
10. **compassion**	comfortable	compassion	companion	consumers	contraction
11. **returned**	retailed	returned	realistic	rotated	relative
12. **tattoo**	tailor	teacher	tattoo	tinkers	taboo
13. **skill**	spill	skill	trill	thrill	still
14. **lucky**	lanky	tricky	healthy	hefty	lucky
15. **enough**	eagerly	rough	entrance	enough	eighteen
16. **musical**	mountain	whimsical	musical	musician	magical
17. **pain**	pain	rain	gain	vain	pine
18. **hobby**	lobby	wobbly	handle	handy	hobby
19. **trade**	track	tread	trade	steal	trail
20. **interrupt**	industry	infirmary	infinity	interrupt	inflate

Time: _____ seconds

Number correct: _____ /20

Record results in Column 13B of the Word Recognition Progress Chart on page 199.

Word Recognition Exercise 13C

KEY WORD

1. **inspired**	instilled	inspired	infected	infamous	inexact
2. **perform**	payload	prefers	perform	performs	patents
3. **upper**	other	regular	offers	upper	uglier
4. **enjoy**	employ	enjoy	entry	occupy	enzyme
5. **better**	batter	putter	butter	better	letter
6. **duo**	due	two	duo	demo	dug
7. **worried**	wailing	waters	waiting	worried	married
8. **maybe**	maybe	meals	midway	master	mayor
9. **subject**	substitute	sergeant	subjects	subject	supplied
10. **shelter**	shelter	shouted	sailor	shaver	skilled
11. **express**	expires	impress	distress	explain	express
12. **distracted**	displayed	destroyed	distracted	disappoint	detained
13. **talent**	target	tangent	tearful	teenager	talent
14. **dreams**	doubts	double	dreams	drains	drowns
15. **focus**	final	finale	found	focus	fussy
16. **attention**	attitudes	altitudes	attention	attractive	attentive
17. **front**	faint	front	knife	float	fleet
18. **along**	aloud	atone	along	around	altars
19. **thought**	though	through	thorough	thought	threats
20. **experience**	exposures	expiration	experience	entirely	entertains

Time: _____ seconds

Number correct: _____ /20

Record results in Column 13C of the Word Recognition Progress Chart on page 199.

Word Recognition Exercise 14A

KEY WORD

1. **place**	palace	plate	please	place	glaze
2. **lyrical**	lately	lyrical	musical	political	radical
3. **project**	protect	preface	profess	project	parent
4. **acquainted**	acquired	alternated	acquainted	acknowledge	addresses
5. **sounded**	rounded	pounded	sounded	bounded	listed
6. **packed**	backed	picked	peeled	packed	tacked
7. **modest**	modern	models	western	eastern	modest
8. **instrument**	imperfect	impulses	instrument	infamous	institute
9. **industrial**	industries	instruments	insiders	industrial	indefinite
10. **kitchen**	chicken	kitchen	children	kidneys	kindly
11. **cots**	cats	cuts	rots	cots	pots
12. **pizza**	pizza	piece	pizazz	dizzy	pasta
13. **future**	failure	feature	future	funnier	foolish
14. **agreed**	around	agreed	abound	agrees	atlases
15. **chili**	china	chilly	chili	child	chair
16. **relaxing**	relating	retails	relaxing	relaxed	rhythms
17. **empty**	entry	empty	apply	essay	edgy
18. **space**	stage	space	chase	speak	spoke
19. **warehouse**	wherever	weather	warehouse	welfare	weekday
20. **comfortable**	countries	conversation	constructs	comfortable	countless

Time: _____ seconds

Number correct: _____ /20

Record results in Column 14A of the Word Recognition Progress Chart on page 199.

Word Recognition Exercise 14B

KEY WORD

1. **hammer**	handle	hunter	hammer	manner	winner
2. **nails**	mails	trails	nails	pails	tails
3. **friendly**	fountain	failing	friendly	lengthy	feathers
4. **surprise**	surface	supplies	suggests	surprise	suntanned
5. **palace**	police	pounce	places	palace	galaxy
6. **dressed**	dreamed	pressed	messed	blessed	dressed
7. **manages**	managers	manages	maintains	mountain	mailbox
8. **kidding**	wedding	getting	keeping	kidding	bidding
9. **introduce**	interview	entrance	intellect	intercom	introduce
10. **carpentry**	counseling	cautionary	carpentry	cornerstone	capitalize
11. **hurts**	holds	hurts	helps	loaves	hates
12. **finally**	finishes	finalize	partially	finally	finance
13. **drift**	draft	drift	doubt	dream	drill
14. **herself**	herself	himself	oneself	hateful	healthy
15. **smiled**	snowed	smoked	smiled	soaked	smelled
16. **theater**	throats	theater	threaten	theory	therapy
17. **donation**	detailed	downtown	donation	dealership	defeated
18. **heart**	health	breadth	harmed	heart	least
19. **pitched**	pitched	patched	perched	gathered	painted
20. **feeling**	failing	feeling	flowers	leaping	peeling

Time: _____ seconds

Number correct: _____ /20

Record results in Column 14B of the Word Recognition Progress Chart on page 199.

Word Recognition Exercise 14C

KEY WORD

1. **evening**	envelope	entirely	entertain	evening	eastern
2. **energy**	entertain	energetic	energy	synergy	emerge
3. **volunteers**	vacations	volunteers	valentines	vehicles	vagabond
4. **hearty**	healthy	healing	hearty	lengthy	hairy
5. **apron**	about	around	again	apron	agony
6. **corner**	counter	calmer	normal	cover	corner
7. **meal**	nail	mole	meal	note	mail
8. **greet**	guest	great	grant	green	greet
9. **counted**	counter	counted	counts	mounted	rounded
10. **loaded**	leader	founded	loaded	kinder	sounded
11. **milling**	willing	mining	milking	milling	winning
12. **beating**	boating	dating	beating	heating	boasting
13. **lighter**	latter	lighter	brighter	lengthen	together
14. **appeared**	approached	appendage	appetite	appeared	attention
15. **faces**	laces	fines	races	fairies	faces
16. **simply**	simple	single	simply	singing	steeple
17. **proud**	ground	trade	round	pound	proud
18. **tonight**	tongue	tonight	tonnage	totally	timbers
19. **stage**	steal	steep	stooge	stage	tragedy
20. **promise**	pleases	promote	grimaces	promises	promise

Time: _____ seconds

Number correct: _____ /20

Record results in Column 14C of the Word Recognition Progress Chart on page 199.

Word Recognition Progress Chart

Number correct

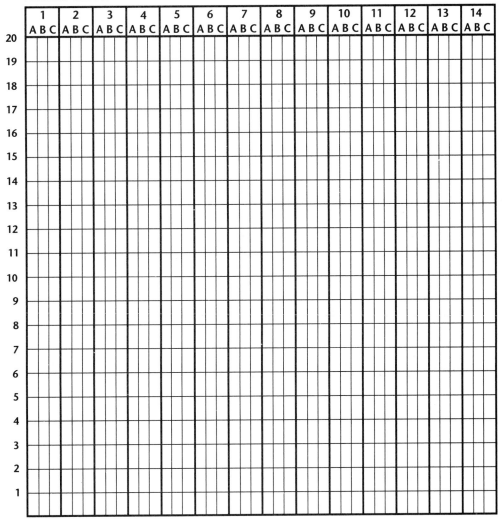

Time (in seconds)

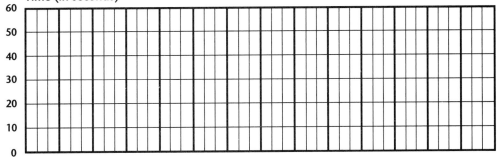

The Whole Story

CHAPTER 1

A Weekday Morning

The radio clicked on. The rock music was loud. Sandy heard the music and woke up like a bullet. She looked at the clock. It was 6:15 A.M. Sandy sang along with the words. She was listening to her favorite radio station.

"Sandy," shouted her father. "Sandy, turn that music off." Steve Finch came into her room. "Why do you have to listen to such weird music? It's the same thing over and over. I'm not sure that is really music. It does have rhythm, though. Hmmm. No, it isn't really music. It's terrible. It is definitely terrible music."

"I like that music, Dad. It's my favorite group, Green Waves. Listen for a minute, and I'm sure you'll like it. It has a really powerful message. Didn't you ever listen to music like this when you were younger?" Sandy went over to the radio to turn it up louder.

"No, no, don't do that. I can't stand it. The music I listened to had a message too. But the words were clear and the groups didn't use offensive language. Turn the radio down so your mother and I can't hear it. I'm sure that music is hurting your ears as well as your brain. Now would you please turn it off and get ready for school? You'd better hurry up!"

Sandy walked into the bathroom. She turned on the shower. At first the water felt cold. This helped her wake up. Then the water got hotter. "This shower feels great," she thought. "A place where I can be alone and sing. No one bothers me in here." She grabbed the soap and washed thoroughly; then she shampooed her hair. If she stayed in the shower too long, her mom or dad usually banged on the door to hassle her. Time to get out of the shower. She grabbed a towel and dried off.

After her shower, Sandy brushed her hair. She put on her old green T-shirt and some jeans and wrapped her sweatshirt around her shoulders. Then she put on her makeup and a pair of earrings.

She looked at the clock again. It was late, and she didn't know what to have for breakfast. She poured a glass of milk and ate a piece of toast while standing by the sink. Her mother, Jane, came into the kitchen.

"Sandy, why don't you sit down and eat breakfast? It isn't healthy to eat breakfast standing up."

"I know, Mom, but I'm already late for school. I don't have time to sit down and eat."

"Did you finish your homework, dear?"

"Yes."

"Do you have your flute?"

"Uh-huh."

"And your lunch?"

"Yup."

"Did you brush your teeth?"

"Mom, I haven't finished eating breakfast yet. I'll brush my teeth after I finish eating."

"You should brush your teeth when you wake up and then brush them again after breakfast. Sandy, why are you wearing that old T-shirt? It has a hole in it. I know you have some nice blouses in your closet."

"Mom, please stop."

"Stop what, dear?"

"Stop nagging me."

"Sandy, are you wearing eyeliner?"

"Yes, Mom, I've been wearing eyeliner for months. Isn't it pretty? It's called French Lilac Blue. I just love it." Sandy pretended not to notice that her mother was a little annoyed.

"Sandy Finch, you're too young to wear that much makeup. Please go upstairs and wash it off."

"Mom, I'm fifteen. I'm old enough to wear makeup. Believe me, all the girls at school wear makeup. They have tattoos and pierced ears, noses, tongues, and everything. Listen, Mom, I don't have time to talk about this now. I'm late and I've got to go. See you later." Sandy kissed her mother quickly on the cheek, picked up her school books, and ran out of the house.

Sandy ran to catch the bus. While she was running, she thought about her older brother, Bill. Bill was away at college, and Sandy heard from him often. When they talked, they shared their problems. But she hadn't heard from him for a while. She missed him. Since Bill had gone to college, her mother nagged her much more than before. And she was arguing with her mother a lot more than usual too.

CHAPTER 2

Jane and Steve

After Sandy had gone to school, Jane Finch sat down to drink her coffee. It was quiet at the table. She sipped her coffee slowly and began to read the newspaper. She was distracted. She was trying to read, but she was thinking about Sandy. Her husband came in to join her.

"Would you like some coffee, Steve?" asked Jane.

"No thanks, honey, my stomach has been acting up. I feel like there are ten thousand knots in my stomach. It's probably that awful music that wakes me up every morning. I can't stand the music Sandy listens to on the radio. I don't think I'm old-fashioned, but hearing that tuneless, offensive language over and over makes my blood boil. There is no message to the music either. I can't believe that Sandy really likes it."

"You know, honey, different generations have different tastes," said Jane. "Remember some of the music we used to listen to?"

Steve smiled as he remembered. "You're right. Maybe I'll just have some apple juice and toast today. Maybe eating breakfast will help me get rid of some of the knots in my stomach."

"I'll get you some juice," she said, starting to get up.

"That's okay," said Steve. "I'll get it. You're reading."

"I'm not really reading. I'm distracted. I've been thinking about Sandy too."

Steve went to the kitchen to prepare his breakfast and returned to sit down with his wife. She gave him a section of the newspaper and they both tried to read in silence for a few moments. Then Jane looked up.

"Did you notice how much makeup our fifteen-year-old daughter was wearing this morning? When I asked her about it, she told me that she's been wearing eyeliner for months. I can't believe I never noticed. I suppose we should feel lucky because makeup is our biggest problem with her. I've noticed other teenagers walking around town with tattoos and rings all over their bodies: from their eyebrows, their noses . . . what's next? I suppose they're expressing their identity. It's very different from how we expressed ourselves."

"Is it so different?" asked Steve. "I remember when I defied my parents and grew my hair long. Remember, it was so long I put it in a ponytail!"

"And you almost got expelled from school," added Jane.

"That's true. But my ponytail could be changed. These tattoos are permanent. It is different. Tattoos seem radical to me."

"Actually, tattoos can be removed," said Jane. "Not as easily as a ponytail, but they can be removed. It seems that every generation has a need for self-expression. I wonder what our grandchildren will do in the next generation."

"What worries me about today's music," said Steve, "is that it has a very negative message. Sandy hears that message, and it could have a negative influence on her. I don't know what's happening to our little girl. She's changing and I'm worried about her. Makeup, terrible music. Who knows what will be next? We need to have a talk with her. The newspaper often has stories about teenagers who are in trouble and their parents hardly know anything about their problems."

"Oh, I don't think the music is so terrible; I like it," said Jane.

"You like it? I can't believe it."

"You know I like loud, wild music. When we first began dating, you didn't like *my* musical taste either. Anyway, you're right. We need to speak with Sandy, have a talk with her," said Jane, nodding her head. "Remember the problems we had with Bill when he was her age? Oh, so many problems, and his music was much worse. And he played it all night long. I remember when he was up all night listening to music and we didn't even know it. I don't want to have all *those* problems again. The difference between Sandy and Bill is that we can talk to Sandy. Bill would never talk to us. He would never tell us what he was thinking or what he was doing. Even now, he still doesn't communicate with us."

"You're right. We haven't heard a word from Bill lately. I hope he's doing all right in school," Steve said.

"Of course he is. He's a good student; he's intelligent and capable. I wonder if he has called Sandy lately. He usually keeps in touch with her," said Jane.

"Let's check with Sandy. Maybe she knows something we don't. You know, Jane, you're always so sure that Bill is a good student, that he's intelligent and capable. But college isn't easy, is it? I think that Bill may be staying away from us because he doesn't want us to know that he's less than perfect," said Steve.

"That's very possible. We need to connect with Bill. We haven't talked to him in such a long time. I worry unless I know everything is okay."

"Well, let's make sure everything is okay, and then we'll both feel better," said Steve.

Jane looked up at the clock in the kitchen. "Oh dear, I'm late!" she said. "Let's not forget to have a talk with Sandy and to ask her about Bill. Right now I have to run or I'll be late for my first appointment." She kissed her husband quickly, picked up her briefcase, and started to go out the door.

"Bye, honey," said Jane.

"Bye, dear," answered Steve.

Jane Finch got into her car and drove to work. She worked as a chiropractor in an office near her home, helping people with body pain and injury. As she was driving to work, she was thinking. She was thinking about Sandy and Bill. Bill and Sandy. Her two children. They were each growing up and they were changing. They were becoming adults, and, in her opinion, they needed her.

"Sandy is becoming a woman," she thought. "Soon she'll be dating and going out all the time. I want her to continue to do well in school. I want her to continue practicing her flute. She's a good student and she's very musical. I don't want her to forget about school and music. Some girls waste their time talking on the phone day and night and watching TV. How can I tell her these things? I wish my mother had told me. And yet I don't want her to get angry with me. If I'm too strict, she'll rebel. I always worry that she'll rebel and go too far. So many young girls get wild. They drop out of school and get into all kinds of trouble. Sometimes they even run away from home. I thought it would be easier to raise a daughter, but sons and daughters are both difficult; they're just difficult in different ways. Bill has his problems and Sandy has hers. I must keep talking to her, so that she grows up with a sense of values, with self-esteem. Could she find that on her own? Does Bill have a sense of values? Does he still need my guidance? I couldn't really talk to him when he was living at home. He always thought I was nagging."

"Mothers need to guide their children even though it may seem like they're nagging. Someday my children will be glad that I told them how important it is to study, to stay on the right track. I believe in the old saying: Mother knows best."

Jane knew what she wanted to say to Sandy, what she had to say to Sandy. She was so glad that she and Sandy could still talk things over. After she had decided that she was going to have a talk with Sandy, she felt better. She reached over and turned on the radio. One of her favorite songs was playing, and she began singing along. Yes, she felt better. Mother does know best.

CHAPTER 3

Sharing Secrets

At school, Sandy was usually very busy. She studied hard and enjoyed being with her friends. During lunchtime, she often went to the library with her best friend, Autumn. They sat together and did their homework or worked on research for class projects.

Sandy and Autumn were in the same grade, even though Autumn was a year older than Sandy. Autumn was from Japan. She took ESL classes her first year in the States, so she was a year behind in school. Her real name was Akiko, but when she arrived in the United States and started school, she changed it to Autumn. On her first day of school, Autumn had met Sandy, and they were still the best of friends. They always helped each other with homework and enjoyed talking about their plans together.

After school, both girls participated in many activities. They were in the school orchestra; Sandy played the flute and Autumn played the cello. Sandy worked on the school newspaper too. She also played basketball with Autumn and some other friends. Sandy liked school. She was a good student and she had a few good friends. She was not as popular as Samantha. She was not as beautiful either. Samantha was the most beautiful girl in the school. But Sandy was plain and most of the time that was okay.

Lately, she had noticed that she was changing. Everything used to be simple. She had always listened to her mother and father. She had never disagreed with them in the past. Yet lately it seemed that everything they said upset her. She wanted to wear makeup, but they didn't like her makeup. She wanted to listen to music, but they didn't like her music. She loved music. *Her* kind of music.

Life was growing more complicated. Sandy discussed this with Autumn. She explained to Autumn that her parents didn't like her makeup or her music and that they seemed to be getting very strict. Autumn's parents sometimes seemed more lenient; Autumn had her own car and could drive anytime. Sandy knew that her parents would never let her drive at night by herself. Yet Autumn's parents made her study on Saturday nights. Sandy didn't tell *her* parents about this. She didn't want to give them any ideas!

Autumn and Sandy shared many secrets and trusted each other completely. Sandy often confided in Autumn; she told her about the secret telephone conversations she had with Bill. Because Autumn was an only child, she liked hearing about Sandy's brother.

Sandy didn't tell anyone that Autumn had a boyfriend. Autumn's parents would not permit her to date. They also insisted that Autumn attend Japanese school on Saturdays. During lunch breaks, she visited her boyfriend, Jackson, at The Soda Jerk, an ice cream shop nearby. Jackson worked there making sundaes, malts, and ice cream cones. The first time he saw Autumn, he was hooked. It was love at first sight. Sandy often listened to Autumn describing Jackson. He was a real comedian, always making jokes and making Autumn laugh. After seeing Jackson, Autumn usually shared his jokes with Sandy.

"What do you find at the end of everything?" Autumn asked Sandy.

"I don't know. What?"

"The letter *g*. Ha, ha," laughed Autumn.

"Autumn, that is the oldest joke. I've heard that joke a million times. Did Jackson tell you that?"

"Yes! I love all the jokes he tells me. I'm always laughing when we're together." Autumn suddenly looked sad.

"What's the matter, Autumn?" asked Sandy.

"I wish I could really go out with Jackson, not just see him secretly. I rarely lie to my parents, but I have to lie about Jackson."

"I understand," said Sandy, "but you're lucky. At least you have a boyfriend."

"I feel lucky. And he is so cute and smart and funny. I really like him. I just wish I didn't have to keep secrets from my parents."

"I don't like keeping secrets either. I know what you mean. My brother, Bill, has been calling me, and he doesn't want me to tell my parents that he's called."

"Why not?" asked Autumn.

"Well, he's having a really hard time in school. He's failing one of his classes. It's a really tough class and Bill isn't doing well. I'm worried about him."

"Maybe your parents could help him. He should probably talk to them. What class is it?"

"It's an advanced math class. Math was never his best subject," answered Sandy.

"Isn't he a good student? He always seemed like a really intelligent guy to me," said Autumn.

"That's just an act," said Sandy. "Bill has a very difficult time studying. He doesn't know how to sit down and work things out. He has a really hard time concentrating. You know how you and I spend hours at the library? We help each other work things out and solve a lot of homework problems together. Bill can't do that. He won't let anybody know that he isn't perfect. He thinks he has to do everything himself. That's why he doesn't want me to say anything to my mom and dad, but they need to know. I promised him I wouldn't tell them, so I'm telling you. What should I do? His grades are very low, and if he fails this class, he'll be in real trouble. My parents will be so upset."

"If you promised him, you can't tell your parents. But he sounds like he needs help."

"You're right, Autumn. He's mentioned dropping out of school, and I'm so worried because my parents would feel terrible. I just don't know what to do."

"I don't get it. Why does he have to drop out? He's only failing one class," said Autumn.

"Well, it's complicated. You see, he feels like he just doesn't fit in at college. He's a very quiet guy, a loner who doesn't like to party too much. He likes to sit at home, listen to music, and draw. He's kind of a dreamer."

"Sandy, do you think he's depressed?" asked Autumn in a quiet voice.

"I'm not really sure," said Sandy. "When I ask him, sometimes he says no, but sometimes he doesn't really answer me."

"That's brave of you to ask him," said Autumn.

"I want to know. He's my brother, and if he's in trouble, I want to help him," Sandy said seriously. "He said that college isn't the right place for him; he doesn't like to study. He sounds so unhappy. But I can't tell my parents because they go crazy when they hear anything is not perfect," said Sandy.

"That's probably why he doesn't confide in them," said Autumn. "You know, Sandy, this is a serious problem. Bill is in trouble, and he needs help. Maybe more help than you can give him by yourself."

"Well, maybe we shouldn't have these secret talks, but I'm worried about him. It's so awful when you have to keep secrets. I hate secrets," said Sandy with a sad expression on her face.

"I do too," smiled Autumn, "but I'm glad you told me about Bill. My problem with Jackson doesn't seem so bad now."

Sandy smiled at her friend. "I'm happy for you, Autumn. Jackson is a great guy. But I hope you can tell me a funnier joke next time. I think you need to stop thinking about Jackson so much because if your parents find out, you're going to have a really big problem."

"You're right. Listen, I'd better get going. I'll talk to you tonight. I'll call you at about eight."

"Okay. And thanks for listening," said Sandy.

"Sure," said Autumn, waving good-bye.

Sandy left Autumn and started to walk to her locker. Autumn was lucky to be in love. Sandy hoped that someday she would be in love. Sandy was distracted. She did not want to think about her schoolwork right now. And she didn't want to worry about her brother. She was thinking about music and a boy. A boy named Paul. She didn't even know him, but she had seen him and she knew his name. Paul was older than she was. And he was taller too! He was the tallest player on the basketball team. After seeing him play basketball, she always looked for him on the school yard and in the library. She wanted to meet him. But she didn't tell anyone. It was her secret.

When Sandy got to her locker, she looked up and there was Paul. He was walking down the hall with a smile on his face. "He's always smiling," thought

Sandy. Then she saw that Samantha was walking right next to him. Sandy did not want to stare. Were they really walking together? Sandy's heart was beating so fast. She forced herself to look away. Slowly she picked up her books and closed her locker. She looked down.

As Sandy began to walk away from her locker, she was looking down at the floor. She walked right into Paul.

"Oh, excuse me, I'm so sorry," stammered Sandy nervously.

"No, it was my fault. I wasn't looking where I was going," answered Paul with a sweet smile.

"Hi, Sandy," said Samantha, who looked as beautiful as ever.

They all stood together for a moment. No one spoke, and then, luckily, Samantha saved the day.

"Paul, do you know Sandy?"

"Uh, no, I don't think so, but I've seen her around."

"Well, Paul, this is Sandy Finch. Sandy, this is Paul Good."

"Hi," they both said shyly at the same time.

"We'd better go, Paul," said Samantha. "We're already late."

"Hey, aren't you the girl who plays the flute in the orchestra?" asked Paul.

"Yes, that's me," Sandy replied.

"Your flute makes a really nice sound," said Paul.

"Thanks," said Sandy.

"Well, see you around."

"Uh-huh, see you around," said Sandy.

CHAPTER 4

Making Music Together

Sandy sat in her bedroom with the door closed. She was staring into the mirror. She had been staring for a long time. She was trying to see herself. Sandy was thinking and asking herself many questions.

"Who am I? Am I pretty or just plain? What is going to happen to me in life? Will I ever fall in love? Will I ever do anything important in life? What will I do? Will I help the world? Will I ever travel anywhere?" Sandy asked many questions as she continued to stare into the mirror.

"I look so serious," she thought. She looked at her face in the mirror. It wasn't an extraordinary face. What were the thoughts behind the serious face? Serious thoughts of sadness in the world. She thought of her brother, Bill, and she worried. But there were happy thoughts too. She remembered meeting Paul. Her serious face changed into a smile and she saw her face light up like a flaming candle, warm and bright.

"I may not be as pretty as Samantha," she thought, "but when I smile, there is a definite improvement." Sandy laughed and thought about Paul's beautiful smile. She was happy that he knew who she was. He knew that she played the flute. But Sandy also worried that Paul was Samantha's boyfriend. Samantha was so pretty. If Samantha wanted Paul as her boyfriend, did Sandy stand a chance?

"Well, maybe if I keep smiling and playing the flute," she thought. She smiled into the mirror and began to do her homework.

Sandy didn't see Paul for several days. Then one Thursday morning he walked into her orchestra class. He was wearing a pair of baggy pants and a T-shirt. She was surprised to see him. He was speaking with the teacher, Mr. Gambera. Paul seemed to know Mr. Gambera well.

"Class," said Mr. Gambera, "this is Paul Good. He writes songs and plays the guitar. He wants to sing one of his new songs for you. Maybe you'll be able to accompany him with your instruments."

Sandy was thrilled. She thought that Paul was a basketball player. She didn't know that he liked to make music too. She was so happy. She loved to make music. She loved playing her flute and singing. Sandy loved music. Sandy sat very still, waiting to hear Paul play his song. He sang:

> When I see you smile,
> When I see your face,
> When I see you walk,
> When I see your style,
>
> Then I'm happy,
> Yes I'm happy.
> Then I'm happy,
> Oh, so happy.
>
> When the sky is dark,
> When the day is gray,
> When the flowers die
> And love goes away,
>
> Then I need you,
> Yes I need you.

Then I need you,
Oh I need you.

You—you're the one I see through the chain-link fence.
You—you're the essence of innocence.
You—you can turn my world all right.
You are a vision of silken light.

Sandy was in a dream. The song was so romantic. And Paul sang the song in the same way he smiled: beautifully. Sandy wanted to sing with him and play the flute to accompany his guitar. Everyone in the class applauded. Sandy looked across the room to see if Autumn had also enjoyed Paul's song. Autumn was smiling. Sandy smiled too.

"Paul has a music club that meets after school," said Mr. Gambera. "The club meets twice a week, on Wednesday and Thursday afternoons, right here in the music room. It's a serious commitment. If you're interested in joining the music club, sign this list." He gave a sign-up sheet to one of the students to pass around. Sandy waited to write her name on the sign-up sheet. She wanted to join the music club and sing and play with Paul.

"Who was he? Males are so different from females," thought Sandy. "This guy is such a mystery to me. I have no idea how he thinks." Sandy didn't know very much about guys. She knew her dad and her brother, Bill, but Paul was different. Paul was special. Maybe he would be that special new person in her life.

After class, Sandy left the classroom singing . . . "Then I need you, make me happy." She was walking on a cloud. Suddenly, she saw the clock in the hall. It was late. She started to run. She didn't want to be late. Whenever she was late, her mother got upset. She didn't want her mother to be upset, because she wanted to talk to her about the music club. She ran faster. If her mother was in a good mood, maybe she would be happy about the music club. She wished she could talk to Autumn. Autumn usually had helpful advice. She would call Autumn tonight. She ran faster.

CHAPTER 5

Experiencing the Generation Gap

Sandy arrived home out of breath. But she was on time. Her mother was waiting for her. Her mother was smiling, so hopefully she was in a good mood.

Sandy planned to tell her mother that she had signed up for the music club. She wanted to tell her mother how much she loved to sing. And how she wanted to sing with Paul. (But she wasn't going to tell her mother about Paul!) While she was running home from school, Sandy thought about how much she liked Paul's voice, his smile, the words and music he wrote.

"Hi, Sandy," said her mother. "Wow! You're out of breath. Have you been running? Sandy? You look so dreamy. Is your head up in the clouds?" Jane was trying to sound casual before she spoke to Sandy about her makeup, her music, and Bill. But she was tense. Sometimes she planned to say certain things to Sandy and then she said something different, something that made Sandy upset.

"I'm fine, Mom," Sandy answered. She was still daydreaming.

"Sandy?"

"Yes, Mom?"

"Are you sure you're all right?"

"Yes, Mom." Sandy waited for a moment. Maybe this was a good time to talk to her mother about the music club. "Oh, I was just thinking about a song I heard at school today." She began to sing, "When the sky is gray . . . " but her mother interrupted her. Why did parents always have to interrupt? Sandy wondered. Didn't her mother want to hear the song Paul wrote? Wasn't she interested in what was important to Sandy?

"Sandy, I don't think this is a time for singing. Do you have any homework?"

"Yes, I do. I have a lot of homework and I'm going to do it right now, Mom. But I wanted to talk to you for a minute." Sandy paused. "Guess what? There's a new club at school and I signed up to join it. It's a music club."

"Don't you think you should have asked your father and me for permission before you joined?"

"Maybe. I didn't think about it. Sorry. I know you're happy about my musical interests, so I thought you'd be happy if I joined a music club."

"I am. I am. But, well, what kind of music club is it? What kind of music do they play?"

"I think it'll be fun, Mom. It's not the kind of music I usually go crazy for, but Mr. Gambera recommended it and the guy who played in our class today was really cool."

"A guy? A really cool guy?" Jane said, sounding like Sandy.

"Mom, I don't think you need to make fun of me. You know, if you were a little more understanding, we might get along better."

"I don't like you talking like that. I also don't like you forgetting to ask for permission. And I don't like you talking about cool guys. You're too young!"

"Mom, I'm fifteen years old. Get serious!"

Jane Finch could feel herself changing from tense to angry.

"Don't talk like that, Sandy Finch!" Jane said in a stern voice. "Your father and I need to talk to you about your behavior. Your father has told you to turn down the weird music, but you continue to argue with him and talk back over and over again."

Sandy interrupted her mother. She knew she shouldn't, but she couldn't help it.

"The music I like isn't weird, Mother."

"I know it isn't. It's not the music. It's your attitude."

"Oh, now it's my attitude. First it was the music, then it was . . . "

"Sandy, don't interrupt me. And don't correct me either."

"Well, I remember how you were always upset with Bill when he was listening to music and staying out late at night. After a while, Bill stopped coming home at all. You didn't know what he was doing and then he left. Now that he's away at college, are you going to start picking on me?"

"Sandy, I don't like the way you're talking to me. You have a bad attitude."

"No I don't. I just wanted to tell you about the music club. I was excited. Listen, I have a lot of homework and I'm tired of arguing with you about music, especially when I love music so much. I'm going to my room."

"I don't think you should talk to me like that, Sandy. I'm your mother. You should be respectful. I have some things to say to you."

"Oh Mom, you just don't understand anything."

"Sandy, don't talk to me like that. It's disrespectful. You're beginning to sound exactly like your brother, and I don't like it. Have you been talking to him? We haven't heard from him, but maybe he's been talking to you. Have you spoken with him, Sandy?"

"Mom, why are you asking me all these questions?" said Sandy, looking down at the floor. She did not want to answer her mother. "You just don't understand me. I try to talk to you, but you don't listen. You only want to tell me what to do, just like you did with Bill. But you can't. I'm growing up and I have my own ideas, my own opinions. I'm a person, a person separate from you." Sandy's voice was shaking, but she tried to control herself. "Maybe I'm not perfect, Mom, but nobody is perfect. Still, you can trust me. I'm a good student and an honest person."

"I'm glad to hear that, Sandy," said Jane, trying not to be angry. She knew that if she wanted to communicate with Sandy, she had to stay calm. "I know that you're growing up, dear, and that you have your own ideas. I'm glad that you have your own ideas and opinions."

"And the makeup I wear is not a big deal. Neither is the music."

"Maybe not, but I want to be able to trust you and to trust your decisions. Can I trust you, Sandy? You say that I can."

Sandy felt uncomfortable. She had never actually lied to her mother and now her mother had asked about Bill and she was avoiding answering. Jane continued. "It's just that you're changing; you're different now and I don't want to have problems with you like I had with your brother, Bill. I want us to communicate. Remember how he used to listen to music all night long? Soon he stopped studying. Then he failed some of his classes. The situation was terrible. Your father and I had a really hard time with Bill. I don't want that to happen again. I don't want you to stop studying. Your studies are very important."

"They're important to me too, Mom. Look Mom, Bill and I are different and I'm a different kind of student. I like studying; I like school. I know a lot about the situation with him, believe me. But I'm not Bill, I'm Sandy. I'm not doing drugs or drinking or anything like that. And neither is Bill."

"Why did you say that, Sandy? Have you spoken with Bill?" Jane looked worried.

"Mom, you have to let us grow up. Both of us. Okay?"

"I don't know, Sandy. I hope everything is okay, but, um, but you're dressing differently, you've been wearing makeup, and I don't know what you and Autumn are talking about on the phone for hours."

"Well, mostly we're talking about our own lives. Mom, stop worrying and everything will be just fine. Relax."

"I'll try. But what about the music?"

"What *about* the music?"

"You know, Sandy, I'm so proud of the way you play the flute. You're so talented. The music you play is really nice. But the music you've been listening to lately is too angry. It makes you angry."

"The music I listen to is *beautiful*. I love it. And if I'm angry, it's only because you and Dad don't understand me, don't let me be myself. Forget about the music. I'll put my headphones on so you won't hear it."

"No, Sandy, that would be worse. Then I wouldn't know what you're listening to. I want to know."

"Well, Mom, I think I need to have some privacy, don't you?"

Jane stared at her daughter. Privacy? Sandy wanted privacy? She didn't know what to say.

"Well, Sandy," she stammered, "you have your own room and . . ."

"And I play my music and study. Mom, there would not be a problem if you would relax. Aren't you glad I love music? You love music, don't you?"

"That's not the point. I'll discuss this with your father, and then maybe we can all talk it over. In the meantime, no headphones. Is that clear?"

"Sure Mom. No problem." Sandy did not want to argue with her mother anymore; she did not want to talk to her either. She was glad that she hadn't told her about Bill. She didn't tell a lie, but she didn't answer her mother either.

"I need to do my homework now, Mom." Sandy weakly tried to smile, then turned and quickly walked to her bedroom, closing the door behind her. She sat down on her bed and quietly began to cry. "My parents do not understand me," she thought. "I'm sick and tired of my mother attacking me. She wants me to be perfect. And she wants me to tell her what I know about Bill, but I can't. I promised. She never leaves me alone. Parents just don't understand anything. It isn't surprising that so many teenagers run away from home." She was grateful for having her own room and a little privacy. Then her thoughts shifted to the music club and Paul. She wiped away her tears, feeling better, thinking about playing music, about Paul. She opened her school books and began to study.

CHAPTER 6

A Telephone Call

"Dinnertime!" Sandy's father called. "Come help, Sandy." Sandy went into the kitchen where her mother and father were preparing dinner.

"Hi, Dad," said Sandy, kissing her father's cheek.

"Hello, sweetheart. Could you make a salad?"

"Sure, Dad. Oh, what's that?" asked Sandy looking at the pot on the stove. "It looks yummy." Sandy took out a bowl from the cabinet and prepared to make the salad.

"Your mother and I made a new dish with pasta, garlic, and mushrooms."

"A vegetarian dinner?" asked Sandy.

"Is that okay with you?" asked her dad.

"It's great. Our health teacher told us that being a vegetarian is a thinker's lifestyle."

Her mother smiled and nodded her head in agreement. "Vegetarians usually have healthy diets, but it's important to get enough protein too. Vegetarians need to eat . . ."

"Right now! Now let's eat. I'm hungry enough to eat a bear."

"That's an animal, Dad, not a vegetable . . ."

"I hate to interrupt, but let's sit down and eat. I'm very hungry. We can discuss the pros and cons of being a vegetarian during dinner or after dessert."

Everyone laughed and dinner began. After a moment, Sandy's father declared, "I hope the idea of vegetarianism is not turning into another teenage fad. Sometimes teenagers are just imitating other teenagers. Becoming a vegetarian is a big decision. It requires a lot of thought."

"You're right, dear. As a chiropractor, I have many clients, both young and old, who don't eat meat. Planning vegetarian meals is sometimes simple, but it can get complicated. I know vegetarians who often have difficulty ordering at restaurants."

"I don't think it's so difficult to order vegetarian food. Most restaurants usually offer vegetarian meals. If not, there's always the good old reliable grilled cheese sandwich," said Steve.

"And when the grilled cheese sandwich is accompanied by a salad, you have protein and green vegetables, all you need really," added Jane.

Steve and Jane were busy discussing vegetarian lifestyles for a while when they noticed that Sandy had hardly spoken.

"You're so quiet, Sandy. What are you daydreaming about?" asked her father.

"I'm not daydreaming, Dad. I'm thinking about how many people in the world are starving while we're sitting here talking about food lifestyles. It's simply criminal."

"Now calm down, young lady. You sound like an angry teenager," said Steve.

"Well, maybe I am. But we can't just live our lives ignoring the fact that people are hungry," said Sandy. "Not just in faraway places, but right here."

"You're right Sandy. This is something for us to reflect on. We can't solve all the problems of the world, but we can find solutions to some problems if we work at them. People can make a difference, don't you agree?" asked her father.

Sandy didn't have a chance to answer. The telephone rang and she quickly got up to answer it. When she picked up the phone, she could hardly believe her ears. It was Paul!

"Hey, Sandy," said the voice on the telephone. "I hope you don't mind my calling you. I got your phone number from Samantha." Amazing! She didn't know that Samantha even had her number.

"No, that's cool. No problem," Sandy answered, trying to sound relaxed.

"There's a group that's really great and they're singing on TV tonight. I know you'd really like them. They're called Starfish. They've got a super flautist. That's why I thought of you. They're on tonight at nine o'clock on Channel 1."

"That sounds super, Paul, super cool," said Sandy. Her heart was pounding.

"Thanks for thinking of me. For sure, I'll watch them. Thanks a lot."

There was a pause on the telephone. No one spoke. Finally, Paul said hesitantly, "I was also wondering if you were free on Friday night. Maybe you and I could go to McBane's. There's a group that's playing there . . . " his voice trailed off.

Sandy couldn't believe it. Paul was asking her out. Ever since she first saw him, she had hoped for this. And now her dream was becoming a reality. She took a deep breath. Although she was very excited, she pretended to be calm. "Um, hey, that sounds totally *cool*, Paul. I'll have to ask my folks and get back to you. Is that okay?"

"Oh, sure. I'll call you tomorrow, okay?"

"Okay, sure, Paul. Cool."

"Well, bye."

"Yeah, bye."

Sandy hung up the telephone very carefully. She loved the telephone. Paul had called her!

"Sandy, who was that? Come back to the table and finish your dinner. I think you said the word *cool* more than twenty times. At least ten!"

"That was a guy named Paul, Dad. He's *very* cool." Sandy laughed, and her dad laughed too.

CHAPTER 7

Talking with Friends

As Jane was getting ready to leave for her monthly meeting, the telephone rang. She went into the kitchen to answer it.

"Hello," she said and waited.

"Is Sandy there?" Jane paused for a moment. The voice was so familiar.

"No, Sandy's not here right now. Who is this, please?" she asked.

Click. The telephone went dead.

"I know that voice," thought Jane. "Oh, no! That was Bill, but he was disguising his voice." She thought for a moment and then she felt her stomach knot up. "He doesn't want to speak to me. I'm his mother, yet he doesn't even want to speak a word to me." Jane tried to stop the tears that were filling her eyes. She grabbed her jacket and ran out of the house. She drove to her friend Sun's house, trying not to cry.

On the first Thursday of every month, Jane attended a meeting of her women's group. She had been meeting with the same four women for more than six years. They got together regularly and discussed whatever was on their minds. The women had many common concerns, but they also appreciated each other's different approaches to solving problems. Because they came from diverse backgrounds, they enjoyed sharing what was similar, what was different, and what was helpful.

Tonight Jane couldn't wait to get to her meeting. She really needed to talk about Sandy and Bill. She was thinking about how much these women had helped her in the past when Bill had had problems. Now maybe they could give her advice about both Sandy and Bill. She felt as if Bill had something to tell his sister, something that he didn't want his parents to know.

Jane was the first woman to arrive at Sun's home, and Sun greeted her with a warm hug. Sun was from Korea and often spoke about her family's customs and traditions. Jane especially enjoyed hearing the sayings that Sun had learned from her grandmother. Her favorite saying was, "Always try your best and you can't go wrong."

"Are you all right, Jane?" asked Sun. "You look a little tearful."

"Well, I've had a big shock. My son, Bill, just called and asked for Sandy, but he hung up without telling me who he was! He even disguised his voice. Can you believe that?"

"Oh Jane, you must feel terrible," said Sun.

"I do. I really do. I'm his mother."

They began to talk and soon Jane felt better. As other members of the group arrived, they caught up on news about mutual friends. When everyone was finally there, they began the meeting. Sun served snacks and tea. Jane was glad to see her good friends again.

"Thank goodness for this group," Juana began immediately. "I'm having so many problems at work. I can't complain to my family anymore. My husband and children are tired of hearing about my boss. I complain every night at the dinner table. But you know, my boss never stops thinking of new tasks for me. He never says 'thank you' for anything. I can't imagine him telling me that I've done a good job. And believe me, I'm trying all the time to do things right. I try so hard."

"That's so tough," said one of the women. "We all need to feel like we're doing a good job, no matter how old we are, don't we?"

"What do you think might help?" asked Ellen. "What could Juana do to help her boss become more understanding?"

Juana asked, "Has anyone had an experience like mine?"

For a moment, there was silence. Each woman was thinking about her own past and working life. Nearly all of the women worked. Because she worked for herself now, Jane didn't have a boss. In the past, she had worked for a difficult boss. She tried to remember what had helped her.

"I don't think it's a gender issue. The problem might be because I'm from Costa Rica. Sometimes he tells me he thinks my accent is cute, but I know he doesn't really think so," Juana said thoughtfully.

"That's ridiculous. You speak English beautifully," said Ellen.

"I agree," said Silvia, who was from Mexico. "I still have a lot of problems with *my* English, but you speak English perfectly. I can't hear any errors at all."

Jane spoke quietly. "You know, in the past I worked for a boss who sometimes treated me like dirt. It was tough, really difficult. I tried a lot of things: I had a heart-to-heart talk with her, I ignored her, I invited her to my home. Nothing helped. Finally, I decided that it was not my problem. That helped. Eventually, I found a way to work for myself. I guess that doesn't sound very optimistic, does it? But people can be difficult sometimes and you can't always make things work. Sometimes there's bad chemistry. Whatever it is, you try and try and then, if necessary, you move on."

The group was silent again for a few minutes. They were thinking about the different solutions that they had heard. At last, Juana said, "You've given me real food for thought. I'm going to experiment with your ideas and keep looking for a way to make things work."

"Keep us posted," said Sun. "We all want your problems to work out for you. That's the important thing. Since I'm a stay-at-home mother now, I don't think I'm very helpful with work-related problems."

"That's not true. We all have different ideas to contribute, and we all find different things helpful. But we can find common ground too," said Juana.

"Well, what helps me the most is to listen," said Sun.

"Listening is so important, isn't it?" agreed Juana.

"Yes, it is," joined Jane. "And that's what I'm having a hard time doing. Listening."

"But you're such a good listener, Jane. You always listen to us. Even now, when I know you're very upset about what's happening with your kids," said Sun.

"I need to listen to you," Jane said. "Your advice is always helpful. And I hope you can help me now. I'm having so much trouble listening to my daughter, Sandy. I know she's trying to talk to me, explain herself to me, but when she talks, I get so upset that I stop listening. She puts up a wall between us; she wants to be totally separate from me, and secretive."

"I know exactly what you mean. That happens to me with my son," said Sun.

"I want to trust her," Jane said. "I think she's a good person. But maybe I'm wrong. She's talking on the phone to Bill and not telling me about it. I'm worried that something is wrong with Bill. Why don't they want me to know? And she's started wearing a lot of makeup. She's watching dumb TV shows and talking on the phone about nothing. She has her own language with her friends, so I don't know what they're talking about. Some of her friends seem to be so materialistic. They want cars, they want clothes, but there is no struggle, no challenge. As a result, something is missing. I'm sure that some kids at her school are using drugs. Do you think she is too? Am I blind? I want Sandy to continue to be a serious student, to learn about helping others in life, not to hurt her own life."

"You know, Jane, I don't think you need to worry about Sandy. I think you need to give her a lot of attention and try not to criticize her too much. Teenagers need some freedom to become adults," said Silvia. "Sandy also needs to be able to have her own relationship with her brother, don't you think?"

"Do you think so? Excuse me, but I see it differently," said Sun. She was speaking quickly. "Jane, I worry about my son. I don't want him to use drugs. I know many of his friends take drugs, and I talk with him all the time. I try to keep my eyes open for any changes in his friends or the way he acts. He's very active on the basketball team, and that helps. But he's also under a lot of stress to get good grades. Teenagers have a lot of energy. They need to use it positively. They also need us to hug them often and to listen to them. I know one thing that helps: to turn off the television. If we turn off the TV for only an hour every day, it gives us a chance to speak to each other."

"That's a good point. But my family won't let me turn off the TV. We fight about TV all the time," said Juana.

"Well, sometimes you have to fight because you care. You have to fight to help your children develop strength and to keep the family together. Today there is so much divorce, so many problems, so much materialism. Cars, stereos, computers, VCRs, and expensive clothes that nobody can afford. At our house, we struggle with all these issues during a weekly family meeting. We try to find solutions and make decisions together," said Sun.

"That's a great idea. I might try that," said Juana. "But I don't know if anyone in my family would be willing to turn off the TV."

"They would for one hour," said Sun. "You have to keep trying. Make it fun. Make it positive. Don't criticize. Listen to your family. We don't want to lose our children, our husbands, or ourselves, do we?"

"I know I don't," said Jane. "The world is a difficult place to live in right now. Thank you all for some great ideas. I'm going to talk to Sandy tonight and make sure everything is okay with her and with Bill."

"Hang in there, Jane. You're a good mom and your children love you. Sandy's having growing pains. Just hang in there. That's what I try to do: Be patient and be a good listener," Juana said.

"I hear you. Thanks to all of you for listening to me," said Jane.

CHAPTER 8

It's Hard to Be Young

Sandy went to school on Friday with a light feeling in her heart. She had attended the first meeting of the music club the day before. They sang, played their instruments, and talked about music. They were a diverse group with different talents and tastes. Some played piano and guitar, while others sang. One girl played the drums. Some liked rock and heavy metal, others classical, others reggae, others rap. There was one thing they all had in common: They all loved music. They wished they could listen to music all day long.

While sitting in class, Sandy thought about her date with Paul. Her parents had said it was okay to go out with him. Of course, she had to follow the rules. She could go out with Paul if he came to the house and they could meet him. And if she promised to be home by eleven o'clock! Rules, rules, rules. Her parents always had so many rules. They were too strict with her. It was probably because of her brother, Bill. Ever since Sandy could remember, Bill had broken the rules. She remembered how he would come home really late when he was a senior in high school. Her parents were awake, waiting and worrying. Once he had come home at 4 A.M., and then, another time, he didn't come home at all! Sandy had been in her room when Bill finally showed up the next day. She heard her parents arguing with Bill, asking him a lot of questions. Later, when Sandy had asked her parents why Bill hadn't come home, why they argued with him, and why they asked him so many questions, her parents had told her that she was too young to know about these things. She had asked her brother too. He had smiled a strange smile, but he didn't give her the answer that she was looking for.

"I'll tell you all about it when you're older, Little Sister," Bill had said.

"Tell me now, Bill. And don't call me Little Sister."

"No, not now. You're still too young, Little Sister," he had said, teasing her.

Well, now she was old enough—old enough to know how to play the game, and she had learned the rules. Sandy didn't want to fight with her parents as her brother had. She wanted everything to go smoothly between her parents and Paul. She wanted her parents to see that she was mature and trustworthy. She was different from her brother.

She thought about Bill. She hadn't been able to speak to him lately because her parents were always watching her. They never seemed to give her any privacy. Maybe she needed to talk to her mom and dad about Bill. Sandy knew that school wasn't going well for him. Couldn't her parents help? What could she do?

Sandy tried to stop thinking about Bill. She began thinking about the future, about Paul. She was looking forward to being with Paul, talking to him. She tried to pay attention in class and do her schoolwork, but she was distracted. Her thoughts kept wandering. She imagined that she and Paul were at McBane's listening to music. It was noisy and she was feeling light and free. Paul was smiling at her. . . .

Sandy felt the teacher looking at her. She tried to bring her thoughts back to her schoolwork. She also tried to concentrate and listen to the teacher. The teacher was dividing the class into groups. Sandy was glad. She could pay better attention in a group and stop thinking about Paul for a while.

After school, Sandy hurried home to get ready for her date. She was excited and happy. Her mom and dad were both at home and she laughed with them for a few minutes, listening to her dad's jokes. Everyone seemed to be enjoying Sandy's good mood. Sandy thought for a moment about talking to her parents about Bill. "Why not? Everyone is relaxed. This might be the perfect time," she thought. And then she changed her mind. "No, I'd better not," she decided. "I'd better not take a chance; I might upset them and I don't want anything to go wrong today. It'll be my first date with Paul, and I hope it won't be my last."

"Sandy seems really happy today," Steve said to his wife.

"Doesn't she?" answered Jane. "I hope her new friend is as nice as she says he is."

"Well, I trust Sandy's judgment. She's like you: She has good taste in men." They both laughed. Steve liked to make little jokes.

"It's because she has such a good father to give her inspiration," Jane said with a smile. She walked over to Steve and kissed him on the cheek.

"We're lucky to have a daughter like Sandy, aren't we?"

"I think so," agreed Jane. "She gives us a few surprises, but she's not like the kids I keep reading about in the newspaper, so I'm grateful. Maybe we're doing something right."

"Maybe. Or perhaps it's just luck. Whatever it is, let's keep our fingers crossed that Paul is a nice guy and that he and Sandy have a good time."

The family had a light dinner together. Sandy wasn't very hungry; she was a bit nervous. After they finished eating, they got up to clear the table. Jane Finch looked at Sandy with approval.

"Sandy, you look lovely," said her mother. "Your hair looks so nice." Jane didn't mention the holes in Sandy's jeans. She knew that Sandy wanted to wear jeans with holes in them. It was the style these days.

"You do, Sandy. You look great! I agree with your mother. You're my favorite little girl," said Steve.

"Dad, please don't make jokes now; I am not a little girl. . . ."

"Oops," said Steve, interrupting his daughter. "Excuse me. I meant, my favorite young lady."

"That's better, Steve," said Jane. "Sandy's growing up and becoming a mature young woman." Jane made an effort to support Sandy; she remembered the advice her women's group had given to her.

Everybody was trying to get along tonight. A knock on the door made the family quiet for a moment.

"I wonder who that could be," said Steve with a wink.

"Dad, don't be sarcastic, please. Not tonight," Sandy said with a pleading look.

"Don't worry. I'll be good. I promise," said her dad.

Sandy quickly walked to the door. She could feel her heart beating fast. She opened the door and there was Paul with a beautiful smile on his face.

"Come on in, Paul," said Sandy, returning his smile.

Sandy and Paul walked into the living room, where Steve and Jane were now sitting on the sofa. Sandy introduced Paul to her mom and dad. Steve stood up to shake hands with Paul. Jane shook hands with Paul too. There was silence for a moment, and then everyone began to speak at once. Laughter.

Paul spoke. "Thanks for letting me take Sandy out tonight. We're going to hear a really special band at McBane's."

"I understand you play the guitar, Paul," said Jane. "Oh dear," she thought to herself, "I sound so stuffy."

"That's right. I also write songs sometimes, when the inspiration hits me."

"What kinds of songs do you write?" Steve asked.

"Oh, all kinds. I sometimes write songs about world problems, the environment, the homeless, and you know, some political songs. I guess I worry about how the world is changing. There's hardly any green left except for golf courses and stuff like that. Right now I'm working on a song about the pollution problem. The environment is really messed up everywhere and people need to do something about it. That's why I'm writing a song, so people will really think about how pollution affects our lives."

"Why don't you sing what you've written for us?" asked Jane.

"Really? Do you want to hear it? It's not finished yet," said Paul.

"Sure, Paul, we'd love to hear what you have," said Jane.

Paul began to sing:

> We need a revolution now!
> We need to turn the tide.
> The pain of pollution, now
> Has taken all our pride.
>
> Cars grow old but they don't die!
> Styrofoam cups with no place to hide!
> Teenagers committing suicide!
> Homeless folks can't go inside!
> I don't know if I can take this ride.
> Something crazy is turning inside.
>
> We need a revolution!
> A green revolution, an evolution revolution,
> What do we need?
> We need a solution.
> We need a revolution, now.

The whole family applauded. Paul smiled. He was glad that they liked his new song. He liked it too. He was always thinking about ways to change the world. And he hoped that the songs he wrote could help somehow.

"That song has a powerful message, Paul," said Jane, interrupting Paul's thoughts. "Songs like that help people think about change."

"I liked your song, Paul," said Steve. "I'm not sure we need a revolution, but the song has some interesting ideas."

"I'm glad you liked it. I hope we don't need a revolution, but we certainly need a change. Look around. There are many, many people who don't have enough money to buy food. And there are homeless people in the United States, one of the richest countries in the world. Some people really don't care. They buy much more than they really need, while other people are hungry. They don't do anything to help the environment, and they don't care at all about global warming. We've got to do something to protect the world."

"I believe you, Paul," said Steve.

"So do I," said Jane.

CHAPTER 9

In the Real World

Sandy and Paul said good-bye to her parents and walked outside. Paul seemed a bit nervous now.

"I hope you don't mind this car, Sandy. It's not mine. My friend Dave let me borrow it. I don't have my own car."

"Neither do I, Paul," smiled Sandy.

"But you're not sixteen yet, are you?"

"Well, no. But I can tell you, I won't have a car for a long time. My parents are worriers. I know they'll worry when I have my own car and I want to drive wherever I want. Anyway, I guess we're lucky that Dave loaned you his car and we're going to McBane's together."

"And that you look great tonight. And you smell good too. Mmm, very nice scent." Paul appreciated her taste. She didn't put too much perfume on, just a little. She wasn't sure if Paul would notice, but she didn't want her perfume to smell so strong that Paul was overpowered. She hated when girls wore a lot of perfume in class. Sometimes the perfume gave her a headache when she sat near them.

"Well, thanks. You look pretty good yourself, Paul. I like your shirt." Paul had dressed carefully for Sandy. He wore a long-sleeved green shirt that covered the tattoo on his left arm. He didn't want her to see his tattoo until he knew her better. Sometimes girls were turned off by tattoos.

Paul and Sandy got into the car. On the way to McBane's, Sandy was thrilled to be sitting in the car next to Paul. "Wow! We're here, together. This is so cool!" thought Sandy. As they drove along, they talked easily about music and the concert that they were going to hear. Sandy could see that Paul was feeling as good as she was.

When they got to McBane's, they locked the car and walked toward the entrance. They got in line to pick up their tickets. As they stood there, together, a voice drifted up to them.

"Hey man, can you help me out? I'm flat broke."

Sandy looked down and saw a man sitting on the ground. He didn't look too clean. Paul was looking down at the guy who had spoken, but he didn't look away. He spoke to the man on the ground.

"Here's a dollar, buddy. I'm sorry, but that's all I can spare."

"Hey, that's okay. Thanks. Every little bit helps, you know."

"Glad to help you, buddy," said Paul.

"My name's Wes. Wesley North," said the man on the ground, reaching up to shake hands with Paul.

"Good to meet you, Wes," said Paul, shaking hands with him.

"You know, Paul," Sandy whispered, "we don't know what he's going to buy with the money."

Wes heard Sandy and said, "Don't worry. I'm homeless and broke and in a bad way. And I sure can use this money. It's going to a good cause, young lady."

Sandy and Paul looked at each other for a moment. Then Paul looked back at Wesley North with a smile. She realized that Paul shared his beautiful smile with the world. He told Wes his name and said they would be back after the show at McBane's. She knew he meant it. The line quickly began to move and soon they were in their seats for the concert. The music was beginning.

During the concert, the group was unbelievable. They sang many of Sandy and Paul's favorite songs, and both Sandy and Paul sang and yelled with the crowd in the audience. The group was really putting on a great show. Paul took Sandy's hand and she felt they were so close, the two of them, enjoying the wild and wonderful music. For a moment, she was distracted by thoughts of her mother and father: "Why," she thought, "do they think this music is so weird? Oh, I don't want to think about them now." Sandy tried to forget about her parents. She wanted to just listen, sing, be with Paul, and feel the music.

Paul was enjoying the concert and Sandy, but he was also thinking about Wesley North. He couldn't help it. Every time he saw someone on the street, without a home, he felt helpless. How could he do something meaningful?

The concert lasted for more than two hours. Sandy and Paul were having a great time together. After a lot of screaming and shouting for the band, they walked with the crowd out of McBane's. Paul had his arm around Sandy's shoulder; she had her arm around his waist. For a moment, they looked at each other and for that moment, everything stopped.

CHAPTER 10

Sandy and Paul Together

Sandy had forgotten the incident with Wesley North, but when they got outside McBane's, who was waiting for them? Wesley North.

"Hey, Paul. How was the concert?" asked Wes.

"Oh, hey Wes. It was incredible! It was great, wasn't it, Sandy?"

"Uh-huh," said Sandy quietly. "Why is this guy here now?" she wondered to herself.

"Listen, Paul, maybe you want to come with me to meet a few of my friends."

"No, I don't think so," said Paul. "Not tonight. Sandy and I have to be somewhere. Maybe another time."

"Oh, yeah, sure. Well, they aren't far away. You see, we've got a couple of tents by the freeway over there. If you want to come over, there's a campfire going and . . ."

"Not tonight, Wes. Sorry. Maybe another time."

"It's not far. Just across that street over there," Wes said. "See that bright glow? That's the campfire. Can you see it?"

Sandy and Paul looked at where Wes was pointing and saw something shining brightly.

"You *live* there?" asked Sandy in a surprised whisper. She was sorry she had spoken. Paul looked at her.

"Hey, it's not so bad, sleepin' under the stars. I don't live there all the time. Sometimes I go to the downtown shelter and sometimes I sleep here and sometimes . . ." Wes didn't finish his sentence; instead he just waved his hand in the air. Sandy saw that he didn't really have a place to call home. "I like it by the freeway," Wes continued. "There are a lot of noisy cars going by though, so I pretend that I'm listening to the ocean roar."

Sandy and Paul laughed with Wes. He was a funny guy.

"Hey, we'll see you another time, Wes," said Paul.

"Right," said Wes.

"See you," said Sandy.

Sandy and Paul waved good-bye and walked to the parking lot. The crowd had thinned and they were practically alone.

"You know, Sandy," Paul said, "I really feel like we're having our own adventure here, a special night."

"You help me see things differently, Paul. I don't usually talk to people I don't know. Wes scared me at first. But being with you and seeing you talking to him, I saw that he was just a regular guy. I don't know, I guess I just don't have enough faith or trust in people. You have ideals. I haven't been out in the world, to learn and understand. I want to see more, do more, learn more."

"So do I, Sandy," said Paul. "There's so much to see and do. And you're right; there's a lot to learn. People don't feel safe in the world anymore. Nobody trusts anybody, it seems. Everything you read in the newspaper or watch on TV makes you afraid. And yet you have to talk to people. I don't think the world is really like what they show on TV. TV makes life look too superficial, too materialistic. Life has to be better than what you see on TV. Is a person with a home better than a homeless person? I don't think so. Think about the concert tonight; there were lots of different people having a wonderful time. Everyone was great. It was like a beautiful party. You never see good news like that on TV."

Sandy looked at Paul. He was definitely different. He made her ask herself questions. Questions that she had never thought about. Paul was a thinker, and he was very perceptive.

"You know, Paul," said Sandy, "I feel like you're the first person, except for my friend Autumn, who I can really talk to. My parents and I don't always communicate, if you know what I mean. They don't understand that I'm changing, and they worry about me. But I can talk to you about my ideas, all kinds of ideas."

"Let's go for a walk, Sandy," said Paul taking her hand. "I want to tell you about my plans to change the world." He smiled at her with his beautiful smile.

"Oh, Paul. I'd really like to, but I'd better go home. I'm sure that my parents are sitting on the sofa waiting for me. They won't like you if I come home late. They'll blame both of us."

"But I need to talk to you. I have so much on my mind."

"I do too. I'd like to talk to you about so many things, Paul."

"Like what?" he said, still holding her hand and walking slowly.

"Well, one thing I'd like to talk to you about is my brother, Bill," Sandy blurted out, and before she knew what was happening, she was crying. "I'm sorry, Paul. I don't know why I'm crying. It's just that my brother is having a lot of trouble at school. I think he's failing and he doesn't want me to tell my parents. I feel terrible about keeping this a secret from them."

"Wow, Sandy, I can see why you're crying," said Paul. He thought for a moment, and then slowly and carefully said, "But there's only one thing to do. Tell the truth. Explain the situation to your parents. They're good people, and they'll help you and your brother. Things always work out, once the truth is told."

"Do you think so?" asked Sandy. She listened to Paul's words.

"Telling the truth helps everyone," smiled Paul.

"You're so right," said Sandy, wiping her tears.

Sandy looked at Paul. He looked sad and sweet and funny.

"I hope we can see a lot of each other, Sandy," Paul said seriously.

"I hope so," said Sandy. He turned to look at her and their eyes met. Sandy could feel her heart beating as she looked into Paul's eyes.

"We'd better get going," she said softly. They got into the car. "Thanks for helping me with my problem, Paul. I feel better knowing that I'm going to tell my parents the truth," said Sandy, taking a deep breath as Paul started the car.

"And you'll feel even better when Bill gets some help from them," said Paul. "He needs them."

"I hope you're right."

They drove in silence for a while, and then Sandy spoke.

"You know what, Paul? I used to think you were Samantha's boyfriend," laughed Sandy.

"Well, I was Samantha's boyfriend for a little while. I really liked her, but she's had a problem with alcohol. She was drinking a lot. I tried to help her by taking her to a self-help program, but she told me not to bother. I really like Samantha. Don't be jealous, Sandy. I'm only interested in you. I want to spend a lot of time with you. You're so special, so understanding. And so musical."

"Really? I didn't know I was so valuable."

"Well, you are. I have plans for this world, and I want you to be a part of them. I know you have dreams too, and I hope we can share our dreams."

"I do have dreams and big plans too. It would be wonderful to share our dreams."

They arrived at Sandy's house and Paul parked the car.

"I hate to leave you. We have so much to talk about," said Paul. "But now you need to go in and talk to your parents. They're probably waiting up for you."

"Good idea."

"I'll call you tomorrow morning. But don't worry. I'm sure it'll be okay."

"Thank you, Paul. And thanks for a special night."

Paul walked her to her front door and they parted.

CHAPTER 11

Sharing Problems

Sandy put her key in the lock and turned it. Very slowly and quietly, she opened the door. She was hoping that her parents were asleep and that she could sneak into her room without disturbing them. Unfortunately, her parents were sitting in the living room, waiting up for her. Sandy collected herself. Perhaps this was the best time to talk to them. She was still on cloud nine.

"Sandy, we've been waiting up for you. Did you have a good time on your date, honey?" asked her mother.

Sandy smiled. "Oh Mom, Paul is a really nice guy."

"He seemed like a nice guy to your mother and me," said her father. "He was genuinely friendly, and I think he likes you. I like your taste, honey. And how was the concert?"

"Oh, you know, that group is always amazing. They rocked."

"They rocked?" laughed her dad. "Well, I guess that's very cool."

Everybody laughed. Sandy took a deep breath and thought, "Well, this is it. It's now or never. I've got to tell them the truth about Bill."

"Listen, Mom, Dad," she began bravely, "there's something I want to talk to you about. It's about Bill."

"Well, Sandy, we just got off the phone with Bill. He called about an hour ago and we had a long talk. You know, I think he really called to talk to you, but since you weren't here, your dad started talking to him and told him not to hang up on us. We knew there was something wrong, but we didn't know what it was. Did you know he called here last week and hung up on me? His own mother?" Jane said. She looked sad and upset.

Sandy nodded her head. "I know, Mom. But he asked me not to tell you what was going on, so I couldn't say anything," explained Sandy. "I felt so bad, so torn between my parents and my brother. I want to be loyal to all of you."

"Well, we had a long talk with Bill and finally found out that he's failing a class."

"I know," said Sandy sadly. "He doesn't have any confidence in himself as a student."

"I could hear that when he was talking," said Jane. "I found out that he's having a very hard time in several of his classes, and I know he feels just terrible."

"You know, Mom, college isn't for everybody. Maybe college isn't the right place for Bill. He has lots of other talents. He can build anything; he can grow anything. I think he feels like a fish out of water in college," said Sandy.

"You might be right. Bill's talents and interests are a little unusual. Remember when he grew all those different kinds of tomatoes and made his own special sauces? I know he'll be successful once he decides what he wants to do. You both know that I've always wanted the best for our two children," said Jane. "But maybe I've been too rigid in my ideas. Maybe I haven't listened to Bill carefully enough. I always thought he was a capable student, but as I was listening to him tonight, I heard him say that he doesn't feel comfortable in a college classroom. I was so surprised, but he said it, and we listened, didn't we Steve?" said Jane, looking at her husband.

"We did. Your mom and I have suggested to Bill that he take next semester off and do some thinking. He's going to speak to his counselor and ask if he can do that. He's going to fail one of his courses, and it will be on his record."

"Oh Dad, I feel so bad for him. Is he upset?"

"Of course he is. We all are. But it's not the end of the world, is it? Some people are meant for college, but others aren't. He's hardworking and capable, but his interests aren't really academic. You know, Sandy, you're the real student in this family, aren't you?"

Sandy looked down and nodded. "I do love school," she said quietly.

"People are different. Even though you and Bill are sister and brother, that doesn't mean you're the same," said her dad. "I'm just glad he was finally able to tell us what was going on. He's been so unhappy for the last few years, and I could never get him to communicate with us. I told him that he could live at home next semester and we can help him figure out what he's going to do. It might be hard for all of us, but we'll learn a lot from each other; we always do."

"You're great parents," said Sandy.

"We try," laughed her mom. Her dad laughed too. Sandy hugged them and said good night. She went to her room, feeling much lighter. Although Bill still had big problems at school, at least he was facing them. And he wasn't facing them alone; his whole family was behind him.

"Good night, Mom and Dad. Good night, Bill. And good night, Paul. I'll dream about what happened tonight," said Sandy to herself as she got into bed.

CHAPTER 12

A Family Man

Steve Finch was forty-one. He was attractive, and he had dark hair and a big, bushy mustache. He worked out at a gym regularly and maintained a healthy diet, so his body was strong and trim. Steve worked as an administrator in the Palace Forum, a popular theater downtown.

The Palace Forum was an old Victorian building with wood floors and high ceilings. It was very elegant but often needed repairs because it was so old. Steve's job was to manage the theater—to make sure everything was working, including the electricity and the plumbing. Steve also booked the performances that were presented at the Palace.

The Palace Forum presented an annual Shakespeare Festival during the summer. There were three Shakespearean plays performed by actors and actresses who came from all over the United States. During the winter months, local actors, poets, musicians, and artists used the Palace to present their work.

Steve Finch wore many hats at work. He was the handyman, so he was responsible for fixing what was broken. Because he was also the administrator, he was responsible for booking winter performances and setting up auditions for local performers too. With the artistic director, he sometimes sat in on auditions. Steve had trained for his job. He had gone to graduate school and earned a Ph.D. in the history of theater. He was always busy at the theater and he loved his work.

Lately Steve had been especially busy. There was a problem with the ceiling in the theater, and a section of it had fallen down onto the stage. Steve had needed to hire a construction crew to repair it because he couldn't fix the damage alone. For five days, Steve had worked with the crew repairing the ceiling. He was very tired when he left work on Friday afternoon.

"I'm really looking forward to this weekend," thought Steve. "I'm going to play tennis, go to the gym, and try to relax. Maybe I'll take Jane and Sandy out. They'd like to go to dinner and maybe see a play." Then Steve remembered that Sandy might have a date with Paul. Sandy had gone out with Paul twice since their first date two weeks ago. "Or maybe I'll just take my bride out for a date," he thought with a smile.

Steve and Jane met when he was twenty-three and she was twenty-four. They had met as students in graduate school. They didn't have a lot in common at the time, because Steve was so involved in being an actor, director, and stage technician in the theater department. Time had changed their lives a lot. He still worked in the theater, but he was also a devoted husband and father. Jane and Steve had been married for almost twenty years. He treasured his wife and considered her his love and his friend. Steve was a family man.

When he arrived home that night, Steve was glad, as always, to see Jane and Sandy. They both greeted him at the door with hugs all around. Jane and Sandy were busy preparing a care package to send to Bill at school. Bill had called and explained that he had spoken with his counselor, who had helped him make arrangements to finish the semester.

Sandy and Jane thought it would help Bill feel better if they sent him a package with his favorite cookies and a new sweatshirt. They also added some recent photographs, one including Paul.

"How was work, honey? Is the ceiling at the theater fixed yet?" asked Jane.

"Oh, there's too much to do, and too little time. And that theater is so old. Of course, there's never enough money. I'm tired. But something in this house smells good."

"I'm baking something. It's a surprise," said Jane with a smile. "Why don't you go into the kitchen, get a drink, and relax? Sandy and I will join you in a minute."

Steve went into the kitchen and got some drinks for everyone while Sandy and her mom continued preparing Bill's care package.

"Do you think Dad will guess what's in the oven, Sandy?" asked her mother.

"Of course he will. He always knows, by the smell, what's cooking. He's a perceptive guy."

They heard Steve in the kitchen. Without opening the oven door, he said, "Oh boy! Chocolate chip cookies. They're Bill's favorites, but they're mine too."

"They're not done yet," said Sandy.

Jane added, "You can't eat too many. They're for Bill. He needs his favorite cookies to cheer him up."

After Sandy and Jane had finished preparing the package for Bill, they all sat down together in the living room to relax and talk. Steve discussed his problems at work with his wife and daughter.

"Sometimes I wish we could build a new theater," he said. "The ceiling is falling apart, and the plumbing is so old-fashioned; everything in that theater is ancient! It seems that every week something needs repairing."

"That theater is an antique, Dad. Maybe someday it will be a historic landmark. It's such a beautiful theater," said Sandy. "I think it's wonderful that you maintain it and keep it functioning."

"So do I," said Jane. "Nobody else could do that job. You and that theater are like an old married couple." Jane paused; she was thinking. "You know, I just had a thought."

"What's that, honey?" asked Steve.

"Maybe Bill could work with you for a while, helping you fix up the theater," said Jane.

Steve's face brightened. "Hmm," he said. "That sounds like a neat idea. We'll have to think about that." Steve thought for a moment and added, "Maybe Bill could help with the theater. He'd make some money and we could work together. He's always been a good carpenter."

"Maybe," said Jane. "But we don't want to push him into anything right now. And you work so hard at the theater. I'm not sure if that would be the best thing for Bill. He's having a hard time."

"You take your job so seriously, Dad," said Sandy. "I don't know if Bill could handle the pressure."

"Well, maybe you're right, but you know, Sandy, it's important to do work that inspires you, to have a job that you love and care about. And sometimes I worry, but a little stress helps get the job done. You can't live without a little stress and worry. It's human nature. I feel fortunate that your mother and I both have work we enjoy and take seriously. I hope you and your brother find meaningful work in your lives as adults. Your mother helps people, and by working in the theater, I help people too—in a different way. Going to the theater helps people laugh and cry and forget about their own lives for a while. But I'm talking too much. Hey, could we think about food for a minute? Is anybody hungry?" Steve asked.

"I am," said Jane. "I'm starving." Jane, Steve, and Sandy sat down at the table for dinner.

"You know, I think if I didn't love the theater so much, I would have been a chef. I love to cook, and I love to eat," said Steve as he began to eat. "Maybe tomorrow night I'll take you two out for dinner. After all, it's Saturday night."

"That sounds great, honey," said Jane with a smile.

Sandy said, "Well, actually, I need to talk to you both about tomorrow night."

"What is it, Sandy?" asked Jane. "Is everything okay?"

"Yes, everything's okay with me. But you know, things are not okay with the world. Paul and I have been talking and we've decided to do something about it."

Jane and Steve exchanged looks.

"Are you and Paul a couple now?" asked her father.

"Well, we're sort of a couple. We want to, um, we're going to play for a group of homeless people," Sandy stammered. "We're organizing a benefit concert for a homeless shelter, and we have to rehearse tomorrow night. We met a guy from the shelter named Wes, and he inspired us to do something to help. So we're going to try to raise some money with our music."

"Sandy, you always surprise me. That sounds like a really interesting idea. Tell us more. As I told your brother, all you need to do is talk to us, dear. We always like to know your plans, and we just want you to be safe. Will the concert be at the shelter? Is it safe there?" asked Jane.

"I think it's safe Mom, but you know, life isn't always safe. Sometimes we need to take chances. I think we can help with our music."

"Is this your idea or Paul's?" asked her mother.

"We thought of it together. We have a lot in common. We both love music and we both want to help the world. This is a way to make music, share music, and help the world a little."

Steve looked at his daughter. "I think it's very generous of you and Paul. Such big ideas. Why don't I go with you and help out? My theater experience might be helpful. You never know."

"That's a generous offer, Dad, but everything is already arranged. Paul and I have worked it all out. For this concert, he's planning on singing a few of his songs with the guitar; I'm going to play the flute and join him in some singing too. Maybe you and Mom could come and see the show."

"And then we'll treat you two to dinner."

"Oh, Dad," said Sandy, "you don't need to do that. We need to raise as much money as we can for the people at the shelter. I'm glad you both want to come."

"Sandy, we're interested in everything you do. And we feel the same way about Bill. Now that we're all talking again, I'm sure things are going to be better, much better. We've always been on Bill's side, and we're on your side too, Sandy."

"Absolutely!" said Jane in agreement.

CHAPTER 13

How Can We Help?

Paul and Sandy had a rehearsal for the benefit concert. They rehearsed for several hours. They prepared ten songs for the performance. Paul had invited two of his friends to join them. One of them was Samantha, who played the drums. The other, Keith, played the bass guitar. Sandy was tense. They were performing some of Paul's new songs and she wanted them to sound good. It was fun to harmonize with the flute. Sometimes Sandy and Paul sang together too. Paul had a strong voice and he sang on pitch. Sandy could harmonize with her voice and together she and Paul made a strong duo. After they finished rehearsing, Samantha and Keith left.

"I'm tense because I feel like I don't know the music well enough," said Sandy. "I get so worried before I perform, and I haven't had much experience. It's great to have Samantha and Keith as a backup team. They're really supportive. They both play well too."

"You don't mind that Samantha is playing with us, do you?" asked Paul.

"No. Why should I mind? Because she's beautiful?" They both laughed.

"You're beautiful to me," said Paul.

"Thank you, Paul," said Sandy with a smile. They both laughed again.

"Samantha seems to be doing better with her drinking problem, and I thought that playing some music with her friends might be positive for her," said Paul.

"You're always so busy helping people, Paul. You helped me when you told me to talk to my parents about my brother. It really helped all of us. We've all spoken with Bill, and we even sent him a care package. I hope he's feeling better."

"He has to feel better knowing his family is on his side. And I'm sure he knows that now," said Paul.

"I hope so," said Sandy. "Well, it was your idea and you really helped. By the way, I heard a rumor that you have a tattoo. Actually, Samantha told me. Does your tattoo say *May I help you?*"

"No. Anyway, I don't really help people, Sandy; they help themselves," said Paul, feeling embarrassed for a moment. "Don't be a tease." Paul rolled up his sleeve, and on the inside of his upper arm, Sandy could see his tattoo. It had a vertical line with a diagonal line balanced on top of it. There were two horizontal lines to the right of the vertical line. The top horizontal line was shorter than the bottom horizontal line.

"Well, what does it mean? I've never seen anything like it."

"It's a Japanese character," said Paul.

"A Japanese character?" asked Sandy.

"That's right. It means *compassion* or *benevolence*. My Japanese friend Isamu helped me design it."

"That's a very interesting tattoo, Paul," said Sandy. "I know that *compassion* means when you share another person's pain. Does *benevolence* mean the same thing?"

"*Benevolence* means an act of kindness. I want to remember to be kind, and the tattoo might help me remember. I guess it's a private tattoo between me and myself," said Paul with a smile. Sandy returned his smile. They shared a moment of quiet understanding.

"It's a cool tattoo, Paul. Some people like tattoos and others hate them. I like your tattoo; it fits you. Hey, did I tell you that my parents are going to come to the performance?"

"That's great. At least someone in the audience will think we're good," Paul laughed. "You know," continued Paul, "Wes has been on my mind lately; I've really been thinking about him a lot. I'm glad we're going to have this special event for the homeless shelter. I know Wes is glad too. But I wonder if we could help in an ongoing way, in a real, long-term way."

"What do you mean, Paul? Don't you think we're helping in a real way?"

"I guess so. But wouldn't it be incredible if everybody at the shelter had more than just one night of music? It would be a shame if we had just one night of fun and then everything went back to normal."

"This event we're putting together for Wes and his friends will really help them, Paul. They'll get some money, and I'm sure they'll all enjoy hearing our group and having a night of music," said Sandy.

"I hope so. I just wish there were something more we could do. Something ongoing, something enduring," said Paul. He was still thinking.

"Like what?" asked Sandy.

"Well, everybody needs work. Everybody needs to have a skill of some kind. My skill, my gift, is music, but not everybody has that. I feel really lucky to be musical."

"You *are* lucky, Paul. Music is a special gift. But you've also worked at it for a long time. You're always working at it. You know, it's not enough to have talent. You also have to work hard."

"I agree. You're lucky, Sandy, because you have a musical gift too. But every person needs to express himself or herself in some way—through a skill, a trade, a hobby, or something. I'm not sure how that happens."

"Well," said Sandy thoughtfully, "I'm not sure either. I know that we're always learning a lot at school. Learning about different ideas in different subjects helps us to see what we like, what is interesting to us. Activities outside of school help too. I know for me taking music classes and then music lessons has changed my life."

"And our parents, our friends, and our life experiences have given us so many opportunities to learn," Paul interrupted her.

"I guess you can learn from anything if you're open to it, if you have an open mind."

"People teach each other in a lot of ways. How could we do that for Wes and his friends? How can we help them? I'm sure they teach each other and take care of each other too. But maybe we should start some kind of school or club at the shelter." Paul was getting ideas. He was feeling inspired.

"Why don't we think about the long-term possibilities after the performance? Right now, I'm worried about the performance, and I'm afraid of being distracted. We have to perform in front of all these people who I don't know, so I really need to focus my attention. You're used to it, but for me it's a new experience."

"That's true. It will be a new experience, but don't worry, you'll be fine, and you'll love performing, Sandy. It'll be great to perform together." He smiled at her. "And aren't you glad that your mom and dad will be there? I know they'll have a good time."

"You like my mom and dad, don't you? You make me feel better about them. In fact, we all seem to get along better since you've been around. You have big dreams, Paul. I think that's one of the things my parents like about you. Hey, maybe my dad could help you with some ideas for the homeless shelter."

"Maybe he could," said Paul. He was quiet again. He was deep in thought. Sandy felt very close to him.

CHAPTER 14

Making Our World a Better Place

On the afternoon of the performance, Paul and the other musicians went over to Sandy's house for their last rehearsal. They played for Jane and Steve, who thought that they sounded very lyrical. The group packed up their musical instruments and went over to the homeless shelter to set up. Wes was there to meet them and was glad to see them.

The homeless shelter was a modest one-room building. There was a big industrial kitchen used to prepare food for the many people who ate there. There was also an area with cots where some of the homeless people slept.

"This time you have time to look around," said Wes. "It's cozy here. We've made it really nice."

"You have. You've made this into a great space. It looks like you've done a lot of work on it," said Sandy.

"You're right. It was a small, empty warehouse, but Lyle and Jim, my buddies, are pretty good with a hammer and nails and they helped to make it more comfortable. It's a friendlier place now."

"Your friends, Lyle and Jim, should meet Steve, Sandy's dad. He runs the Palace Forum. Do you know the place?"

"You mean that beautiful old theater downtown? That building must be at least 100 years old," said Wes.

"It is. It's 101, actually. I think it's a city landmark. It's Victorian, and because it's so old, it always needs work. Steve manages the theater," explained Paul.

"No kidding. Maybe you could introduce him to Lyle and Jim. They're two good guys who know a lot about carpentry. Maybe Steve could find them some work."

"Maybe," agreed Paul. "It never hurts to ask."

"I'll introduce Lyle and Jim to my dad," said Sandy. "He's always looking for skilled workers."

"Thanks," said Wes. He smiled at her. Sandy and Paul continued talking to Wes for a few minutes. Sandy was relaxing and beginning to enjoy herself.

"Since this is a benefit concert, we're going to put a box for donations by the door, so people can donate a few dollars to the shelter," said Wes.

"That's a great idea," Sandy said. As the afternoon wore on, other people began to drift in. There was a special feeling in the air. People were excited about an evening of music, a live performance.

Sandy wandered over to the kitchen area, where volunteers were making a hearty meal. She put on an apron and pitched in to help prepare a big pot of chili. Soon the food was cooking on the stove and it was time for Sandy to change hats. She left the kitchen and went to the stage to make sure her music was all in order.

As the day wore on, many more people appeared at the shelter: homeless friends, volunteers, and others who simply wanted to hear some live music. Then Sandy saw her mom and dad walking in. She was happy they had come and walked over to greet them.

"Hi, Mom, hi Dad. You guys look great! You got all dressed up."

"And guess what? We have a surprise for you," said Jane.

"What's up?" asked Sandy.

"It's a surprise, so I'll tell you later," said Jane.

"Oh Mom, you always like surprises. Anyway, it's cool that you two are here."

"Yeah, cool," winked her dad. "We wouldn't miss it. Hey, this is a neat space." He was looking around, noticing everything about the shelter. Steve always liked to inspect buildings. "Where's Paul?" he asked.

"He's over there setting up. There isn't a real stage here, so we're trying to make a space for the band," explained Sandy.

Soon the shelter was filled with people. All kinds of people. Sandy saw lots of people whom she didn't know and some whom she did. There were Autumn and Jackson. Sandy walked up to them.

"Do your parents know you're out with Jackson? Is it okay?" asked Sandy.

"Well, I told them we were working on a school project. That's kind of true, isn't it?"

Sandy and Autumn laughed.

"Hi, Sandy. It looks like it's going to be a good concert," said Jackson.

"Look," said Sandy, taking Autumn's arm, "there's Mr. Gambera! He's here with his wife, and they're talking to Paul." Sandy knew that Mr. Gambera was proud of his students. Everyone was talking, laughing, and having a good time. The energy was building in the room. Sandy could see that it was a special night, a real concert. It was time to begin making music.

"I'll see you guys after the show. Thanks for coming," said Sandy to Autumn and Jackson. She walked over to Paul.

"I'm going to turn off the lights for a few seconds," Paul told her. When I turn off the lights, you, Samantha, and Keith walk up to the stage we've set up. Get your instruments ready, and then I'll turn the lights back on, okay?" asked Paul.

"Okay," said Sandy. She was excited now, but she wasn't tense.

Paul went to the corner of the room. People were milling about. He turned off the lights and it grew silent in the shelter. Sandy, Samantha, and Keith walked onto the stage to get their instruments. Paul quickly turned the lights back on and ran up to join them. Sandy's heart was beating so fast. She was so excited. The audience cheered.

Then the group began to sing. Their first song was a big hit. The audience shouted for more. Sandy looked into the audience and smiled. For a moment, she couldn't believe her eyes. There was her brother, Bill! So that was the surprise her parents had mentioned. Bill waved at her, and Sandy walked up to the microphone.

"This song is for my brother, Bill," said Sandy. "He's here tonight and we're so glad." The crowd welcomed Bill with applause. And then the band sang a quiet ballad for Bill.

> Things may not always go the way we plan them.
> Hey, but that's okay.
> People tell us truths and we can't stand them.
> Hey, but that's okay.
>
> I look out at the road ahead,
> It's staring back at me.
> Tomorrow I might be dead.
> But for now I can see . . . that
> Hey, it's okay.
>
> This life is what's unfolding.
> This life is what I'm holding.
> And hey, hear what I say.
> It's okay.
> Yes it's okay.
> Hey, it's okay.

For more than two hours, the band sang and played music while people in the audience listened, sometimes joining them by clapping or singing along. Looking at the audience, they saw a group of friendly faces. Bill was sitting in the front row. Sandy was happy that he had come home. The concert was a big success, and people stayed for a long time, enjoying the music, enjoying being together.

Finally, it was time to leave. The group had said their good-byes and put away their instruments. Wes walked up to the group with a big smile on his face.

"Well, almost everyone has left," he said. "I really want to thank all of you for what you did. Did you see all the money we collected? We made a pile of money.

I haven't counted it yet, but it looks like a lot more than we expected. I hope we can all do this again soon. It was great!" he said. "This money will really help the shelter." Wes shook hands with everybody.

"I think we should plan to do it often," said Paul. "We raise some money, we get to practice our music, and everyone has a good time."

"I agree," said Steve, joining the group. "Anyway it's getting late, and I think we'd better get going. I hope to be seeing you and your friends again, Wes. It was good to meet you."

Sandy and Paul loaded their instruments and equipment into Steve's car. Steve, Jane, and Bill helped them. They all went back to the Finches' house. Autumn and Jackson came too, so everyone had a chance to talk with Bill and welcome him home. Everyone was very hungry after a long night of making music, so Steve brought in some pizza. They all sat around the kitchen table eating pizza and talking about the concert and the future. Life seemed a little lighter tonight. Paul and Bill were getting acquainted and talking about Bill's plans. Under the table, Paul and Sandy held hands.

"It's been a wonderful evening, full of promise, promise for each person here, promise for those at the homeless shelter, and promise for the future," said Steve. "It would be great if tonight never ended."

"Somebody turn on the music," said Sandy and Bill at the same time. Everybody laughed.

THE END

CERTIFICATE OF COMPLETION
READING AWARD

This is to certify that _____ has completed

Changing Generations: A Story for Developing Reading Skills

CONGRATULATIONS!

You're on the road to successful reading. Keep up the good work!

_____ _____ _____
Teacher's Signature School Date